UNEXPECTED JOURNEY

WALKING HOME ON THE APPALACHIAN TRAIL

CHRIS JOHNSON

UNEXPECTED JOURNEY

WALKING HOME ON THE APPALACHIAN TRAIL

Cover photo by Chris Johnson

Library of Congress Catalog Number 2012931091

ISBN 978-0-945980-97-1

For Chris (Fuzz) and Becky, my terrific kids,
Although I'm not always around, I'm always here
My love, hopes and dreams for you are ever present

And for every soul everywhere
Don't fear this event called life
Hike your own hike
Follow your dreams.

FOREWORD

Why hike the Appalachian Trail? Why would anybody put him or herself through such an ordeal and endure separation from family and friends, solitude, strain and pain, long days of tough physical exertion, inclement weather, filth, and all the "unpleasantness" of long distance hiking?

For me, it was not so much for the love of hiking – although I've always very much enjoyed hiking, nor for the love of backpacking – up until preparation for and hiking the AT I had never done any. The answer was simply, "Because I always wanted to." Whenever I asked another AT hiker why they were hiking the trail, their answer invariably would be the same, "I always wanted to." And no further explanation was needed, we understood what was meant.

I suppose hiking the AT is a personal conquest or achievement, much the same as, say, wanting to make a million dollars before you're forty; or going to college, being established in a career, getting married and having a nice home and family by the time you turn thirty. Why do any of that? It's something you strive for, a personal goal. The answer is as unique as the individual, yet, at the same time, as simple as, "I always wanted to." And no further explanation is needed.

My hike of the Appalachian Trail became, as it probably is for many who do it, an inward or spiritual journey. I don't know that anyone could undertake and accomplish such an adventure and not change, re-define, or re-establish who they are. During my hike I encountered great hardships, but was blessed with incredible beauty; I experienced every emotion, often quite deeply, that is known in the human condition.

By nature I'm a rather reserved person; I like my own company, my own routine or rhythm, and the company of a few close friends. But in hiking the trail I met many wonderful people

– fellow hikers, trail angels, clerks, waiters and waitresses, random passersby – folks from all walks of life (pardon the pun). Some of these folks I met only briefly, some whose company I occasionally enjoyed, a few I felt a strong connection to and felt a loss from when we were finally separated by nature of the trail. All the folks I encountered from hiking the trail added to and enhanced the experience of the hike.

While on the trail I experienced life more deeply than I had at any other time. Hiking the Appalachian Trail became a life-altering event for me – it was the best thing I have ever done for myself. And it all started with, "Because I always wanted to."

1

THE BEGINNING

Just when I was taken by the notion of hiking the trail I cannot say. What I can say for sure is that I had wanted to do it for quite some time. I suppose I knew all along that at some point in my life I would hike the trail.

Along about 2004 I started talking more seriously about it, gearing myself up mentally. Some of the folks I had mentioned it to were supportive and encouraging, others not so much. I had been asked how I was going to manage such an undertaking, considering the condition of my knees (at the time I was having persistent pain in my left knee). Oddly, even though my left knee is not what it ought to be (residual effects from the second time I was hit by a car), I had no doubt that my knee would hold up just fine. Even my wife at the time told me, "You can't do that, you can't leave your job!" But what's a job, I thought, compared to following a dream and doing something you've always wanted to do? Besides, there'll always be other jobs. For a while little else was said about it, though I continued to think about it.

In 2005 my life as I had known it for the past sixteen years was unraveling. I had moved out of my home, my wife and I had come to an impasse and pretty quick we were headed for a divorce, in April 2006 it became official. Since I now had only myself to answer to there was no reason for me not to seriously consider hiking the trail.

One day it came to me. In 2008 I would turn fifty years old – it seemed like that would be the perfect time for me to go for a walk. The more I thought about it the more sense it made.

Fifty. A half a century. Half way (if I dared to think that I would live to be one hundred) through my life. In some aspects, I was indeed half way through my life. I couldn't think of a better way to usher in the second half of my life than to pursue my dream of hiking the trail.

The big job I held with the state had played out for me a couple years ago, I had absolutely no desire to continue working at something that I felt was draining the life out of me. Money and benefits, no matter how good they may be, cannot, should not, certainly in my case would not, be exchanged for living life. I had no debt what-so-ever and I did not have to stay at the job for need of the money. I was as free as I had ever been.

So, doggone it, in the year I turn fifty – 2008 – I'll hike the AT!

As it always seems to be, the most difficult aspect of doing anything is deciding, for sure, that you are going to do it. Once the commitment is made everything falls into place.

Okay, so now I had to plan on getting ready for the hike. I needed to acquire the necessary gear for such an undertaking. I had hiked a number of the trails throughout my home state of Maine, but they had been just day hikes – I had no experience backpacking. Fortunately, my oldest brother did. He loaned me some of his gear – a couple of different stoves, sleeping pads, a backpack – so I could try out different equipment and see what would work best for me. Bit by bit I started figuring out what I wanted to take with me on the trail. Now, this process may have gone better had I read up on the different types of gear and had spoken to other folks about what they had used and how well it worked, but that wasn't my way. Through the fall and winter of 2007 and 2008 I assembled my gear, getting the final touches done days before my departure.

My backpack was an el-cheapo model purchased over the phone (more on that later); my sleeping bag I happened to find in a discount bin at L.L. Bean; my cook set consisted of an alcohol stove homemade from a set of plans, an old aluminum pot, a cup that was graduated so as to double as a measuring cup, a plastic spork (spoon on one end, fork on the other), all of which I could carry in the pot with the base/windscreen for the stove. My clothing consisted of two pair of hiking pants with zip-off legs; some sort of polyester blend t-shirt; a silk underwear top; lightweight wool long johns and sweater; a fleece jacket; a wool stocking cap; moccasins with two pair of hiking socks and one pair of waterproof socks; and a rain suit. As it has been my habit to be cheap (thrifty is a kinder term, but not necessarily accurate) I did not buy any high-tech, light weight clothing when I already owned perfectly good, adequate clothing.

Now, maybe you're wondering about the moccasins. You see, I enjoy hiking barefoot (I enjoy the feel of the earth beneath my feet), so I figured I'd need the moccasins only for sharp rocks (at least until my feet toughened up in good shape) and, along with waterproof socks, for any snow I might encounter. But mostly I figured on being barefoot.

The remainder of my equipment consisted of a 35-mm camera and film, old school stuff I already owned; water purification filter; two 1-liter water bottles; a 20-ounce soda bottle for alcohol for my stove; pack cover; first aid kit; small flashlight; a Leatherman multitool; writing tablet and pen; toothbrush, toothpaste and floss; a roll of toilet paper; soap; a backpacking towel; a lightweight tarp; a length of parachute line; some few things that I thought would come in handy; and the 2008 Appalachian Trail Data Book, which contains useful trail information such as the distance to, say, the next water source, lean-to, or town.

My very dear friend, Stef, (my girlfriend at the time) said she'd mail all my re-supply packages to me along the trail, so I figured I had everything in order. I had given my boss a month's notice so I could wrap up all the business with the job and leave them in as good standing as I could.

I got done work on Thursday, April 3, 2008; I would be flying to Atlanta, Georgia, the following Wednesday, April 9, to start my walk back home from Springer Mountain, Georgia, the southern terminus of the Appalachian Trail, to Mount Katahdin,

Maine, the northern terminus, a distance of nearly twenty-two hundred miles.

I flew out of Portland, Maine, on a cool, damp morning, being of two minds. Of course, I was excited to start my adventure, but I was also in a quiet, reflective mood as I was leaving my girlfriend behind. And so I boarded the plane for an uneventful flight to Atlanta.

There is the shock of leaving one climate and soon entering another quite different one. Naturally, it was warmer in Atlanta than it was in Maine. Since it was already warm and humid, I wondered what I would encounter on the trail – I never did care for hot, humid weather. I guessed I'd soon find out.

The following pages are from my journal, written every day I was on the trail. I wrote about what I did, what I saw, how I felt, and about any aspect of the hike that was particularly notable. This is a more or less complete account of my hike on the AT. In reading these pages, you may catch a glimpse into the everyday world of a long distance hiker. I hope I am able to pass along to you, dear reader, some comprehension of experiencing a journey on the longest marked footpath in America – the 2175 mile Appalachian Trail.

2

GEORGIA

Wednesday 4/9/08

Not really a good night's sleep – something on my mind? Up at 4:30, left for the airport about 5:30. Got checked in easily and got in the security line. Just a few minutes left with Stef – a hug, a kiss, and a good-bye. My last sight of her was through the glass – a smile and a wave. I got teary eyed. Shoot, I'm teary eyed now.

The flights to Baltimore and Atlanta went very smoothly. In the air I was thinking about what I left behind, and what's to come. I believe I'm much more fond of Stef than I realize. Mixed emotions… sad for leaving, excited about starting this adventure.

Walking through Atlanta Airport terminal it dawned on me – really hit me – It's begun, I'm living my life! I expect only great things now.

So I'm just sitting here in the warm Atlanta sun waiting for the Greyhound Bus office to open so I can get a ride up to Dahlonega, the closest town and jumping off point to the trail. Yeah, but Greyhound doesn't go to Dahlonega, they go as close as Gainesville. It was suggested I try the shuttle services. They don't go to Dahlonega, either. I found one that was soon leaving for Gainesville, so I took it. In Gainesville I got a taxi for Dahlonega and went to the Hiker Hostel, which was full. The fellow at the hostel suggested I stay at Motel 8 in town, and he would pick me up in the morning to take me to the trail head. Back to Dahlonega I go. Tonight I will have a good meal, and I'm hitting the hay early. After breakfast tomorrow, the fun begins.

Thursday 4/10

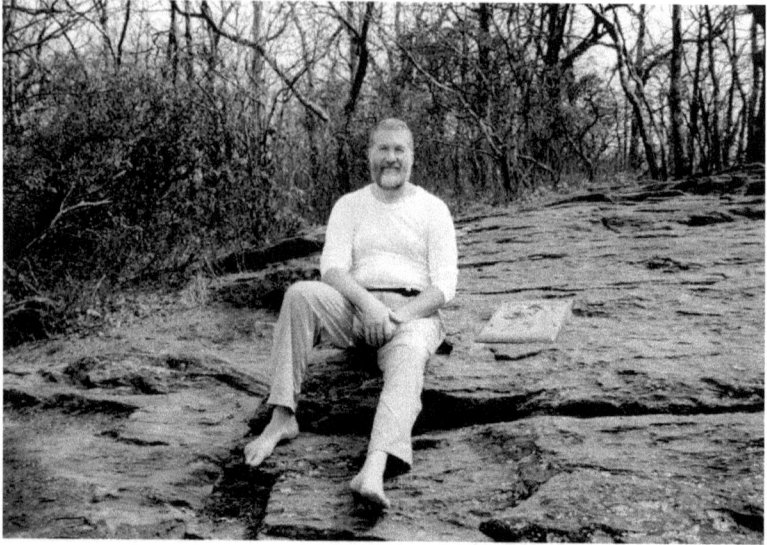

The first day on the trail

Up about 5:30 and a nice hot shower. Stef called at 6:30, it sure was good to hear her voice. Off to an okay breakfast about 7:30. Back to the motel about 8:30 for my ride. I got a ride to the Springer Mt. parking area with Long Distance Man, a former thru-hiker (a thru-hiker is someone who has hiked the entire trail in one season) I met the night before at the motel. I walked the 9/10 mile to Springer Mt. – the official start. Some say the real start is at Amicalola Falls State Park, but in my data book Springer Mt. is listed as "Mile 0" of the trail. Six of one, half a dozen of the other.

What did I feel? Tremendous joy, exuberance, knowing I was finally getting underway. A gorgeous day, maybe 70°. Three young folks on Springer, one from Camden, one from Canton, all headed to Maine. Some pictures and I'm on my way.

The trail is great, very easy compared to trails in Maine. It's early spring, nothing yet in bloom, but the forest is beautiful old-growth hardwood with some hemlock and pine. With the trail so nice I move right along. Before long I meet up with D, a thin fifty-three year old guy with piercing blue eyes and a quick smile, a very pleasant guy. He says he's looking for a change and he's going all the way. As we hiked and chatted we discovered that we have many similarities and share many of the same viewpoints about life. I don't necessarily take to people right away, but I did with D. We hiked and chatted together for a few hours, but after Long Creek Falls, in my enthusiasm to hike, I got ahead of him. I'm not fast, but I'm faster than he is.

I'm on top of Sassafras Hill for the night – I pushed too long, too late. A lesson there. Also, more importantly, camp where there's water. It's not like in Maine – there isn't water everywhere here. Supper tonight is rather blah – couscous with dried vegetables, dulse, and protein powder. Not gourmet fare, but nutritious. I'm beat, I'm turning in early. About eleven miles today, pretty good considering the late start.

A couple things learned today: Plenty of water is crucial, so is good footwear.

Friday 4/11

Today's lesson was about arrogance and humility.

I drank right from streams yesterday, but I chose good ones. In the night I was quite sweaty and all I could think was giardia, an intestinal ailment caused by drinking bad water. I'm sure I didn't contract any, but it was enough to make me pay attention and take care of myself. Also, I was overly ambitious about the barefoot hiking business. As I hiked today, I realized that my feet were just plain sore, and that my feet being so sore led to an overall fatigue. It's one thing to do a five to ten mile barefoot hike for one day, quite another to do it for an extended period with such a load. I guess it was arrogance that made me think I could do it easily. Also what I found was that I had to focus so much on the trail and my footing that I was missing the view. Fortunately, it's early on and I can correct the situation.

These Georgia mountains sure are pretty and the trail is quite nice. Mostly, it's mature hardwood forest, but now and again there are groves of hemlock and pine or of rhododendron not yet in bloom. I well imagine when I get to see them in bloom they will be very lovely.

Today I hiked by myself and encountered few people. I finally got to Woody Gap about 3:00 and decided it was time to eat an early supper. Called Stef about shipping my boots to Helen, about three days away at my present rate. I'll hike with footwear so I can enjoy the trail and the scenery. The fellow who let me use his cell phone to call, a real nice guy, told me there was a storm blowing in bringing rain and thunderstorms. Trail angels. Thank you.

For those who don't know, a trail angel is someone who helps you in any way, be it by leaving food along the trail, giving you a ride to or from town, or in this case, letting me use his phone. And anything bestowed upon you by way of an angel, food, ride, etc., is known as trail magic.

So I loaded up with water and decided I'd make camp early. Since I've been setting up camp, thunder has been rumbling in the distance. With my inadequate footwear, sore feet, and early camp I didn't make too many miles today. I'm not sure just where I am tonight, but I figure I made eleven miles. With boots and a lighter pack I'm sure I'll do better. I'll have to, or I'll never make it all the way this year.

Saturday 4/12

Last night's thunderstorm wasn't much, but I was glad I put up the tarp. Showers off and on this morning, but by the time I put on the pack the sun poked through. I started off quite enthusiastic and soon realized I was moving too fast. Today's lesson – pace yourself! The land is very hilly, it seems I'm going up or down. My feet are tougher today than yesterday, or the trail easier, and the hike is going very well.

Along the way I met Hal who had thru-hiked in '05 at age sixty-one, a very nice fellow. We hiked for a number of miles to Neel's Gap. He informed me a lot on what to expect as far as towns to re-supply. Before we parted he gave me his phone numbers, saying that if I needed anything for the next few weeks to give him a call – he would be within a two hour drive.

Up on Blood Mt. there was a family out on a day hike, and before they left the woman made us cheese sandwiches and gave me granola bars and raisins. Trail angels. Apparently they're all around.

The day is just beautiful, sunny and 60°. The country is lovely mountain land that just seems to go on in every direction. The trees aren't yet budded, so the views are lengthy. Once I get my pack and footwear squared away, this will be a breeze. A couple times today I got a little teary eyed thinking how fortunate I am that I'm out doing this – living my dream.

Sunday 4/13

I spent last night on Rock Spring Top, but Hurricane Hill would be more descriptive, as about 8:00 last night the wind changed and roared through camp all night long. My tent is pretty noisy in the wind, so I did not get much sleep. The other fellows in camp, Blaine, a tall, broad, lanky, quiet kind of guy in his mid-twenties and Shawn, of shorter stature with a tremendous pile of dreadlocks, and a very unassuming, easy going nature – both from Topsham – said they did not sleep well either. I was up shortly after sunup and, having had enough of the wind, broke camp without breakfast. I hiked about four miles down to Hog Pen Gap and had breakfast by a spring. This is where I learned to mix the dry meal ingredients then add water and let it set a spell before cooking. This works as well as boiling the water first, but takes less cooking time and uses less fuel. Today's lesson was camp efficiency.

The day is mostly clear, the sun has warmth to it, but the strong wind that continues to blow is mighty chilly. The first and last parts of the day's hike were steep and twisty, but in between there were a couple lengthy stretches that were relatively level, which made for easy going. All along the trail are great views of the Georgia countryside which, for the most part, is pretty rugged mountain country. It really is quite pretty, but there is a definite lack of water. There always seems to be enough, but you have to plan your breaks by watering holes. Some different from Maine where good, fresh water can be had most anywhere.

So tonight I'm camped on Blue Mt., elev. 4000', and it is spitting snow. They say tonight and tomorrow night is supposed to be cold, so I'm wearing my cold weather clothes to bed. A bit of a lesson in getting here tonight – I pushed hard about the last three miles so I could get here in good time. Too hard, in fact, because when I stopped, fatigue and a chill set in. Once into my warm clothes and a hot supper I feel pretty good. But I'm ready for bed. My first fifteen mile day.

Monday 4/14

Chilly overnight, a little ice in my water bottles. No breakfast, just got up and got going figuring I'd eat a breakfast in town. Over two miles to the road, then a hitch to town. At the road I hadn't gone a hundred feet when I got a ride from the first vehicle along – a wrecker truck – driven by a very nice fellow who let me out right at the post office. The boots came at a good time as the trail is getting rockier and steeper. The boots came with a letter from Stef that brought tears to my eyes. Whatever it is between us, it's strong.

After postal business is done, I walk up the street to Huddle House for breakfast, though by now it's nearly 11:00. Helen is a very touristy town with nearly everything within a half mile on the main street. Breakfast done, I pick up just a couple items from the store for mid-day meals. Called Stef, but only got her answering machine, so I'm placing an order for better contact.

The fellow who brought me to town was on his way back and asked me if I was ready to go. That was just before I called Stef so I had to decline his ride. But as I was leaving, I bet I didn't walk a mile before a young lady picked me up and dropped me back at the trail. Trail angels, highway angels – they're all the same. Thank you all.

The day is overcast, windy and chilly. Back on the trail there is intermittent snow and hail, though little accumulation. The terrain is much steeper and higher than it was a couple days ago, and will stay this way through North Carolina, I'm told. Tonight is chilly on Tray Mt. at 4,233', and I'm ready to hit the hay. My first night in one of the trail shelters. Two other hikers with me – Bear Meister and J.J.

This afternoon was rather emotional, and as I walked along the trail I was crying about Mom and her death, about Dad, Jake (an old dog), and even a little about my ex-wife. Old issues...

Tuesday 4/15

Cold overnight, didn't sleep well at all. After breakfast D came walking into camp looking for water. He left before I did, but I caught up with him fairly quickly and we hiked the whole day together. Unlike yesterday, the day is sunny and warm, and the hiking is terrific. Hiking with D, I don't get as introspective as I do when I'm alone.

Nothing very special... No, scratch that – today was just a glorious day to hike. Tonight I'm camped on a ridge, there is no wind and it is much warmer than last night was. It is so peaceful here I believe I will sleep well. I'm pooped, it's time for shut-eye.

Wednesday 4/16

A good night's sleep. My knee, which was aching pretty bad when I went to bed, felt good. Got up about sunrise, had a bucket of oatmeal, packed up and got under way. I broke camp before D and never did see him the rest of the day. The day is beautiful with a gentle breeze, cloudless skies and warm temperatures. The trail is getting steeper and hillier than at the start, but as I'm heading into North Carolina, and the highest point on the trail, it has to start climbing.

Needles, Mountain Lion and I cross the Georgia/North Carolina border at 1:00. We stop for pictures and a quick break, then press on. The hills are definitely more work, and Bly Gap proved to be a doozey. But we make it, just like all the others – one step at a time.

Needles and I stop at Muskrat Creek and briefly debate going on, and when I decided to go another five miles to Deep Creek, so did Needles. We're camped in a lovely little glade with a nice little stream just below. Tomorrow we start the day with an 1150' climb in 2.4 miles – the hardest climb yet. Today was a 14.6 mile day; I'll bet tomorrow won't be anywhere near as lengthy.

3

NORTH CAROLINA/TENNESSEE

Thursday 4/17

A dreamy, but restful, night. Up and going in good season to get over Standing Indian Mountain. But the mountain was pretty easy! On top of the mountain I pause to look up the hill and the countryside around, then start to continue on down the trail only to be called back. I walk the couple hundred yards to the top to find an open, grassy spot maybe sixty feet across. This place is sacred – it is a place of much energy.

I approach the opening with great reverence, and before long I'm crying tears of joy. Thank You, thank You, thank You for bringing me to this spot, and on this journey. I practiced Tai Chi, then just lay against Mother Earth absorbing her energy. As I said, there is much energy there, so much so that there are daffodils in bloom on this high mountain top so early in the year. Stopping there sets my mood for the day, and as I walk I often find myself crying tears of joy as my heart is full. Stef, how I wished you were there to share it with me, but we both know this walk is for me. And when we re-re-unite, I will have much to tell you about.

The trail around and down the mountain is absolutely lovely as I walk down a lane shouldered with laurel and rhododendron. Today's trail is the easiest one yet, and with my joyful mood, is pure pleasure. After ten or so miles the trail starts to climb, drop and climb again, often through groves of rhododendron, but mostly it is beautiful, mature hardwood forest. The day has been sunny with a light breeze making for excellent hiking. Often I find myself getting choked up and teary eyed at my fortune to be able to be here and experience this grand adventure.

The last part of today's trail was up over Albert Mt., the toughest quarter mile scramble over rocks I've had to do so far. Tonight I'm camped at Big Spring Shelter; tomorrow I will make for Franklin for a motel room, hot showers, laundry, good meals and re-supplying – as is the plan for many of the other hikers camped here tonight. I think I will figure on an early start tomorrow.

Friday 4/18

Got up in good season – before sun-up – skipped breakfast, packed up and got under way. I've decided I want to get early starts as I enjoy seeing the world wake up from the trail. This morning is the first time I've seen any game – a rabbit and a deer. A hawk flew overhead at one point – an omen in native lore as a bearer of messages. Most of the nine miles to the highway are pretty level and easy going through still mature hardwoods intermixed with rhododendrons and some hemlocks.

My lesson for today is to take my time and enjoy this journey – it's not just a hike. Funny, but it seems I still have had some sort of schedule. I passed up a night at Muskrat Creek, a beautiful, peaceful spot, so I could get nearer to Standing Indian Mt. I took some time up on Standing Indian, but I could have stayed longer. My strained ankle and sore knee are telling me I'm hurrying too much, that I need to slow down and enjoy.

About noon I got to the highway and was greeted by Ron who offered to bring me to town. Turns out Ron also owns two motels, but after seeing his I told him I thought I'd rather be at the Franklin, so he brought me to it. A genuine nice guy. But then, all of the folks down here have been very nice. Today I've laid low, iced my sore spots, got scrubbed up, did laundry and rested. I will pick up a few provisions for the next five days, get a good supper and breakfast, and I'll be ready to get back into the woods. This noisy city life is no life for me.

A typical lean-to.

Saturday 4/19

A lousy night's sleep, I rest far better in the woods. Called Stef about 7:00, we talked for about an hour. Missing her becomes harder the more I talk to her.

A cloudy, cool start to the day as I walk over to a restaurant for breakfast. I find that my right ankle is very sore, so I decide to give it a test and I walk the mile to Outfitters for a food bag. Outfitters is closed until 10:00, but right across the road is a drug store; I went in and got some glucosamine/chondroitin for my joints and tendons. The sky cleared up pretty well on my walk back to the motel, and my ankle limbered up. I went next door to the hardware store for some alcohol, but the smallest size they had was a quart and I didn't need that much. But here's the kicker – a quart was $6.99, but they filled my bottle from a can (I took about 16 ounces) and they charged me $1.07?! Shrewd. Having all my chores done, I walk up the hill to get a shuttle ride. I got dropped at the trail about noon, filled my water bottles and started walking.

Siler Bald Shelter was four miles away, so that seemed like a good destination. Along the way I started becoming unraveled. I was missing Stef, physically hurting and felt like quitting. I started crying and asked – almost pleaded – for Spirit to help me. I was instructed by Spirit to go to the shelter for two nights. Once at the shelter, I spread my tarp on the grass and cried. Before long more hikers arrived and it looked like a party was brewing. I set up camp at the far end of the grass to be away from the ruckus. In a bit D came along and set up camp beside me.

Sometime later, Shawn and Blaine rescued us and invited us to camp up in a field with them. D and I moved. From our new campsite there was a half mile walk up to the bald for tremendous views of far reaching mountain ranges all around. Had it not been for Shawn and Blaine, I undoubtedly would have missed the spectacular views from the bald. Time for supper, so we went back down to the site, ate well, enjoyed a great fire and had pleasant conversation. I played out and turned in first.

Sunday 4/20

I woke first, but got out of my sleeping bag just to pee. I crawled back in my bag, cried some and again asked Spirit for help. Again, I was instructed to move to the shelter. And this is where I am, and will be until tomorrow, at the Siler Bald Shelter – writing.

It's a mostly overcast day, breezy and chilly. I wish it were sunny and warm so I could lay comfortably on the grass. I've been here all day, writing, thinking, resting. Some campers have been coming in all afternoon. There are now six other tents here. I'm back down at the end of the field, right where I was last night. I'm not feeling sociable at all. In fact, I'm in a very quiet mood – pensive, I would say. Here I sit, by myself, enjoying my little campfire. Before long I am visited by another hiker, Michigan Wolverine, a pleasant, enthusiastic, energetic, excitable guy full of life and trail stories who chats for a while before going back to the crowd. Quiet again...nice.

Monday 4/21

Slept very well last night and woke this morning feeling very good. As usual, I was the first one up. I debated having breakfast right away, but I did, and as soon as camp was torn down I was on my way. The morning is cool with a little breeze, very nice for hiking.

The tendons in my right ankle, which have been swollen and painful for the past couple days, are feeling much better, but I am still mindful of my footing. The meltdown I had Saturday, and the subsequent day off for rejuvenation yesterday, were the best things that could have happened to me. I now have my head on straight, my heart is light and my spirit soars.

The trail today is very easy, perhaps more so because of my re-alignment, but I walk along effortlessly. At one point I was thinking about Stef, and I paused to say, "Stef, you're a beautiful woman, and I love you." In the next breath I said, "Chris, you're a beautiful person, and I love you." I meant it and it brought me great joy.

The day is warming pretty well and I hike in shorts and short sleeves, though on occasion there is a chilly breeze. The forest is changing slightly. The once abundant rhododendrons are still about, but not nearly as much. There are now more beeches, yellow birch and hemlock along the way. I imagine it's because I'm staying more to the four and five thousand foot elevations. From one overlook, I could see in the distance what I supposed is Clingman's Dome, the highest peak on the trail. According to my trail book, it is about seventy miles from where I am. I will be over it within a week.

Today has been a truly magnificent day, and I wouldn't be anywhere else. Tonight I'm camped right alongside the trail near a little spring. I could have gone on further, I was feeling so good, but 14.3 miles is good enough for today, especially since I'm still mending sore parts. Oh, today's lesson was gentleness. Walk gently on Mother Earth, let your movements be smooth and fluid. But most importantly, be gentle with yourself.

Tuesday 4/22

Slept very well last night. Unsure of the time when I got up, but it felt late. The morning is clear and bright, but despite the early chill, it feels like it will warm up.

I feel like I am moving in slow motion today compared to yesterday's boundless energy. I go along at a good pace and before long I am up on Wesser Bald, and the tower/platform up there. Being the only one there, I practice Tai Chi. It is obvious I haven't been doing it much as I forgot the order of some of the moves. Priyadarshi would not be so pleased. But I run through the whole thing, do some energy work and leave feeling better.

The trail so far today is pretty good, but I still feel as though I'm not doing much. Even so, I don't hurry. Come late morning the day is indeed heating up. About 11:00 I start a descent that seems to go on and on. It does. I started the day out at about 5,000', but by early afternoon I have dropped to 1,740' at Nantahala River. The day seems quite hot now. At this lower elevation most all the trees are leafed out, and there are wildflowers growing about.

I pick up some food for the next few days, then go to a restaurant. There's always talk on the trail about upcoming places to eat and such, and I had it in my mind to get a hamburger, so I did. It was listed as a half pound burger, though I didn't know if I could eat all that. It came with a very nice salad, and I ate every bit. Mmm, delicious. It was about 2:30 when I got back on the trail, I had already done nine miles.

Of course, as much as I came down, I went back up. The climb this afternoon was a real workout – especially in the heat and having little water. I finally got nearly on top of the mountain, and with my knee putting up a fuss, I made camp in a rhododendron grove about 1.5 miles from the shelter. It has been a long, hard fifteen miles today – I'm sore and tired. The sleeping bag will feel some good.

Wednesday 4/23

Slept great last night on my bed of rhododendron leaves. The first of the day's trail was three miles up – the last mile UP. The day is sunny and warm, hopefully won't be as hot as yesterday was. After the hike up Cheoah Bald, with terrific views of surrounding mountains, the trail is pretty level for a distance, then starts to drop gradually.

My knee and ankle feel pretty good after yesterday's grueling run. I'm some glad because they sure were hurting last night. The morning is so beautiful and peaceful that I feel no need to hurry it. I'm kind of in an odd frame of mind in that I don't seem to be thinking of anything at all. I'm just walking and gawking. The land really doesn't seem to change much, it's just mountain after mountain that seem to stretch on and on. The trees are budding and leafing out, and the trilliums are now blossomed.

At 2:00 this afternoon I was hunting around for some water. I drank the last of what I had an hour ago, and where there was supposed to be some at a spring, there wasn't. The next water supply was 2.5 miles away, mostly uphill. This is where I stop thinking and focus on putting one foot in front of the other. I shoulder my pack, put my head down, and plod along like a buffalo. That aspect of me is strong and sturdy so that I pass younger folks on the hill who started before me.

I finally got to the water source, which was not much more than a trickle, but got a good drink and filled water bottles. From there it was 2.5 miles to where I'm camped tonight. I quit about 5:30, it's been a long enough day – about thirteen miles of up and down. Tomorrow I'll be in Fontana Dam for cleaning and re-supplying.

Thursday 4/24

I don't like camping around a lot of people – too much noise – especially when some come in at 10:00 pm and go stomping around my tent. But all's fair in love and war. I'm up before the sun and the birds and start my day. Oh, you wanted to sleep in? Gee, sorry about that... I like camping by myself, it's so quiet.

The day is clear and bright and will be warm again. This country is dry, it needs rain. The land really doesn't seem to change, it's up one hill and down the other side. Then up again and down again. But the forest is changing, more beeches, birches, hemlocks and pine, less rhododendron and laurel. The land is also getting higher, I'm often at 5000 feet or more. Then back down to 2000 or 3000, and back up to 5000. Hey, it is mountain country after all.

Today will be an easy day, just into Fontana Village for re-supply and cleaning. The trail is easy, just a couple hills have me breathing hard; the rest is down to the highway. It's a quiet, peaceful walk today; I've only got to go nine miles today. Mostly I take in what is around and don't think about much else. Stef, of course, comes to mind – Good morning, Babe – I wonder what she is doing today. So I get down to the highway at some time, I figure it's early afternoon and I check out the marina at the lake. There's not much to see from the shore, but from high up the lake formed by the dam is expansive with many bays and coves. From my guess, the lake is down twenty feet. This country needs rain!

I catch a ride to the village in the back of a pick-up and go to the post office to get my package. In the store I get chocolate milk and a Klondike bar, and request a shuttle to the lodge. I check in, it's only 1:30?? The room is $60, which seems pricey, but the room at Motel 8 in Dahlonega was $54, and this is much nicer! There's a nice, firm, king size bed, a little balcony and a bubbling brook right outside my door. I'm pampering myself tonight! Only thing is, I wish my hottie was here to share it with me – that would be perfect!

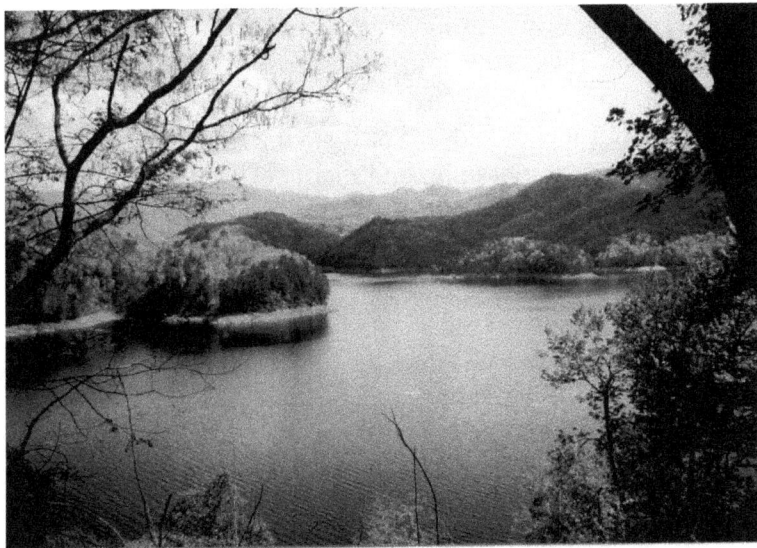

Fontana Lake

In a bit I will walk down to do my laundry, maybe take a swim in the pool, and get a supper in the restaurant here tonight. I called my ex-wife to wish her a happy birthday, and spoke with her for a half hour or more. The talk was nice, I was glad I called. Then I called Stef about 8:45; she had just gone to bed, but got up to get the call. We talked for about an hour, but the later hour left us both a little dopey. Breakfast in the morning, send a package home, and I'll be back in the woods for another week or so.

While in my room, I went through my pack to figure out what I needed for re-supply, what I needed for day food, and to get my journal pages and rolls of exposed film together to mail back home. I should have had three rolls of film, but I could find only two in the pack. I tore the pack completely apart looking for that third roll, but it just was not there. Then I remembered where I changed it – I remembered taking the exposed roll out of the camera and setting it down beside me while I put a new roll in.

I'd have sworn I put that roll into my pack, but as I searched high and low, it was not with me. My pictures are precious to me; needless to say I was quite blue at the prospect of having lost that roll. But no point in crying over spilt milk – it's gone. And then I got calm about it, I talked to Spirit saying that I knew, through Him, all things are possible, and that I really would like to get that roll of film back. And that was all I could do, I let it go.

Friday 4/25

Despite being in a king size bed in which I could sprawl all over the place, I didn't sleep all that well last night. Called brother Herb at 6:00 this morning, he was getting ready to go to work. We had a pleasant talk and I informed him of the goings on. I wanted to call Stan, my buddy of almost 30 years, and called his wife, Carol, because I couldn't remember Stan's cell phone number. She was glad to hear from me. Called Stan's cell phone, but got his voice mail. At 7:00 I called Stef, we spoke for about an hour and a half. Not much to say… It's hard, this journey I'm on, when just not too long ago I fell in love with her. But as hard as it has been, I'm ever so grateful for her. Sometimes I think it is harder when we talk – I always miss her real bad afterward. I miss her anyway, and dream of being with her, but after we talk it's worse.

After our talk, I got breakfast, checked out, got my outfit together, and headed to the post office and store. I got the package taken care of and went to the store because I had only twelve pounds of food and needed more. Obviously. All the business done, I got a shuttle to the trail head.

It is sunny and warm today, though not as warm as it had been. I talked with a couple hikers about the trail and such, and got going. I was entering Smokey Mountain National Park. Of course, the trail started off uphill, but the newly-acquired knee brace helped a lot. I met a couple of AT trail workers and got information and the required back-country permit. The forecast calls for some rain, so I thought I'd try for the shelter eight miles away. I was hurrying along when I caught myself and realized I need to slow down and enjoy the hike.

Glad I did. At one stretch of the trail I heard leaves rustling and stopped to see a bear – my first of the trip. It was a female with two cubs, and she didn't see me until I spoke to her. She hurried about to gather up her young, then sat placidly and watched me. They were about seventy-five yards uphill of the trail, and I stopped just long enough to take a picture. Had I been moving right along, it might never have happened. Then I got to nearly the top of the hill, the AT went left and there was another trail going straight ahead towards the top – I took that one. Glad I did. At the top was a fire tower that afforded incredible views of the dam, the lake and beautiful mountains all around. Again, had I been hurrying right along...

The last few miles to the campsite – I nixed the idea of going to the shelter – were slow and easy. Got to the campsite and very casually set up, got supper and chores done, and got into the tent to write. I hiked just over five miles today – it was great!

Saturday 4/26

Slept very well, woke early, and a few taps of rain on the tent urged me to get up and get going. Tore down camp, got breakfast and packed up before any rain. About twenty minutes down the trail and the thundershowers commenced. Surprisingly, they didn't last very long, certainly not as long as they should have considering how dry it is. This rainy/foggy morning is very peaceful, a great time to be hiking. There is nothing for a view, but walking through the shroud of mist feels like walking in a fairy land. A fellow I met said he had just stood and watched a couple deer, one of them thirty feet from him. Before long the clouds broke and provided a partly sunny day, cooler than what they have been.

The trail is pretty easy today, and I make decent time. At 1:30 I met a couple south-bound (SoBo) hikers who told me it was due to storm in a couple hours, so I made for the next shelter. It was about 3:00 when I got there, and since I was hungry I got supper. I made just eleven miles today. I had planned to do more, but with the forecast I think I'll stay put for the night. After this stormy weather comes through, it is supposed to cool down, which ought to make for pleasant hiking.

I really enjoyed the hike this morning in the fog with all the ghostly shadows all around. There was no visibility beyond fifty yards or so, and it made me feel as though I was the only one out there.

I saw two bears today. I watched the first one squeeze itself into a hole in a hollow tree that I wouldn't have thought he could put his head in, but he got completely inside! The other one I startled as I rounded a bend in the trail, so all I got was a glimpse of the south end of a north bound bear as he took off in a huff. I didn't have the opportunity to get a picture of either one of them.

I feel like I'm just poking along, having made only five miles yesterday, and just eleven today. But it's not a race, and I have plenty of time. I suspect the next couple of days are going to be some tough hiking, seeing as how I have so many big hills to get up. But I've been surprised before.

Sunday 4/27

ReeRee's (my ex-wife's) birthday. Happy birthday, I wish you the best.

First one up after a rather restless night. An older guy in the shelter snored very loudly most all night. At one point shortly after turning in, my ear was ringing briefly, so I listened for a message. Metaphysically speaking, when my ear rings it's because someone is trying to tell me something. What I got was, "Have compassion." I had been a little annoyed at the snoring, but learned to cope with it.

When I got on the trail, I noticed that it seemed to be an effort to hike. I got to wondering where my head was and came back to last night's conversation with the snorer about the trail. In a nutshell, he said it was all up and down, and all hard. Maybe that set my mood for this morning. Then I got thinking about the guy – maybe all he has known in his life is hardship, maybe that's why his breath does not come easily. So I wished him peace and that he may know joy in his life. I guess that's what the lesson on compassion was for. And after that, the trail got easier. Then I got thinking about Stef's comment about the bears – she said I needed to go inward. So, much of the morning I was in my head. Trouble is, I couldn't find anything.

The trail is fairly level and I make five miles pretty easily. But the weather changes and it starts to rain, then in a few miles it starts to rain hard. I make it to a shelter just about the time it cuts loose, so I pause for some food and put on my rain suit. Since I had been only six miles and wanted to do thirteen, I kept on. At mile eleven, I stopped in a shelter for a hot meal. When that was done, I went the last two miles to Double Springs Gap Shelter, the nearest one to Clingman's Dome. I will be over that in the morning.

An interesting thing about most of the shelters here in the Smokeys is that the fronts of them are closed in with a chain-link fence to keep you safe from bears. Kind of a reverse theory on zoos, I think. Oh, early on this morning I saw three wild hogs. Not much of a view of them either as they did not stick around long to socialize.

Monday 4/28

Raining pretty good this morning, had been most of the night. Just the Wolverine and I stayed in the shelter. Oatmeal for breakfast, pack up and underway. Only three miles to Clingman's Dome, rain most of the way. At the top it is so cloudy the visibility is about two hundred feet. From the top of the tower, the trees below are just shadows. Well, I'm over the highest point of the trail now. The trail is wet, of course, with many puddles and running water. This section of the trail is rockier than it has been, but good going. After the dome, the trail looks more like one in Maine – rough, wet and with fir trees grown up close to the sides of it. With the clouds so low and the trees so close, there isn't much for views today. Mostly, today was a slog with little to see.

We hit Newfound Gap about 3:00 where a ridge runner (trail worker/assistant) informed us it was going to get cold tonight – in the 20's, maybe the teens. He would have taken us to town, had we wanted to go, rather than stay out in such cold weather. Perhaps if he was going to Cherokee, North Carolina instead of Gatlinburg, Tennessee, I might have gone, but Wolverine and I make for Icewater Shelter three miles away. We arrive about 5:30, get supper and ready to call it a night. The sky is clearing and it will get chilly, but certainly not life threatening.

A young fellow from Maine just got in – he's finishing his hike started last year going north to south. He'll be done in a couple weeks. Well, I'm done for the day.

Tuesday 4/29

It got cold overnight! And it snowed – about two inches around the shelter. I figured around Clingman's Dome I'd see snow, so I wasn't disappointed. The morning is cold, so breakfast and dishes were done in the sleeping bag. Wolverine and I got on the trail around 8:00. I thought the trail would be slow due to snow and ice, but it really was pretty good. The worst part of it was having to put on cold, hard, frozen boots, but after a mile or two they were reasonably comfortable.

As the morning progressed and the clouds started to lift there were very nice views of surrounding mountains, the higher ones covered with snow. One of the interesting things about this section of the hike is that if you look over your left shoulder, you're looking at Tennessee, whereas if you look over your right, you are looking at North Carolina. Pretty neat. About 11:30 we met three hikers; one of them said the temperature was a balmy 33°.

Fun in the snow.

I don't know what it was about today, whether it was the third day in cold, wet boots, the cold wind that seemed to be constantly blowing, or the trail that seemed to be all uphill, but by mid-afternoon I was not enjoying it so much. But the scenery is beautiful! The forest looks more like Maine with thickly growing soft and hard woods. By mid-afternoon the sky cleared and there were many nice views – still something about it was not that enjoyable. I guess in everything, even a hike in paradise, you can have a down day.

Around 3:00 we got to a shelter thirteen miles from last night's. I debated pushing on, thinking about the timing and getting to the Hot Springs post office, but given that today is Tuesday and I still have about three days of hiking to get to Hot Springs, I decide to call it a day. Besides, this shelter has a low, brown, metal roof that the sun is beating down on, so I'm taking the opportunity to do some washing and drying. Even with the sun out, the air is chilly – it could be cold tonight! Another interesting thing about the shelters here is that most of them have fire places built in. So with some enthusiastic firewood gathering (tree climbing included), a nice warm fire goes a long way to driving chills from the bones as well as the spirit.

Wednesday 4/30

Yeah, it got cold last night, but not as cold as the night on Tray Mt., Georgia. One guy in the shelter had a cell phone with a thermometer (?) that put the temperature at 26° at 7:00. I got breakfast, packed up, and was on the trail by 7:30 on a beautiful, bright, clear morning. I hiked alone this morning, enjoying the solitude.

The high elevation forest is primarily fir with some hardwoods, and grows close to the trail. Now and again the trail approached an edge close enough to allow a view. Quite literally, the right side of the trail is North Carolina, and the left side is Tennessee. North Carolina is still high mountain country, whereas Tennessee drops into an expansive valley. In any direction, the land is very pretty.

Early afternoon I come to the Mt. Crammerer side trail which I was advised, by Wolverine, to take for an awesome view. I did. It was. At the end of the side trail is a stone fire tower appearing to sit out on the very end of the Earth. The 270° view of surrounding mountains was breathtaking. It's too bad, but it is often the case, that the AT does not go to these spots of incredible vistas. To see them you have to take side trails, and sometimes after hiking so many miles you don't feel like doing another half mile or mile. This sight was definitely worth the extra time and steps. And the day is beautiful! Sunny and warm with a gentle breeze. As far as I'm concerned, this is hiker heaven.

I was joined by a woman as I was coming down the mountain, and we hiked together to the next lean-to; a very pleasant woman out on a solo ten day hike. She was hiking with the most enormous external frame backpack I'd ever seen, and although she said it didn't weigh much, it was at least ten pounds heavier than mine. It fairly dwarfed her small stature. At the lean-to she told me about her regime of at least wiping down her body every night to remove the day's sweat and grime, and about clean clothes and dirty clothes. Very sound information, and a practice I adopted for myself.

The trail is easy today, mostly downhill and in good shape, and I make eight miles in four hours. Slow by some folks, a good pace for me. For the first ten miles there is no change in the forest, but after the Mt. Cammerer side trail, the trail starts dropping steadily. At about 4,000' the forest starts to change again, becoming more hardwoods and rhododendrons. At about 3,000', trees are leafed out and flowers are in bloom – quite a change from the high country of 5,000 to 6,000 feet. And, surprise, surprise, it's noticeably warmer. It really is a different world here compared to up high. Tomorrow I will hit the hostel for a few groceries to get me to Hot Springs, and maybe a shower. Hot Springs is thirty-seven miles, or three days away; I ought to be there Sunday afternoon.

Thursday 5/1

Woke to a bright, sunny day. The trail to the highway was quite easy and very pretty, especially down near the highway where the stream joins the Pigeon River. The forest is very pretty at this lower elevation as everything is in bloom, some different than the high country. I got to a hostel at the next road in good time, picked up a few groceries and called my babe. Back on the trail I start climbing as I head up Snowbird Mt. at 4263', and find the forest changing back to hardwoods not yet budded out.

The climb up was warm, but once on top I cooled quickly with the wind that was blowing over the bare top. I feel motivated to get some miles behind me as the past few days I don't seem to have hiked many miles. And another motivator was seeing an entry from D in one of the shelter logs that said he was hoping to meet up with me again, maybe by Hot Springs, as he missed my company and conversation. That made me feel awful good. Well, I'm certain that if I don't catch up to him in Hot Springs, I will in the near future.

I'm in Brown Gap tonight, twenty-three miles from Hot Springs, and am hoping to get into town fairly early Saturday. We'll see. I'm camped with Rance, a very nice fellow from Florida, originally from upstate New York, and his great old dog. We enjoyed our suppers and wonderful conversation by a warm, crackling campfire. A real nice guy, his company is quite enjoyable – a very pleasant camp mate.

Friday 5/2

Fell right off to sleep real quick and slept very well. I find I sleep best in my tent. I got going early and said so-long to Rance. Since I move faster than he does, I doubt I'll see him on the trail again. The start of the day's trail was uphill for a mile. I don't particularly like to start my day off going uphill, I'd rather ease into the day and allow my body to warm and limber up before anything strenuous. But once beyond the first mile, the trail got pretty easy and I started making good time. Before long I'm on the summit of Max Patch, a wide open mountain meadow probably a mile long, presenting terrific views of the surrounding countryside. What gorgeous country this is!

I'm feeling motivated today and I move right along. As is typical this time of year, the low elevations are in bloom while the upper lands have not yet budded out. I'm noticing even more changes in the forest now – there are more pines and hemlocks mixed in with the hardwoods. Though even in the course of a day the forest can change greatly – sometimes open hardwood ridges, sometimes softwood thickets, sometimes a mixture of both, sometimes groves of rhododendrons, no matter what the flora in an area may be, this land is always very lovely.

At Walnut Mt. Shelter I stopped for a rest and a snack. I met two ladies, Grace and Stardust, in for the same. They are thru-hiking as well. Grace is from the area, Stardust is from Boston via Bar Harbor. A couple times Stardust said maybe we'd hike together along the trail, or maybe in Maine. Never say never, but at the rate they moved I'd be surprised if I saw them again. While at the shelter, I heard from another hiker that there is a nuisance bear in the area that likes to rob hiker's back packs. In fact, one hiker, who had hung his food bag above his tent for the night, had a rude awakening when the bear, in an effort to get his food, lost his footing and fell on the fellow's tent – with him in it! Some people have all the fun…

Today I have climbed over two high mountains, plus all the little hills and valleys in between, and have traveled twenty miles. It was a good day to make some miles, my most to date, but I don't know that I'll do it again anytime soon. When I got to the shelter at 6:00, I had had enough. I didn't even bother to cook supper, just ate the last of my day food. I'm camped yet again with Wolverine, who I will be hiking into Hot Springs with in the morning. Hot Springs means a shower, laundry, groceries, mail and phone calls. It is rumored there are no rooms available in town due to some festival, so I don't think I'll stay the night. But that may change.

Saturday 5/3

Got up and going, skipping breakfast, and headed for town. I will never again believe anyone when they say the trail is all downhill. I'm hiking with Wolverine this morning, and he has hiked this section of trail before. He assured me that it was an easy downhill to town. It wasn't. The trail to town is just over three miles, but I'd say a mile of it was uphill. Not steep uphill, but when you're expecting something else, it seems harder than it is. So it goes.

The Wolverine and I got to town just about 8:30 and went straight to the diner for breakfast. Breakfast was good and we met up with a number of other hikers, one of whom was Needles, whom I hadn't seen for more than a week. He was staying in town, so I asked if I could shower in his motel room – he said sure. When done at the diner, I took care of business at the post office, then went to Needles' room to shower. Man, did that feel good!! While at the motel, I chatted with another couple hikers, and one of them showed me his cook pot that a bear had bitten through while he was camped at Walnut Mt. Shelter – the same place where the fellow got sat on by a bear. A weasel-y looking fellow drove up in a battered pick-up delivering something in a paper bag to the other hikers. They told me it was moonshine (no doubt), and that the bootlegger was none other than the town mayor. They swore it was so!

After the shower, I put in laundry, picked up some groceries, and called home. Stef was running frazzled, so she cut me short; sister Kath and Fuzz, my son, could not be reached, but I left messages saying all was well. Laundry and re-supplying being done, I sort of dawdled around trying to decide if I was going to stay the night, or move on. Come about 3:00, I'd had enough of Hot Springs, a rather dumpy, red neck town, so I got a meal at the diner, a couple more food items, made calls to Stef and Beck, my daughter, said good-bye to Wolverine, and headed out of town.

Now, when I say that Hot Springs is a dumpy, red neck town, I'm referring to the west half of town. The east half, just as soon as you cross the bridge, is an array of neat, upscale shops and eateries, and has an entirely different air about it. Still, no place I wanted to be.

About three miles out of town I started to feel at ease, like I had my mind back. For today, I did eight miles, not bad considering the time I spent dubbing in town. I came out of town with a different, or rather re-confirmed attitude. For many hikers the chance to get to town is a big event, one that is much looked forward to. For me, getting to town means cleaning and re-supply – I'm just not much of a social butterfly, I don't like all the commotion of a town. For all the talk and enthusiasm I'd been hearing about going to Hot Springs, I found it to be an uneasy place – one where I didn't want to spend any time – and I was pleased to be back in the woods.

Sunday 5/4

My plan to sleep under the stars came to an end with a few raindrops pattering on my head. I jumped up and hurriedly set up the tent, and got my gear under cover. It didn't rain a lot, but I'd have been wet for sure. The day dawned clear and bright and the trail started off gently, but a few miles into it, something happened. The trail didn't change significantly, my outlook towards it did.

It seemed like all at once my knee started hurting, and I felt like I didn't want to do this anymore. Right away I asked myself where my head was – it sure wasn't on the trail. My first thought was that having a conversation with Stef is difficult, what with all the emotions involved. That was just part of it. Mostly, I just didn't feel like trudging up another hill. Then came the conversation with myself about getting my head on the trail. It started with,

"You're walking the Appalachian Trail. In the Appalachian Mountains. The APPALACHIAN MOUNTAINS, what did you expect?!"

I guess I had had the notion these mountains were more rolling hills, but they're not – they're steep, rugged mountains. And I'll be hiking in them the whole way, so I'd better get used to it.

The change wasn't instantaneous, but I felt it. After a while I was gawking at the landscape, noticing the bird song and the breeze in the trees, and I remembered why I was here. The rest of the day's hike, though often steep and rather dry, went well. I stopped about 5:00 this evening having done fifteen miles, and other than tired from the work, I feel good.

Monday 5/5

I slept well. Up and going in good season, the first one out. As I expected, the trail started right off uphill, and stayed that way for maybe a mile. The day is clear and bright, but cool, though in a short amount of time I am warmed up.

What an unusual trail day! It started with a long, gradual rise, leveled out some, then went up onto the boney spine of the mountain range. This narrow ridge literally separates North Carolina and Tennessee. Looking right you looked into North Carolina, looking left you looked into Tennessee. And the trail was rocky! It was a scramble up, over and around rough rock. It reminded me of trails in Maine. Once over the spine, it dropped and leveled out, only to repeat the process a little further on. Still the trail dropped and rose, dropped and rose, sometimes through ridges of hardwoods, groves of pine and mix, or groves of rhododendrons. A couple times the trail rose over balds – long, grassy meadows up on the hills – and for quite a stretch the trail was part of an old road.

Anyone home?

After leaving camp this morning, I briefly encountered six other hikers, but mostly I hiked in my own solitude. I like it that way. I almost made camp at 4:00 thinking the next water supply was six miles and a 1500' climb away – more than I wanted to do after having already come thirteen miles. So I was trailside cooking my supper when a hiker I'd past earlier came back by and told me of a nice stream just over three miles away. Thinking that 4:00 was too early to quit, I finished supper and got under way. Now, I'm not a fast hiker, but I can make tracks when I want, and this afternoon I wanted to.

Tonight I'm camped at the site of an old homestead with a nice stream across the trail. Why the data book didn't list this water source – a beauty – I'll never know. The three buildings that were part of the homestead have long since given themselves over to the forest, and what remains is a nice, peaceful place with scattered remnants of a previous occupation. I always wonder what might have befallen the homesteaders to make them give up on their home, their livelihoods. Only the forest knows now.

Oh, another thing about today – I passed four grave sites, at what seemed to be just random places in the woods, where folks were laid to rest. One of them, a Millard Haines, born 1850, died 1863, is very much tended to as there are newer flowers, flags and notes left at the site. The graves just seemed to be out in the middle of nowhere. As good a place as any, I suppose.

Tuesday 5/6

Slept well last night, cowboy camping as I did. Woke to another bright, clear day. I was a little lazy getting going, but not very much so. The day started with a climb, but a gentle one. For as much as yesterday's trail varied, today's trail does not seem to change much.

A little bit onto the trail I heard a dog bark. The bark sounded just like Hannah's excited voice when she was after something. Hannah was my dog I had to give up when I took to the trail as I could not find anyone to take care of her while I was gone. I got thinking about her and wondering, praying that I had done what was best for her. And then I started crying. It seemed that once I started, I was crying about all sorts of things. I realized I had made some unwise decisions in my life, and these decisions were based on a lack of respect, and not listening to my heart. From now on, decisions will be better thought out, will come from the heart. That was the big time for today.

I hiked nineteen miles today, and apart from being up on Big Bald, a high, expansive mountaintop meadow, the scenery never really seemed to change much. The woods are getting thicker, so views from the trail are not as frequent. At one point I learned I was hours behind D, so I moved right along in hopes I would catch him. At 5:30 I found I was four hours behind him, and instead of calling it a day where I was, I decided to go another three miles to the next campsite in hopes of catching him. If nothing else, maybe I'd close the gap by a couple hours. Well, he wasn't in camp, so maybe I'll catch him tomorrow before Erwin, Tennessee.

I'm a day or more earlier than I thought I'd be – I hope I'm not too early to get my packages at the post office. I'll get a place in town tomorrow night, but I don't want to stay two nights.

I never wore my knee brace today because when I got up this morning my right knee and ankle were sore. I think I considered the brace a crutch, and so I favored my left so much I think I put a strain on my right. After nineteen miles, my left knee still feels good, so I think I'm going to use both legs equally and see how that goes. Yeah, I know, but I'm listening to my body.

Wednesday 5/7

A restless night, it seemed I just couldn't get comfortable. I wonder if it was due to pushing a nineteen miler yesterday. So I rolled out a little later and was slower getting going. The morning is a little cloudy, wet weather coming? The trail is pretty easy today, but I kind of feel like I'm struggling. It's only thirteen miles to Erwin, so I'm in no hurry.

The scenery changes quite a bit today – sometimes mature hardwoods, and then you round a bend and it's pine and hemlock. The changes are nice, I like them. There was quite a lengthy section where there were many dead trees, mostly pine, which left the canopy open and the land hot and dry. For quite a distance the forest was burned – a controlled burn – in order to minimize the chances of a serious fire. As I tottered along, I realized the reason I wasn't moving well today was in part due to having pushed hard yesterday, but mostly I hadn't drank enough water – either yesterday or today.

It wasn't long before I got to the last shelter before Erwin. I had done eight miles, and had five to go. But those last five miles, especially the last two, seemed to take an awfully long time. I got down to the road crossing about 3:30, which would have been about right for a fifteen or sixteen mile day ending about 5:30. So, all things considered, I wasn't as slow today as I thought.

Right away you come to Uncle Johnny's Hostel, and I met a few of the speedy hikers who took off and left me in the dust a week or more ago. They hike fast, but stop often and for longer periods than I do. The old tale of the tortoise and the hare. I asked about D, but they said he barely stopped and was back on the trail. Also, I had heard that Wookie and Wasabi, formerly Blaine and Shawn, had asked about me – they are a day or more ahead of me. Perhaps I'll catch up with those characters by Trail Days in Damascus. I'm looking forward to Damascus, I think it'll be something of a milestone for me – by then having three states behind me.

I went to the post office, no package, then went to start laundry and go to supper. I'm now in my hotel room in Erwin, it's 9:40 and I'm done in. I never stay up this late on the trail, typically I turn in by 8:00, but I've had phone calls to make and my journal to write, so I'm up late.

While I was going through my pack tonight, I was pulling out the rolls of exposed film so I could send them home. To my initial astonishment and great pleasure, I "found" the roll of film I had lost back in North Carolina. Sure, you could say it was there all along, but I'm telling you the truth, the roll of film was nowhere in my pack when I first searched for it. Asking for its return, and my belief in the works of Great Spirit, is what returned that roll of film to me.

Thursday 5/8

I walked into town light yesterday, and out heavy today. Eight day's worth of food – ugh! All business taken care of, still no package at the post office (another request to have it forwarded to the next town I would visit), I got back on the trail about 12:30. The trail out of town was very pretty and easy through tall, straight hemlock, pine and maple. The trail followed a meandering stream where at one foot bridge I stayed a short while to watch a trout that was in a clear, shallow pool.

As I continued on, I realized I was in love – with life, Spirit and myself. It is such a glorious event to be on this walk – undoubtedly it is the best thing I have ever done for myself. Thanks again, Spirit!

The trail today is very nice and I'm shooting for Deep Gap, twelve miles from town. About 5:00 the sky got real heavy and a light rain started. I thought about continuing, but I decided to quit while it was not raining hard, and I set up under the canopy of a large hemlock. Better to keep my outfit dry, I figure. For the most part I'm staying dry under this tree, so I think stopping here was a good idea. Besides, eight miles since 12:30 isn't bad.

Sitting here writing I realize how much I miss my gal, and how much I would like to be with her. I think of what I enjoy doing with her – the quiet times, the fun, silly times, curling up with her at night. These will be my thoughts when I crawl into my sleeping bag and listen to the rain patter on the roof.

Friday 5/9

I slept well last night under the hemlock tree. I went to sleep with my arms wrapped around my hottie – in my mind. And at some point during the night, I dreamt that Stef and I were making love, but it seemed like more than a dream, like it was actually happening on some level. Cyber sex? I wonder if Stef had the same experience.

Very light rain this morning, had a dry breakfast and got packed up in good season. Since it's still raining I start off with my rain suit, but am soon sweating a lot, so I take it off. I figure, "So, I'll get wet." Dumb move. It is a cool morning as well as rainy, and before very long I'm cold and need to put on the coat for warmth. At Deep Gap Shelter I put on more clothing as I am shivering with the cold and I don't seem to be warming up very quickly. But eventually I come around. The trail is interesting and changes often, but due to the heavy clouds and rain the views are limited. By noon the sky is breaking up and the hiking is good.

But today was much more than just a hike, I went inside my head a lot. The mother of our kids had been in many of my dreams, for some odd reason. I was thinking about that and wondering why and I thought, "unfinished business." I took a moment to think about what had been, and said, "I forgive you and thank you." And I smiled and felt good. At one time I was just enjoying the day and I thanked Spirit for all the gifts. And I'm in love. This walk has opened my eyes, my mind, and my heart. I feel like I've just begun my metamorphosis, and am interested is seeing what a change I will experience. Of course, the hike itself is a grand adventure. I'm so grateful that I'm able to experience this.

Saturday 5/10

I caught up with D at the Clyde Smith Shelter last night – it was real good to see him. He said Wookie and Wasabi had left about an hour ago, and they asked about me. A very pleasant, merry evening in camp catching up with folks I hadn't seen for a while.

I was the first one on the trail this morning – typically – and upon getting to the top of the hill I saw a deer, the first one in a long time. About a mile from camp I saw a nice spot to practice Tai Chi. Halfway through the form I watched a coyote trot up the trail. My thought was, "I wonder what the message is?" The next time I talk to Stef, I'll ask. After a short bit the others from camp came along, none of them had seen the coyote – or me for that matter – as I stood thirty feet off the trail. I spent the day hiking with D, a very pleasurable day.

Today was the steepest, longest climb yet – up Roan Mt. On the trail up Roan, D and I picked a mess of ramps, a plant with a tuberous bulb, and reportedly a flavor something like a cross between onion and garlic. We figured they'd be good in tonight's suppers.

The day that had threatened rain turned out to be quite a nice day. Yeah, the trail up Roan was long and somewhat steep, but not nearly as bad as it was made out to be. Past Roan Mt. was Jane Bald which provided great views of mountains ranging off in the distance all about. Maybe because today is Saturday and a nice day, we encountered a lot of people on the trail. We even got some trail magic – a can of Fresca and a granola bar.

For tonight's supper, D and I fried up the ramps in olive oil and had them in our meals. Yum! However, one aspect of ramps is that they have a tendency to kick the digestive system into overdrive, so the evening was gassy with frequent trips to the potty. Maybe if we hadn't had a quarter pound apiece…

I'm the last one up trying to do this log by what little light is remaining as the sun set a while ago. This trip continues to be – as I expect it will be to the end – an awesome experience.

Sunday 5/11

The wind picked up in a big way last night, and brought rain with it. The shelter we were in faced right into the weather, so there were damp sleeping bags in the morning. A warm breakfast and going by 8:00.

The trail starts easy, but with blowing clouds and rain there are no views to be had. In a couple of miles we come to an open field where the wind is blowing quite strong. The trail ascends to the Roan Highlands, up Little and Big Humps, and the weather is very harsh. The wind is blowing a steady thirty miles an hour, gusting to fifty or more, and with the rain and clouds made for the most difficult walk I have yet to experience on the trail. The wind blew so hard at times that I had to angle and lean hard into it to stay on my feet and make progress. It seemed to take a long time to get across the highlands, and was quite taxing. The unfortunate aspect is that with a visibility of less than one hundred yards, I am unable to take in what must be some fantastic scenery. The hike in that wind gave me some insight into what it must be like for those who climb mountains like Denali or Everest. After being battered about for over an hour, we finally made it down into the tree line into what seemed like a whole different world. What a relief!

About noon, D and I stopped for a snack. Just before eating, there was a thunderstorm very near to us that lasted no more than fifteen minutes. Directly afterward the sky cleared right up – just like that! We had a pleasant walk to a nearby restaurant where D, Geoff, Bad Diner, another hiker and I took in the $10 buffet. For $50 we all staggered out stuffed!

D and I then went to Dollar General to get enough grub to get us to Damascus, then caught a ride back to the trailhead. Shortly onto the trail, the wind picked back up and the rain came again. It was eight miles to the next shelter, but at the late hour we'd never make it before dark. I have a tent, so I can make camp anywhere, but D is without, so I started thinking about shelter. I thought, "Maybe we'll come to a road crossing where there'll be a house, and maybe we'll be able to sleep in a barn." Shortly afterward, we came to a road and there was Buck Mountain Baptist Church, with a meeting in progress. We took off our wet rain gear, went in and sat down. After the meeting I approached the preacher about sleeping on the front stoop as it is out of the weather. He said as long as we didn't make a mess, it'd be okay. I knew we'd find a house where we could sleep out of the weather. Spirit always provides. Thank You.

Monday 5/12

Just a little bit wet last night, otherwise a good night's sleep. We had breakfast, and got underway about 7:30. It's still quite overcast, but the rain is minimal. The trail is easy and we make good mileage. The forest changes a lot today and there are a lot of streams in comparison to what there has been. At some point we came to a small valley alongside a small river – a lovely area. Our intent today is to make it to Moreland Gap Shelter, a fifteen mile hike. About ten miles into it, while standing on a footbridge over a small stream, Wookie and Wasabi come along. It has been a long time since we have seen them. We had a nice reunion.

The day turned clear, or mostly so, about 2:00, but it is still a cool day. As I walked, I was thinking about how my knees have been hurting. Knees/joints represent direction in life, and the ease of change. So I was thinking about what my issue is – my relationship with Stef. I sure do love the woman, she's very special. But I discovered that I still have concerns about commitment. It's a learning event, and I'm learning to receive as well as give love. As I told D today, I'm going to walk myself healthy on this trip. When I get through with this, I'm expecting I'll be ready for anything, and looking forward to it.

Tuesday 5/13

Woke to a still, clear day – what a blessing! The temp is cool, about 40, but holds promise to be a splendid day. Breakfast done and underway about 7:30.

Since we camped in a gap we have to climb right away. The climb is easy and brief, and the trail afterward is very nice. The forest changes as we descend and is beautiful all the way. There is more variety to the land than there was earlier in the trip as there are more rock formations and the growth is more diverse. For the first time on the trip, there were laurels in bloom. They are very lovely in hues of light pink to lavender.

At the foot of the mountain, we come to a field maybe ten acres in size where both D and I stretch out in the grass to absorb the wonderful sunshine. The past couple days were mostly rainy, so it feels really good! Down on the road, we get some magic, converse a while with the angel, then head to the hostel so D can get alcohol. Many edible goodies to be had, a new long-sleeved shirt for me, and we head back for the trail. A little more magic and conversation and we're on our way.

This section of the trail follows Laurel Stream, and is absolutely beautiful. The day is bright and warm, the laurels are in bloom, and the forest is captivating. I took a side trail down to the stream; D came down a few minutes later, took off his boots, and washed some. I took off my clothes for a bath. My first bath in a stream – the water was chilly, but oh so refreshing! The trail follows what might have been an ancient river bed as down in the ravine the stream churns along. It is magical here.

In a bit the trail descends to Laurel Falls, a very pretty waterfall. We spend time here just soaking it all in. Ohm (whom I hadn't seen since Hot Springs?) unexpectedly joins us. The trail follows the stream, nearly right alongside it for a ways, and there are a few wonderful campsites along the way. A mile further and we come to a campsite that is too pretty to pass up. Even though it is only 5:00, we make camp.

Today has been the shortest full day of hiking I've had, just eight miles, but the scenery and the day have been absolutely glorious! Thank You!! When I'm out here hiking, I think a thousand thoughts – many of them good ones – and I always think I'll write them into the journal, but by day's end I seldom remember them to do so. Like yesterday when I was thinking about my knees, what it boiled down to was: It's all about love. Giving and receiving love. I can't begin to express how I feel the change in me, but I'm becoming more at peace, and more in love.

I'm sort of on a schedule to get to Damascus by Saturday morning – I want to be sure to get to the post office before it closes Saturday. Once Damascus is done, I know I will have no more schedule, and I will be wherever, whenever I get there. More important than the beautiful sights I have seen along the trail is the journey I have made, and am making, into my heart and soul. Truly, I am falling in love – with life. I'm walking home to myself.

Wednesday 5/14

Overcast today, high, thin clouds, so no rain. The trail started easy, crossing a stream a couple times before climbing what is supposed to be the last big mountain before the Whites. But don't ever believe foolish talk, especially trail talk. The climb is nice, but the descent is nicer, and we make eight miles before noon. A little lunch on the shore of Watauga Lake, and we press on for another eight miles.

The eight miles in the afternoon felt more like twelve, and D, Ohm and I seem to be struggling. Actually, I've been off kilter the whole day – I seemed to be catching my toe on every rock and root in the trail, and a couple times I caught myself with my head in the wrong place, and dark thoughts plagued me. I don't know where my head was today. One thing I do know is that I thought of Stef an awful lot, and I wished we were together. We are together – I feel her with me – but I mean physically, so I could hold her and kiss her and... I was fantasizing that she would be in Damascus waiting for me at the trail. Man, how I would enjoy that!

Tonight's campsite is up on a ridge overlooking part of Watauga Lake and the mountains behind. Even though it is overcast, it is still quite pretty. My head has been so far in the clouds and elsewhere today that I walked by a lot of stuff without seeing it. What I have seen is all very lovely – this whole country is – and I am very grateful to be here to experience it.

We have thirty-two miles to go until Damascus, we ought to be there by Friday evening. I'd like to get into town soon enough to get settled, cleaned up, and go out for a good steak supper. We'll see how it goes.

Thursday 5/15

A little lazy getting up and going this morning. D, Ohm and I were packed and underway just after 8:00. It is quite overcast with periods of drizzle and light rain obscuring the views. Still, the trail is very easy today, and the hiking quite pleasurable.

I wondered what the difference was between today's and yesterday's hikes, and what I came up with was that I was pushing to meet a schedule. Yeah, I know – I'm hiking the AT with all the time in the world and I'm pushing to meet a schedule! Ohm, who has been hiking with us for the past few days, is meeting a friend in Damascus, so he really wants to be there tomorrow. Being the fastest hiker of the three, I am urged to take the lead and keep the pace for the others. So I have felt some responsibility to get to Damascus tomorrow for myself as well because I figured my meals real close; I ate the last of my breakfast and supper foods today. I just have some day food for breakfast and midday for tomorrow.

We cruised right along today, going further than we'd planned, so the last leg into Damascus tomorrow will be shorter and quicker than expected. I made a pact with myself: after Damascus there will be no more schedules, and no more hurrying to get anywhere by a certain time. And as much as I enjoy D, I want to hike by myself for a while and get back to my rhythm. I came to do this hike for me, and I'm all through letting someone else's schedule dictate mine. That said, I have enjoyed the company of D and Ohm, but I've missed my own.

4

VIRGINIA

Friday 5/16

Woke to light rain and wind, but today we'll make it to Damascus. Three miles into the trip we encounter Wookie, Wasabi and Wolverine at Abingdon Gap Shelter, what appears to be the oldest, smallest shelter of the trail. Another nice, brief reunion, and we move on. The trail is very easy, and I mention to D that at our present speed, we ought to be in Damascus by 3:00. We walk a ridge the whole way and find it real good going. There aren't anything for views early on as the trees are all leafed out, and the clouds are pretty low.

About noon the sky starts to break and it warms up. Through the trees I can see beautiful, lush, green valleys down below. About 1:00 we get to the Tennessee/Virginia state line, and stop for the required pictures. From here, the trail is pretty much a gradual downhill walk to town, and we step onto asphalt at 2:50. Geez, I'm good.

First stop is the post office for packages – I have only the one I bounced forward. I inquire about rooms, but there are none. Following information from others, we make it to the Baptist church tent and… hot showers! Yee-haa!! I find a place to set up tents across the street in some folk's front yard. Tents set, it's time to do laundry. We have laundry done a little after 6:00, and go out to tent city.

What I call tent city is a field where hikers and vendors set up their tents. It is a congested, busy, noisy place, but there's free food. I got a cup of chili, chips and salsa – all in one cup – and some cookies. That done, I go back for some vegetarian stew. All that done, we go back to town and find wonderful desserts at the

Baptist church tent. Warm blueberry cobbler with vanilla ice-cream – yum yum! And then pecan pie – yum! And then the warm apple cobbler with vanilla ice-cream – yum yum! Along with this are the random cookies and other delectable delights. Yes, I do enjoy food, and with the physical demands of the trail, you can't eat too much. I intend to walk out of here as fat as I can.

All of the food, showers, laundry, places to tent, are provided for hikers out of the kindness of hearts of some really terrific people! Trail Days in Damascus is a celebration of the spirit of the hike. Literally, the whole town opens up to hikers of today and yesterday. It is, indeed, a very heartwarming place to be.

But that's it, I've had enough for the night. By 9:00, I'm done for the day and turn in. I did it, I got to Damascus for Trail Days.

Saturday 5/17

Up and out for breakfast shortly after 6:00. The restaurant is not yet open, so D, Ohm and I get hot chocolate and coffee. I called Stef and had a pleasant chat which got teary-eyed when I said I missed her. And I do – a lot.

Most of the day is spent poking around: getting a hair cut – yeah! – looking for new boots, and just checking things out. I'd been hiking since early on in Georgia with an old pair of work boots, and they just weren't cutting it for me – I was looking to upgrade. There are a lot of vendors set up, and everything a hiker could need is available in some tent. Along with vendors, there are performers around all day. Trail Days is BIG happenings in Damascus!

There's a parade at 2:00, and just before it starts I sit and listen to a bluegrass band. The parade was short, but good fun. I had never seen a parade where water balloons and soaker squirt guns were not only accepted, but encouraged. The exchange was equal from both the parade doers and parade viewers. An old woman I was talking with said, with some tone of disgust, that it wasn't always like that, and that every year it gets worse. And then she dashes for a water balloon that didn't break so she could hurl it back into the parade! I wonder why it keeps getting worse…

After the parade, D and I cruised the vendor row where D got footwear and a water filter, I got nothing. Then it was off to the grocery store – a real store with a good selection of dried fruits! I walk out with about fifteen pounds of good food. It'll be a bear to carry for a few days, but worth it.

Trail Days is great fun, and the town folk are very friendly and hospitable. I'm glad I stopped for the day, but I'm ready to move on – I've had enough of crowds and commotion. Tomorrow morning I'll be heading for the trail.

Sunday 5/18

Woke to a pretty, clear morning. Last night was late for me, about 11:00 when I got to sleep, and this morning was early – the birds were singing loudly before the sun even lighted the sky. I got up rather groggy and went to mail a post card and make calls home. I had good conversations with brother Tom, and Stef. The more I'm away from Stef, and the more I talk to her, the more I fall for her. It sure will be great to see her again. After phone calls, I got my pack together and D, Ohm and I went for breakfast. Afterward, D and I headed out of town about 11:30.

Once on the trail I start to settle down and feel at ease. The forest here is lovely, a good mix of hard and soft wood as well as laurel and rhododendron. Also along this trail is more water than I saw in most of North Carolina. We walked along a large stream for quite a distance. Since the day clouded in mid-morning, there aren't much for views. Couple that with the trees being all leafed out, and the view is pretty much what's just in front and beside you. The past couple days, hikes have been much easier than they were early on. I hear that's the way it gets, the trail is more gentle and you start to hike with the ridges instead of crossing them. But don't believe everything you hear about the trail.

D and I get to Saunders Shelter about 4:30, shortly before it starts to rain. Wookie, Wasabi, Nicole, Party Animal and three other hikers all come in a little later. We're glad we're here early, and have our places all set in the shelter. I haven't told D yet that I want to hike by myself for a while, but I will tomorrow. I know he'll understand. I'm looking forward to time by myself.

Monday 5/19

Slept good last night, but I was still up later than I expected. Wookie and Wasabi love their camp fires, so I was up a while enjoying it with them. By the time I leave camp, the sky is mostly clear. I was the first one out of camp, D was right behind me. When I stopped to pee, he'd caught up to me. I told him I needed my own space for a while, and he understood. I enjoy the company of others, but after a while being with someone else so much infringes on my space – I lose my own rhythm and feel out of place.

The day is wonderfully bright and the forest is lovely. There are more little streams than there were in North Carolina. The trail descends into a pretty, little valley with a nice stream flowing through it, and deer tracks in the trail. Before long, the AT joins the Virginia Creeper trail, made on an old railroad bed, and runs alongside a large, fast flowing stream. This area is gorgeous indeed. I think Stef and I need to bicycle this trail.

In what seems like a short amount of time, I come to the next shelter, six miles from where I stayed last night. Being the only one there, and it being very peaceful, I deliberated between staying there and moving on. Toward evening, the serenity probably won't last, and in the interest of getting to the post office in Atkins in time, I move on. Sometimes there are schedules to meet when it comes to making it to the post office in time to get your next re-supply. The trail led me up to Buzzard Rocks where there were terrific views of green valleys shouldered by lush mountain ranges. This land is certainly very lovely, and I feel blessed to be here to experience the splendor that Spirit has provided. Thanks again!

It's breezy and rather cool this evening, and we're supposed to have rain again later tonight and tomorrow. By 6:00 I'm set up in a pretty decent spot, fairly out of the wind sort of under the boughs of a large fir tree. It's not an "official" campsite, but it ought to be fine for me tonight. I'm the only one here. As soon as supper is done, I'm turning in for the night. I'm looking forward to that.

Tuesday 5/20
Didn't sleep real well, not as well as I'd hoped. I think maybe it was due to the highly salted pre-packaged food I had for supper. Wookie walked by before I broke camp, so I walked with him a while. The trail is easy, and I make good mileage with little effort. The forest is much more diverse here than it was in North Carolina, and is very pretty. Before long, I cross a highway and start to climb up a meadow. These high mountain meadows are very pretty, and allow for great panoramas. The climb up Mt. Rogers, one of the highest points on the AT in Virginia, is easy.

Along the way up Mt. Rogers, I felt as though I was hiking a trail in Maine – it was rocky, rooted, muddy and the fir trees would brush your shoulders. While taking a break at Thomas Knob shelter, Wasabi caught up to me, and we spent the rest of the day hiking together. Once past the shelter, the mountain opens to meadows. I just love these open, sprawling mountain meadows. The air is sweet, and the views breathtaking. We are coming to Grayson Highlands State Park. The highlands are known for the wild ponies that roam and graze these meadows, and one of them came right up to me and enjoyed the salt that he licked out of my hand. Another one was quite bold and would try to get into the pack for something to eat. They are beautiful animals in a beautiful place. I imagine the early natives must have felt blessed to live here. This is another place to bring Stef.

After leaving the meadows the trail winds down through some very lovely forest lands. Of the states I have hiked in so far, Virginia is by far the prettiest. And Wasabi is a very good hiking companion – we share a lot of the same thoughts and ideals about life. We are camped together tonight in a hollow between a meadow and a stream. It is a great spot, and we have a nice campfire going. Life is good!!!

Friends in Grayson Highlands

Wednesday 5/21

Woke to a heavy sky, but no rain. The morning is breezy and cool, about 40°. I was on the trail just after 8:00. I don't know what time Wasabi got up and going, he was still sacked in when I left. The first part of the trail meanders through woods and meadows. The meadows have many rock outcroppings, some in strange formations. One looked like a huge egg on its side, balanced on a pedestal. This part of Virginia is very pretty indeed – well worth another visit.

As I walked along, I got thinking about the dreams I had of my brother Jeff the past couple of nights, and decided I needed to call home. Troutdale is sixteen miles from where I camped. I had it in my mind that there was an outfitter that I wanted to go see, so I move along quickly. After three hours of walking, I make it to the next shelter, seven miles away. The day is clearing nicely, and the forest is very pretty. The terrain changes much during the day giving wonderful views of mountains and valleys hereabouts.

In my endeavor to get to a phone so I can call home, I miss a lot of scenery as I hurry along. At one point in the afternoon, I was taking a break and Wasabi came marching up the trail. We sat briefly, then started making for Troutdale, possible outfitter and a meal.

When we arrived, I called home and found that all was fine. I had the extra pleasure of talking with Stef, who was visiting my brothers. There was no outfitter, but I had a great meal of a salad, a jumbo loaded cheeseburger, onion rings, and a great strawberry shortcake for dessert. Everything was delicious, the best hamburger I'd had, and the price was very reasonable. And when we were done, the owner gave us a ride back to the trail. You can't beat that with a stick!

Today's hike was a little over seventeen miles, but the trail is getting real easy and the hiking very enjoyable. Tonight we are camped in a little glade down off the trail, there is a small stream nearby, and we enjoy a wonderful campfire. Tomorrow night, a bunch of hikers are planning on camping at Partnership Shelter and ordering pizza from town, which is less than a mile away. This hiking business is tough…

Thursday 5/22

Well, actually, yeah, this hiking business is tough. You go to bed sore and tired, and you wake up with feet so swollen you have a hard time pulling your boots on, and ankles and knees that are still hurting from the previous days are begging for mercy. And it's like this every day. You force yourself out of the sleeping bag because you have to pee, then you hobble around until some form of life comes to your weary bones. But once you've had breakfast and are packed up, things are moving pretty well, and a mile up the trail you're all limbered up and feeling pretty good again.

And when you get on the trail early, and the world comes to life with you, it is a peaceful, magical time. This is the time you see the most wildlife, listen to the myriad of song birds, smell the fresh, clean morning air – you feel as though you're the only one around, and that all this splendor was created just for you. And you know in your heart that this is where you're supposed to be – this is heaven on Earth. I am so grateful that I am able to be here to experience these magnificent works of Great Spirit. Tears of joy come to my eyes as I hug a tree and thank Spirit for providing all this.

I woke this morning to mostly clear skies; by mid-morning the sky is completely clear, and the day is superb. The forest is bright and clean, and I walk for hours without seeing another person. The trail has become so much easier that before I know it, I have walked four miles. The first live beings that I encounter is a small herd of cows grazing in a field that I pass through. A young one right on the trail is rather skittish, but the others are totally unconcerned with my presence. I suppose they know they could run me over and stomp me into the ground if they had a mind to, but, like me, they aren't about to bother anyone.

The forest and scenery changes often, so there always seems to be a lovely view. My plan for the day was to make about fifteen miles, leaving ten miles for tomorrow to get to Atkins. As I said, the trails are getting easier, so that by 4:30 I'd made seventeen miles. It seemed too early to stop, but I was at a nice campsite with good water close by, and I was feeling a little tired. I cooked my supper which was very good (I had been given a bag of pumpkin spaghetti with a bunch of good stuff in it), filled my water bottles, and I was rejuvenated enough to go a little further.

I went only a mile more and I am cowboy camping on top of a low mountain. The sun is dropping behind me, and I'm hoping for a nice sunset – provided I can stay awake long enough to see it. In the morning, the sun will make its way over the ridge in front of me, so I ought to be able to enjoy a pleasant sunrise. For now, I'm alone on this ridge top with only a breeze that blows over me. Lying here on Mother Earth, I feel very peaceful as a gentle breeze caresses me.

Stef, my love, I have seen so many wonderful sights so far on this journey that I want to bring you to. Many times during the day I think of you and wish that you were here to share this with me. We will have plenty of time to enjoy others together. Yeah, I guess I'm saying it; I'm more in love with you than I thought I'd ever be with anyone so soon after the divorce. I was ready to go for years before I sought out, or got involved with anyone again. And there you were on that fateful day, and I guess I couldn't resist your pursuing me. Many times I've spoken to Spirit about you, and I'm told to just love – openly and fully. I have to admit that I'm still feeling gun shy, but it's not as intimidating as it was. And yet it feels very right. I guess we'll just see what happens when I get back home.

It was a nice sunset. After supper I lay in my sleeping bag watching the golden light fade from the trees, and then the red/orange sun drop behind a deep blue horizon as it turned the clouds pink and lavender.

Friday 5/23

The sunrise was not so spectacular as it had clouded in overnight. However, there was a band of red/orange just on the horizon that was quite nice. This morning's walk was very pleasant as the trail meandered along a stream through a grove of rhododendron. Before long I come to the turn to the Settler's Museum. It's right alongside the trail, so I went for a look. It's really very lovely and provided a glimpse into farm life at the turn of the century. Tomorrow there are big goings on there with craftsmen and speakers talking about and demonstrating what folks did to survive in that time. And there will be food, refreshments and live music all day.

As I left there and headed for Atkins, I thought about staying at the inn so I could go back there tomorrow. The more I thought about it, the more I realized that I came on this journey to see things, so I decided I'd stay in town and go visit the museum tomorrow. The reason I was debating was because I'd want to bring Stef to come see it as well. I thought it'd be something she'd be interested in, particularly the talk they will have on Native American culture in that period. But I can always come back again.

And in a few miles I was in Atkins. I spent the rest of the day getting cleaned up, made some calls, and went to get my mail. I don't know when it was mailed, but my package wasn't at the post office. Maybe it'll be there tomorrow morning, if not, I'll have to re-supply as best I can, and bounce the package forward. So far, however, the postal service has not been very good about advancing packages – a package due to arrive in Hot Springs, North Carolina was not there, and was to be bounced to Erwin, Tennessee. Again, it was not there and was to be bounced to Damascus, Virginia. So I'll see what I see. I went out to eat at The Barn, by reputation the best eatery nearby, as did most every other hiker staying at the motel. It was a lively, fun-filled group of about ten hikers.

Saturday 5/24

Stef called this morning about 6:00. I was awake, but had not yet gotten up. Last night's conversation with Stef was awkward and didn't flow well. I was delighted when she called back. I had been thinking a lot about her while on the trail. Since I've been out on this walk, my emotions have poured out of me – I cry a lot. I cry when I think of Stef and how much I miss and love her. I cry at the beauty of where I am, and out of gratefulness of being able to be here, and that Spirit has provided all this for me/us. Since I've been out here, I'm more in love – with myself, with Spirit, with life, with Stef. My heart has been opened up, and I think I feel more deeply than I used to. And because of this, the way I feel about Stef has become deeper. Our talk this morning was very nice, and I'm looking forward to our re-re-union. After our talk, I went and picked up my package, went back to the motel to put my pack together, and then headed for the Settler's Museum. Within minutes I hitched a ride right to the museum. Wasabi, D, Unicorn and Pegasus were there, already eating. I ate another breakfast – free food you don't pass up, especially when it's as good as this, and I cruise around checking the place out. The day is absolutely gorgeous, sunny and 60ish with a gentle breeze. I ate some more and went on an educational tour of local flora. Back to the farm for dinner, then to the old school house for a talk on native culture in the area prior to the coming of the white man. We arrived just in time to hear her say, "Thanks for coming." We talked with the lecturer for a while, then went back to the farm for more sight-seeing, and, of course, more food. Sufficiently stuffed, and things winding down at the museum, we decide it's time to get back to the trail. This break from the trail was very relaxing and fun.

Sunday 5/25
Woke early this morning, the first one up and on the trail. The day is clear and mild, and the trail is easy. This section of the trail is the prettiest that I've seen yet. The rhododendrons lining the trail are in bloom with large, pink flowers. Virginia is very lovely indeed. The first part of the day's hike is mostly level, then descends to the first road crossing. Just before the road, the trail cuts through pastures which smell terrifically sweet and fresh. Then the trail starts to change and becomes a roller coaster hike, though the hills are not very tall.

About mid-day the weather gets quite warm, nearing 80°, with no breeze and cloudless skies. At one road crossing, there is a small terrier mix running loose, and she befriends me. I made the mistake of giving her some cheese, so she stays with me as I hike. She is a good little dog, friendly, appears quite affectionate and rather intelligent, but I don't want a dog. I ignore her hoping she'll go away, but she doesn't. I meet up with Low Impact, and since he hikes faster than me she follows him. Good, I'm off the hook.

The trail is up and down a few more hills before dropping down to a large stream in a low land setting. It's quite nice, pretty and peaceful, and would be worth staying here, but I have other plans. In just over a mile I come to a forest service road, then the last three miles of the day. I'm already tired. I've done sixteen miles, but I want to get to the pond that my data book says is just ahead. So I push on.

I don't know, sometimes I'm not too smart. I ought to have called it a day by the stream, fifteen or sixteen miles are the end of my comfort zone, but I forced myself to go the last three miles – mostly uphill. I'm getting exhausted and very sore, but now I'm committed as I'm out of water and need to get to the spring. Maybe one day I'll learn. But I make it, collapse and make supper, then set up camp. The pond I strove to get to is small and solid green with algae, so I'm not going to take the swim I was thinking about. It is, however, a great place to camp high up on a meadow with an extensive view. In camp tonight is Serenity, Low Impact, and, yes, the little dog. The sun set a little bit ago, so I write this by my little light. That's it, I'm tired, I'm done, I'm going to sleep.

Monday 5/26

I woke late this morning – I guess I was pretty well beat when I turned in last night. From where I'd camped, the trail rose gradually almost two miles, and came to a shelter. My back was awful stiff, so I took the time to do a lot of stretching. Even though breakfast wasn't very long ago, I eat a little bit. I met a couple that was hiking with their husky, and told them about our little tag along. They said they'd take her with them and try to find her a good home. There, all done with that dog business.

Today's trail is pretty easy, a gentle roller coaster hike, but it seems to be taking forever to get anywhere. At first I thought I was still sore from yesterday's long hike, but I came to realize that my head just wasn't in the hike today. I don't know if it's because today is Memorial Day – I used to go camping with the kids and my ex-wife on this weekend – but my mind is back home today. I keep thinking I'd like to be back home with the kids and Stef. Not having my head on the trail makes for a very difficult hike.

The only thing to do is keep plugging along. And maybe it was because of my frame of mind, but my feet, ankles and knees were very sore all day. No doubt some of it was because I pushed so hard yesterday. And maybe some of it is due to my deteriorating boots which are no longer very comfortable. In any case, I made only twelve miles today, but it sure felt longer.

I got to Jenkin's Shelter about 5:30 or 6:00, and had it all to myself. Not for long as there are now eight of us here. D, Wasabi, Unicorn and Pegasus – with the little dog, Serenity and a few others are in camp. There is excited talk of a free hiker breakfast being put on by a church group, we just have to be at the next road by a certain time and they will pick us up – if it's still going on. That sounds awfully good, and we plan on making it. It's still fairly early, and I'm all through with supper and chores. I think I'll catch up on rest tonight.

Tuesday 5/27

I was in bed in good season, and slept pretty well. In native lore, I wonder what the significance of deer is. Yesterday I watched a doe for a while, the first I'd seen in weeks, and last night I was visited by deer three times. One time there was a deer that stomped and blew not far from the tent, another time one got scared off by the dog, and there was another that was so close to the tent that it got scared off when I looked up from my bed.

I woke about 6:00, had breakfast, got packed and was underway pretty early. D and Wasabi had left already hoping to get magic. The five mile walk to the road is very easy, after the first uphill mile. I met up with the clan before 9:00. Just after

9:00, the church folks showed up, got a count, and came back with a couple trucks to get us.

At the church there was delicious, home cooked food galore. We had sausages, egg casserole, potato casserole, pancakes, biscuits, banana nut bread, homemade molasses, apple and peach butter, apples and oranges, orange juice and coffee until we were full. The food was very good. And after the meal, we had goodie bags to take with us that were filled with cookies and granola. After the feast, we were taken to town to the post office and grocery store, then brought back to the trailhead. This was incredible trail magic!!!

When we got back to the trail, we walked about fifty yards to the first campsite and called it quits. We were all fat and happy and didn't feel like moving. For myself, I'm nursing shin splints, sore knees and achy feet from the other day's hard run. It's not worth it to get the miles, you just wind up beating yourself up. Unless the trail is real easy, I'm not going to push for the miles. I'll get there when I get there. While we were taking our break, I mentioned to the guys that if we were down to the next road crossing tomorrow morning, I bet the church folks would pick us up and feed us again. We hiked another half mile or so to a good camping spot, had a great campfire, sat back and enjoyed the afternoon.

Wednesday 5/28

Overcast this morning, and light rain by the time I got up at 8:30. Packed up and walked out the two hundred yards to the road just before 9:00. Again, the church folks showed up just about that time, and before long we were headed for another free, all you can eat breakfast. The church folks didn't mind a bit that we got breakfast two days in a row; in fact, we were told they'd pick us up every day until they left! This is what they do every year, they said, come up to put on these exquisite breakfasts just to help out the hikers. An awesome group of people, and excellent trail magic! A quick ride to town afterward, then back to the trail.

I felt good when I got started, but before long my left leg starts hurting real bad. When I first woke this morning, I asked Spirit to help me figure out and fix this problem. In thinking on it, I got that everything is about love, and that problems come when dark thoughts or feelings prevail. And then I questioned myself, "Do you feel worthy of love?" So I meditated on that most of the day. Since it's been raining, it's a good day to go inside. Much of the day I talked to Spirit, and cried a lot.

The trail to the next road was seven miles, and I don't remember much of it. When I got to the road, Wasabi and D were there. The next shelter was just two miles from the road, but it was a tough two miles. D was behind me, and one time when I stopped to stretch my back I said, "D, I'm afraid." What I'm afraid of is loving and losing. Fear, being the opposite of love, is the cause of all my pain. I sure love that woman, Stef, but I guess I'm still recovering from the divorce. So what to do? Right along I've been told to, "Love with fullness of Spirit." All I can do is the best I can do. Of course I trust Spirit, more than that I shouldn't need.

Thursday 5/29

Well, here I am on the side of a hill a couple miles out of Bland, Virginia. D, Wasabi and I made it to the shelter last night sometime before 5:00, and it stopped raining when we got here. A big fire going, and spirits are high. This morning I'm really hurting. My left leg, particularly my shin, ankle and foot are causing me great pain. In fact, I'm hurting so bad that I'm not going anywhere today – I'm going to rest up. I don't know how long I've had this pain, but it's probably been longer than I realize.

Hiking the trail is very much a mind game, and I'd better get my mind on this game or I'm not going to make it. I worked on it all day yesterday trying to figure out what is going on in my head. I came up with some things, but I don't know if I hit on the right thing. Then again, maybe I have and I just haven't dealt with it.

The question that came to me yesterday about feeling worthy of love seemed to come from nowhere, yet at the same time, it hit home. Later in the day when I asked myself the same question, I didn't answer right away, as if I had to think about it. Of course, by my very existence, I'm worthy of love. But as I've said before, the divorce really tore me up and left me unsure of myself. This brings me to the second part of the equation – Stef. I love the woman, I surely do, but do I feel worthy of her love? Am I even ready for it? So I've got this big battle going on inside me. Do I feel worthy of a love that I'm unsure I'm ready for, yet I'm into and want? Here I am having a tug of war with myself; it's no wonder that my legs have been hurting.

Wasabi hung around with me after everyone else left. He stayed until the early part of the afternoon, and I was talking to him about all my goings on of late. He asked me about my relationship with Stef, and how it might coincide with what is going on with me physically. There definitely is a connection. More so lately, I have found myself becoming more fond of Stef. The more I think of her, the more I want to be with her. Then you factor in how I may not feel worthy or ready. Legs, they carry us forward in life; ankles and knees, joints, changing direction in life. At the same time, I want to go forward, and I'm hesitating. Then, just for fun, let's throw in the fear of loving and losing. I'm telling myself and hearing "go," then tell myself "whoa." It's no wonder my body is acting up – too many mixed messages.

And the battle rages. What do I do? Tell me, Spirit, help me sort this out so that I may move forward happily and safely on this journey – on these journeys. I'm so tired of living with this pain. Yes, I came out here to find myself, but I didn't expect it would be so hard on me. At this rate, with the physical pain I've been enduring, I won't be able to finish this trip. And I sure don't want to pack it in. I've dreamed of doing this for years, there's no way I'm willing to quit. Please, please, Great Spirit, help me through this. And then Spirit and I had this conversation:

"Okay, so what do you want?"

"I want to be able to finish this trail, pain free, joyously."

"And afterward?"

"Whatever I choose. I want a good woman in my life to live and experience life with, to grow old and die with. I want all the money I need to live in the fashion that I dream. I want to travel and roam to my heart's desire; to see and experience as much of this wonderful world as possible. A good woman, the right woman, is key."

"And what if I said you have all that, and more, now?"

"Then I guess I'd be about the happiest, most blessed person on the face of the Earth."

"Well, son, it's true – what you wish for, you have. Remember the roll of film? It's all the same."

"How is it that I can know something to be true, yet at the same time, forget that it is so?"

"It is the human condition, or as you call it – the great forgetfulness. It is the opportunity to remember the Union. By having to re-learn, you have the chance to experience this process as if it were all new to you, which, of course, it's not. In the Spirit world, you know all there is to know. When you choose to take physical form again, you do so knowing that you have to "re-learn" that which you chose to "forget." That is how we have the opportunity to experience life over and over again."

"But does it have to be so difficult?"

"No, none of it has to be difficult – it's all in what you choose."

"All right then, I choose to walk out of here tomorrow morning with no more pain. I choose to finish this walk home with no more problems. I choose to have all that I desire. I choose peace and joy and love in my life. I choose to live in godliness."

"And so it is. I want what you want for yourself. Choose wisely, for what you think is what you get."

"If it's just that easy, why do I make it so hard on myself?"

"I don't know; why do you?"

"I don't know either. I guess I just forget. You'd think that with the anguish I go through, I'd smarten up."

"Maybe you like the experience. Remember how you felt when you discovered the missing roll of film? You're an experience junkie! (I chuckled at that comment and said, "You have a sense of humor.") Yes, of course I have a sense of humor – who do you suppose invented it?"

"I try, I do my best to remember the pleasure without having to go through the pain. I guess that sometimes I forget a little too good. By the way, that afternoon at The Barn when Blue Butterfly suggested that the waitress put all the orders on one check, that I'd get it, was that a test?"

"Well, suppose you try remembering just as hard, you'll get all the great results without all the grief. Yes, it was a test. If you really knew that you had all the money you desired, you'd have gladly picked up the tab for all the others. But that doesn't mean you won't have what you want, just that it is delayed."

"OK, I get it. Thank You. Now, I'm back to thinking about my body. If I take the ibuprofen, and use the patch, does that mean I don't have faith that my ailments will be relieved by changing my beliefs?"

"No, it doesn't mean that at all. It simply shows that you are dedicated to taking care of your body. Like you using the glucosamine tablets to help your joints work better."

"Do the glucosamine tablets work, do they help?"

"Do you feel that they do?"

"Yeah, I guess so."

"Then they do."

"Thank You, Spirit, for helping me through this. I feel much better than I did. I feel like I need a nap, but I feel good."

"Well, you've done a lot of hard work, a nap will do you good. You're welcome for everything. Remember, I'm in on this experience just as much as you are – I want it to be enjoyable as well. Of course, for me, it's all enjoyable. As well, it can be for you. It's all in what you choose."

Friday 5/30

The sun is just up over the horizon, and I get up to pee. My leg is still very sore, so I guess I need more healing time. I guess the relationship with Stef is not the issue. That's good news, at least. However, of further concern is that I have a small attack of gout. It's in the same place as before, the ball of the big toe on my left foot. It's very mild, but there just the same. If I remember Louise Hay's metaphysical writings correctly, gout has to do with repressed anger. Who is it I'm so angry at? Myself. I'm angry at myself. I came out here to hike and have a wonderful time, and I have, but I also know that I've had a lot of misery that I brought on myself. The words failure and disappointment come to mind. Of course, I'm the only one who would see me in that light. I'm not a failure; I have not, and will not quit. I will work through this and finish this journey.

However, I am disappointed that I'm having this difficulty. The gout I understand, but where has all the other injury and soreness come from? I know that if everything is working properly, there would be no pain. What is it that I'm not dealing with? Schedules, destinations – pressures. It's odd that even out here we put demands on ourselves. Get to Damascus by Trail Days – that was some sort of a mile marker. Okay, did that. Then it's "got to get to whatever town by such a day to get to the post office, make a phone call, etc." I am on a once in a lifetime adventure. That's not to say that I'll never do it again, but I'll never do it again for the first time. This business of having to be some place by some time is so contrary to what this experience is supposed to be about. Could the problem with the injury and pain be so simple that I'm telling myself to relax, to not place constraints on myself? Certainly, this is an effective method of doing that. Since I'm so sore that I cannot hike without causing myself great pain, I have to stop and take time. Perhaps that's the lesson in this for me – that I just need to relax, take time and lighten up.

If so, Stef, I'll need your help here as well. You don't place any burden directly upon me, but you have to understand that I might not be able to contact you on the appointed day. Mostly, I don't want any more appointments. Yes, we will meet up somewhere about the first of July, but beyond that, contact will be when it will be. I no longer want the pressure of having to check in by a certain time. You need to learn that I am safe, that no harm will come to me, that if I don't call by a certain time, I'm still fine. Dare I say that you need to trust the process that I live by. That aside, this hike and these lessons are for me. What I am dealing with is for me. I am so grateful for this opportunity, this journey – I intend to make the most of it. Even if on occasion I have to get knocked down, so I can progress onward.

It's noonish, maybe, as I sit here in this shelter up on a Virginia hillside. I am the only one here, everyone else is hiking. That is just what I'd like to be doing, but at this moment I am unable to. Sitting here in the quiet is not a bad thing, it's giving me time to empty my head. Granted, not a lot of time is needed for that… I trust Spirit to give me what I need, I guess maybe I needed to learn how to sit and be quiet without feeling that I must go. And it's getting so that I think if I can't comfortably hike tomorrow, it'll be just fine. Really, I'm enjoying the serenity – the songs of the birds, the whisper of the breeze in the trees, the wonderful silence when nothing is moving, the warm sun and the soft air. These are also things I came to experience, things that I sometimes overlook in my endeavor to get somewhere further up the trail. So what if I don't do the whole trail this year and have to finish it next year? Far better that I experience the trail more completely than hurriedly. Perhaps it's possible to do both, provided I stop setting unnecessary goals and expectations for myself. I really just want this journey to be enjoyable; after all, that's what it's supposed to be about.

As I was sitting here writing, two guys came in, one for lunch, the other for water and to check the register. The one who checked the register asked what day it was because he is determined to get to Pearisburg in a day or so for magic. He was in such a hurry that he was not going to take the time to fill his water bottles – something essential out here. I told him to take my water as I would be here all day, and could go get water whenever I wanted. Just before he left, he said this would be his longest couple of days yet, his longest being a twenty-four miler – he is determined to make it to the magic. The first guy who stopped for lunch said he did the Damascus 40 challenge in seventeen hours – "It was awesome." Maybe my way of thinking is not so extreme, but was it so different? Was I not setting goals and destinations for myself just the same? Yes, I want to do this whole trail before mid-October, but I want to do it relaxed and comfortably. Now that D, Wasabi and anyone else I was hiking with are a couple of days ahead of me, I'm free to hike at my own pace. Not that I wasn't before, but when you hike with others you tend to move as a unit. Sometimes that works well, sometimes it doesn't.

Now that I'm forced to sit back for a spell, I have time to think about how I'm doing this, and how I want to. The trail is full of compromises. I want to do it all this year, and I want to see it all. There is too much to see in one, or maybe two or three seasons, so I'll have to compromise. I'll do it all this year, that was the initial plan, and I'll see as much as I can in the process. Should I feel I missed a lot, I can always do it again later.

Something just came to me that I really don't want to think about, so it must be something I need to address. Perhaps since I started this hike, I think I've been comparing myself to other hikers, and maybe judging them by my standards. Like those two guys that were just here and their style of hiking. It's fine that they choose to hike the way they do, everyone has to hike their own hike. Early on I wondered if D had what it took to go all the way, that he wasn't eating well and taking good enough care of himself, or physically capable of doing the whole trip. I compared him to myself. Well, now D is two days ahead of me, what does that say about me?

Maybe my head is up my butt, and I have no idea who I am, or what I'm doing. Yes, I came out here to find myself, but it seems that I'm coming up with more questions than answers. The only thing I know for sure is that my leg and foot really hurt and are preventing me from hiking. And that is what I want to do – just hike. Great Spirit, I know that with You all things are possible. Please help me mend my leg and heal my spirit, so that I may do what I came here to do – just hike. In return, I'll do the best I can to be the best I can.

I finished supper a little bit ago, and everything is set to call it a day. I'm sore and tired, and tired of being sore. I've written and cried and talked to Spirit all day, and I'm done in. I have two days of food left, so my options are that I could stay here one more day then go back to Bland on Sunday, or I can move on as the next place to re-supply is just over sixteen miles away. I don't want to go backwards, and there is no guarantee that lying low for another day will help. I was given a dozen or so ibuprofen, so I'm going to dope up, and make my way to Pearisburg. It's forty-one miles from here, and if all was fine, I'd make it in three days. Since, at this point, all is not fine, I'm hoping for the best. We shall see.

Saturday 5/31

I thought I'd be up and going in good season today, but that is not the case. As much as my mind was on hiking last night, it is not this morning. Today my mind is on Stef. I'm in love with the woman, and I'm no longer afraid to admit it, say it, or feel it. So far this morning, all I've thought about is wanting to be with her, hold her, touch her, caress her, make love with her. Today I'm in love, and I'm just lying here enjoying the feeling. Maybe I'll hike, maybe I won't. Maybe I'll eat, maybe I won't. None of that matters, I'm just in love with being. Yes, my leg and toe do still hurt some, but they are greatly improved. I could hike reasonably comfortably, but I want to go out in good shape, not just close enough.

Stef, did I tell you I'm in love with you? I didn't? Well, I'll have to do that one of these days… Chris, did I tell you I'm in love with you? Well, I am, I surely am. Spirit, have I told you that I'm in love with You? What's that, You say I just did?! I'm so in love with life!!!

Two young hikers just walked out of camp. I said good morning, fellas, they said good morning. I asked if they were hiking together, they said yes, I told them to come over. One of them asked my name, I didn't ask theirs. I pulled $20 out of my pants, handed it to them through the screen door, and told them to have a meal on me when they get to town.

One fellow asked, "Are you sure?"

"Yup."

The other asked, "Why, man?"

"Why not?"

"Yeah, but why, man?"

Again I said, "Why not?"

"Well, you've got a good point."

They thanked me, and away they went. In a moment, they were back asking me if I smoked, I told them no. I figured they were asking for a cigarette; they were offering to share their smoke with me to re-pay a favor, that they really appreciated it.

"I know, that's why I did it."

They thanked me again, and said maybe we'd meet up the trail, and walked off.

I knew I was cut out to be a philanthropist. Now, when I have more to work with…

It's nearing noon, I've been out of the tent only to pee. The day is overcast, the sky appears to be thickening, it feels like it's fixing to rain. In a bit, I think I'll pack up and move into the shelter. I have lain here all morning, and suspect I won't do much more this afternoon. There is a great improvement in the condition of my leg and foot. I figured I'd be hiking today, but I think immobility has been very good for me. Tomorrow is June first – already. In a very short time, I will have been out here two months.

I don't know if it will rain today or not, but I think I'll pack the tent and move to the shelter. If nothing else, I'll be that much more ready for leaving tomorrow morning. I'm excited about getting back on the trail – I have a hottie waiting for me on the other end.

A good call on moving to the shelter, a thunder storm rolled through about 5:00, I stayed good and dry. It's a beautiful evening now, warm soft air, and a cool, gentle breeze.

My leg is a little stiff, but pain free, and there is only some tingling remaining in my toe. I guess I needed the break in order to figure things out and mend.

There are three other people staying in the shelter tonight, all south-bound section hikers. A couple started in Harper's Ferry on April 20, but said their first bunch of days were low mileage. I'm quite confident that I'll be there by the end of June – not that I'm setting a schedule. I was also told that the land up there is quite varied and pretty. I'm looking forward to it. This is my fourth night at this shelter, I'm really looking forward to getting back on the trail.

Sunday 6/1

Up early as the sky lightens. I get breakfast, packed up and head for water before most of the others are up. The leg is a little stiff, and the toe sore, but I think they'll come out of it. About a mile up the trail I feel the first few rain drops, and before long I'm walking in a thunder storm. The rain isn't hard, nor does it last long. As filthy as I am and as bad as I smell, it wouldn't hurt me a bit if it rained hard on me. I'd say I'm a mite gamey.

The sky is heavy and low, so the few breaks in the forest provide no views. The trail is easy, gentle ups and downs, and fairly smooth. The first five miles were pretty easy, the next couple a little more difficult, the last three kind of tough. Not because of the terrain, but because of the shin splints. I've worked with a lot of pain in the past, but these things are killers. By the time I made the first road crossing, seven miles from camp, the three days of rest were pretty much a waste of time. So I sat at the road and considered my options. I could get to Pearisburg and set until I mended completely, I could go back to Maine to heal if it acted like it would be a long process, then do Katahdin south, or I could call it quits. There's no way I'm willing to quit on the grandest adventure I've ever been on. Of course, if I did have to give it up, I could always pick it back up and finish it next year.

But I don't need to decide at this moment, and I go the three miles to the next shelter for the evening. Along this last stretch, my leg was hurting so bad that I could not walk down a hill going forward, no matter how gentle – I had to turn around and walk down backwards. Boy, that was fun! I got to the shelter at 2:00 – there's still four good hours of hiking, but I'm calling it quits for the day to give my leg a rest. I'll poke along and make it to Pearisburg, then I'll decide what I need to do.

Monday 6/2

Woke to a clear, cool morning. As usual, I was the first one up, but not the first one out. The shin splint has me moving a little slower. Thanks to the taking of four ibuprofen tablets, I'm moving pretty comfortably. That's a dangerous thing – being hurt and not feeling it, it would be very easy to push harder than what is best. So I poke along, I've got only six miles to go, there's no point in pushing it.

In walking along, I'm thinking about my present condition and how I got here. It occurred to me that three things were foremost in my mind, or in the way I approached this walk, and they were: inadequate preparation, naïveté, and the biggie, arrogance. I never researched anything about the hike, I just went ahead and did it. I had no real idea of what I was getting into, so when I got into it I had some surprises. But most of all was thinking it was going to be a piece of cake, that I could handle it all easily. I had it in my mind that I could do the entire hike with no trouble or pain what-so-ever. The shin splint sure took the wind out of my sails.

I poked along for the six miles today, and made the destination around 12:30 – just over a mile an hour. Not that it matters. The destination is Trent's store and campground in Rocky Gap, Virginia. The campground is not much, a little grassy area between a pasture and a stream. There's a cruddy little shower, just the same, a warm shower, a place to do laundry, and a little store that sells sandwiches and small meals. It isn't much, but it's cheap and fairly convenient as a rest/healing stop.

I called a friend back home, Julie, and was telling her about the walk, and my condition. She read from Louise Hay's book that shin splints were caused by breaking down ideals, that shins represent the standards of life. That seems pretty much on the mark. I came into this figuring I'd be doing X number of miles a day, that it would be easy for me (arrogance), but what I found was something completely different, and it sure kicked the slats out of my ego. The shin splints have been very humbling indeed. Of course, when I recognized all this, I thanked Spirit for the lesson. It was a tough one, but I needed to learn it. I called Stef to let her know where I was, and that I was fine, and I called the kids, but got only voicemails. As soon as I finish my writing, I'll try the kids again, call Stef back, and finish my conversation with Julie. I've got a very busy life…

Tuesday 6/3

I didn't leave the campground today, the leg is not ready. I walked down and called Stef, it was 5:45 (I had no idea of the time) and I woke her up; we talked for about an hour and a half. I called my old work number half expecting/hoping brother Bill would answer, but Adrienne, my former colleague, answered. We had a good, lengthy conversation; and I got to talk to my friend, Denise, as well. As much as I enjoy my old friends, I sure don't miss that world.

I got a couple breakfast sandwiches, then went back to my tent where I just lay around. At 1:30 or so, I went back down for something to eat, and sat around in front of the store watching the goings on until 5:00 or so, then went back to lie down again. I got up off and on, did my laundry, but not much else. About 7:00 I went down and called Stef, and again talked to her for quite a while until I was getting wet and chilly from the light rain. I got something to eat, talked with some other hikers, called and spoke with Beck, then headed back to camp.

Wednesday 6/4

I have been stretching my foot this morning, and have found that I can stretch it down pretty well, but when I lift it up, that's where the trouble is. One of the hikers camped here is a runner, and she said she'd show me some stretches that will help. Today I will work on stretching it out, so that tomorrow I can continue on.

I walked down and called Stef at 7:00, we talked until 8:30. We talk a lot and quite often. I look forward to our conversations very much. There are many aspects of the woman that I admire and want to have in a partner. I certainly did not expect to be in a relationship this soon after the divorce, but here I am. At the same time, I know I'm not fully committed to it, I'm not ready for it. In hindsight, I know that this relationship business is also hindering my hike. I had my mind too wrapped up back home to be fully here. Still, there is the love.

I've been soaking my leg in the stream as I've been writing, maybe for the better part of an hour. It's feeling a little numb from the cool water, so I think it's time for a break. I just came back from another foot soak in the stream. As I sat there, I rolled my foot from side to side as I lifted it up – this gave me the best stretch of the muscles and tendons into the foot. While I was doing that, I was talking with Spirit about this lesson. Arrogance is the key factor in all of it. I understood my attitude regarding how I approached my hike, but then I had another revelation.

I've thought of myself as a non-judgmental person, but I've found that, since I've been on this hike, I've been comparing myself to other hikers. A typical conversation with another hiker would be by asking if they are thru-hiking, and when they started. And from that I would measure my success by theirs. Maybe they started March 30, and are now getting to the place I am. Me, having started April 10, I would think myself a better hiker. Then the opposite may be the case. Maybe they started April 20, and in less time have gotten to where I am now, and I would think myself inferior. Too much crap in my head.

This noon I was sitting down at the store when this young couple of hikers came in, both very fit, he handsome, she really built. He went in the store and came out with two packs of cigarettes, one for him, the other for her. She was talking about the foods for re-supply in the store (of which there isn't a great selection), but commented that all she needed were some cigarettes, and it was all good. Again, I found myself comparing them to me, or my standards to theirs. Why? What difference does it make? I hate to say it, but it comes back to the arrogance issue. There's a saying out hear that you hear quite often – hike your own hike. It's the same as saying live your own life. I thought that's the way I looked at other people, I guess I was wrong. Okay, another lesson to learn. Will there be many more? This is all very humbling.

Well, the good news is that the swelling and pain in my shin is down quite a bit, but there is still a lot of swelling in my foot beneath my inside ankle bone. It causes me no discomfort. However, something is off kilter. I knew this journey was going to be a transformation for me, but I figured it would be a gradual, pleasant event – I sure did not expect this kind of anguish. But then, maybe that's just the way I go about things – bullheaded. Yeah, I guess sometimes I do. And I hear Ma's voice say, "Sometimes??" I'll learn, I'll soften to this life, you just wait and see. And I don't mean that in an arrogant way, it's just inevitable.

It turns out that this dumpy little store and campground is just the right place for me to start to recuperate. Had I gone on to Pearisburg, I would have been laid up in a comfortable motel, and probably would not have been exposed to all the people I have. I'm ashamed to say that I would have labeled most of the folks around here as rednecks, but they're people just like everyone else. The greater majority are real decent folks. We're all God's children just hiking our own hikes. This is something I've known for a long time, but somewhere along the line I forgot it. Thank You, Spirit, for these lessons, and this opportunity to remember. However difficult it might be, it's something I need.

Thursday 6/5

I got up to pee in the night, and when I did my leg spoke to me. It said, "I don't think so, not yet." I sure wanted to hike out today, so when I got back into the tent I asked Spirit to guide me, give me a sign. The dawn broke cooler and drier than the past few, a great day to head out. Instead, I rolled over not feeling like getting up. Here's your sign.

After a bit I got up and walked down to call Stef. She sounded different, almost giddy. She said she wrote a letter to her lover, and asked me if I wanted her to read it to me. Of course. I cannot recall verbatim, but the gist of it is that, in regards to our relationship, she is ready to throw caution to the wind, and allow come what may. So that's it, we're a bona fide couple. A couple of what, who knows...

Here I sit on my flat rock soaking my feet in my gurgling, babbling recuperation stream, grateful for this time and opportunity. I do so want to be hiking, but I'm getting so I'm appreciating the simplicity and quiet of just being. I realized this was also something I needed to learn. I know now that if I have to be here a week while I mend, so be it. I'll hike the AT, the whole of it, as best I can. If it turns out that I can't do it all this year, that I have to finish it next year, that's okay as well. The thing that keeps coming to mind is – I'm living my dream!!!

Friday 6/6

Rocky Gap, Virginia, day 6843. No, it really hasn't been that bad. Had a restless night, perhaps due to the heat and humidity, but probably more so that I'm not hiking. The thought came to me, "It hasn't been that long, be patient." It really hasn't been very long, nor has it been very painful.

I called the chiropractor that I occasionally see, and spoke about my shin splint. He told me the usual stuff, then he told me about massaging the muscle, and a particular stretch that would be good for me. The massaging and that stretch worked wonders to ease the tension.

I got breakfast, hung around in front of the store a while, then went to soak my legs in the stream, then went back to guard the store front some more. While there, I met Charlie, from London, Spider, and eventually Spider's cousin – three fellows in their early twenties on their thru-hike. They had been running high mileage days with some other guys, but were tiring of the pace. The cousin was occupied with an in-grown toenail that was making his hike less than enjoyable. They sat debating how far they were going to go that day, and I said I was going to go swimming at Dismal Falls. The cousin thought he would walk the road as well as it would save him a mile or more on the trail.

We had a very nice conversation on the way to, and at the falls. He was getting even more tired of the pace, and the lack of communication between Spider, Charlie and him. I suggested he leave the other two, and hike his own hike. He said he'd been considering it, but felt he owed something to his cousin, Spider. I told him people fall in and out all the time, and that he had to hike his own hike. At the falls, he asked me if I had any insightful thoughts or moments on the trail. I said, Oh yes, and told him all about my leg issue, and the metaphysical relationships and problems. He readily accepted what I said as the truth, especially when I said that toes represented minor details in the future. He said that Spider was obsessed with trail details, mileage and time, and that was very annoying to him. Again, I suggested he go on his own. I think he was leaning that way all the more. Then, out of the blue, he said to me, "Chris, you've been a breath of fresh air on what was otherwise becoming a miserable day."

Surprised, I said, "Thank you, and you're welcome."

Before he left, I shook his hand and wished him the best of luck. Maybe we'll meet again on the trail.

Saturday 6/7

I've had enough of this place, I've got to get out of here. I got the idea last night that I would hitch into Pearisburg in hopes of getting new footwear for when I get back on the trail. After talking to Stef, I got breakfast then started hitching. I walked for an hour or more, and got just one ride – for about a mile. I got dropped off at the Amish store where I got my day food for when I strike out. It is awful hot, and I was discouraged by the lack of rides, so I went back to Trent's. Upon getting back, I straightened out my food pack, grabbed a bike, and rode up to the falls for a cool swim. Me and everyone else. Too many screeching, bellowing people, so I left.

Presently, I am sitting on my thinking/recuperating rock with my feet in the middle of the stream. I hate to say it, but I'm becoming a little disheartened. This is not at all what I imagined hiking the trail would be like. I expected I'd be hiking and loving it. In the few trips I made to the falls, I spent time walking in the stream. The unsteady footing on angular rocks has been good therapy for my shin, ankle and foot. I still have some tenderness and swelling, but nowhere as bad as it was. In massaging my leg, I concentrate on breaking down the knots, which seems to be helping a lot. I sure hope I can walk out of here in a day or two; I want/need to get back on the trail. But I realize I can't go too soon, and possibly re-injure my leg.

In all of this, I'm reminded of the story, The Alchemist. It's the story of a shepherd boy who sells everything, then loses everything, has to re-plan and work through obstacles in his quest to follow his dream. That is where I feel I am. In the story, he ultimately gets what he dreamed of, and more. The keys to the realization of his dream were persistence and adaptability. One lesson learned right off out here is adaptability – things don't always go as planned.

So I'm doing my best to make the best of a, well, not a bad situation, but an undesirable one. I just need to hold on tight to my dream. And I know – I know – that my dream will come true.

Sunday 6/8

The leg feels pretty good today. There was no more swelling in the leg or foot this morning, and I could stretch it with full range of motion with no pain. I sat in front of the store all morning with Hobo Joe and one of the hikers who stayed here last night. It is still wicked hot today, but it doesn't feel as bad as it has been. As improved as my leg is, barring any turns for the worse, I'll be back on the trail tomorrow.

I came to sit in the stream at 2:30, my foot is just a little puffy. Apparently I'm not 100%, but I'm a solid 90%. Tomorrow morning I should be even better. Anything I feel is in the ankle and top of the foot, so I'm thinking the shin splint is pretty well healed. However, should I get up tomorrow and it doesn't feel quite ready, I'll give it some more time. The last thing I want to do is walk out of here and re-injure myself. Another hiker was saying that in Blacksburg, twenty-five miles east of Pearisburg, there are three outfitters, so I was thinking that when I get to Pearisburg, I might hitch to Blacksburg for new footwear. I'm thinking I wasn't supposed to get to Pearisburg yesterday, only as far as the Amish store, so I think I'm ready to go tomorrow, but I'm prepared to stay longer if need be.

Stef told me today that I can move in with her when I get back, if I so choose. That's a pretty big step, but it's one I had considered as well. It sure feels like we're building something solid, yet we're both aware there are no promises. I have very much enjoyed this long distance courting, except for the distance. Yet, because of the distance, there has been time to muddle things over and take them in. I knew this journey would be one of discovery, enlightenment and healing. Thank You, Spirit, for everything.

Monday 6/9

I called Stef last night, and a couple times during the conversation she asked me if I was all right, that I sounded down. I said I was tired and had a headache, which was true. Even though it was still light, I went to bed after we talked. I did not sleep well at all last night, the headache worsened. When dawn broke, I lay there thinking that I just wanted to sleep. I took that as a sign that my leg was not quite ready to go. But it is not about my leg.

This is hard to write, hard to face. I suppose everyone going on this hike knows it's a mental game, if they don't ahead of time, they quickly learn. I knew it ahead of time, but through my arrogance, ignored it. I started the trail exuberant, I was filled with joy and enthusiasm. A week into the trail and my body is feeling the punishment that it receives on a daily basis. Of course, it didn't help that I started barefoot or with moccasins, I brought on more pain and suffering than if I had come out with good footwear. Add on many more miles of hard work and punishment, and the body develops constant aches and pains. Live with this for a month and a half, and you can start to lose the mental game. That's what happened to me. Remember, when I started this journey, I erroneously thought I could do it easily with no problems. Yes, I had severe leg pain from continuous physical strain, but the mental strain was the root cause.

So I lay here this morning wondering if I even wanted to go on. Not because the leg wasn't ready, but because I was struggling with the mental game. Did I feel like quitting? Honestly, yes. I had to wonder if I even wanted this anymore. And I really had to think about it. Then I remembered this past

March when I was putting up next year's firewood. That is a job I always enjoyed, but it got to the point where I was miserable on the woodpile, and I hated doing it. And Spirit spoke to me, "Do you think it will always be easy on the trail?" I realized that it probably wouldn't, and it changed my attitude about finishing the job at hand. And when the wood was all cut, split and stacked in straight, even rows, there was a great sense of pride in a job well done.

And so the question came again today, "Do you think it will always be easy on the trail?" I now know that it won't. My arrogance and ego have been put in their place, having had the slats kicked out of them. Now it has come to, "Do I want to continue?" Yes, I do. This has been my dream for so many years; am I so willing to throw it away because it can be difficult? No, I am not. Many things in life are difficult, ask any woman who has given birth. But, like the woodpile, there is a great sense of pride in a job well done. Having learned my lesson, I'm ready to continue on the journey. Thanks again, Spirit.

I got breakfast then went to pack up – I was ready, I was leaving. I concluded business with the store, and got underway at 10:30. It's already pretty hot and humid, no doubt it will get more so.

The first eight miles of the trail were pretty easy going. It wasn't flat, but there wasn't a lot of elevation change. With the trail so easy, and my spirits high, I had a very enjoyable walk. About 2:30 or so, I got to Wapiti Shelter and took a break. The next shelter is another eight miles away, but since I had already done eight miles, I didn't think I'd do eight more. The day is indeed quite hot and humid, but underneath the forest canopy it isn't nearly as oppressive. On my walk today, I saw one rabbit and seven deer. I don't know what the significance of a rabbit is, but I remember that deer represent gentleness and beauty. The beauty surrounds me; maybe it's time to be gentle with myself.

After the shelter, I decided I'd go another four miles to the next watering hole. Making twelve miles for not having started until 10:30 is pretty good. My leg is fine, there is no swelling or soreness of any kind. Which is what I expected. I am camped in the yard of what looks like an old forest service cabin. The cabin is still standing pretty square, but the roof is in a bad way, consequently the interior is in bad shape. There is a lot of thunder rumbling in the distance while there are some high, thin clouds overhead. I think I'll put my fly on the tent tonight just to be on the safe side.

Tuesday 6/10

I got going in good fashion, probably by 6:30, and, except for a few rocky areas, the trail was pretty easy. Before very long I arrived at Doc's Knob Shelter, four miles from last night's camp. It didn't seem like I'd covered that much distance that quickly, but I had. After the shelter, the trail got real easy as it followed an old road for quite a distance. I'm in my own world today not having seen anyone else on the trail, either yesterday or today. This very real feeling of solitude has allowed me to get into my own rhythm without having to consider anyone else in any way. I don't know that I'll always want to hike in this solitude, but right now it's good.

After a 2000' descent, a good test for my shin, I come into Pearisburg. It is HOT down here, and makes me want to be back in the mountains. A strawberry shake was first on order, then the post office, an ATM stop at the bank, then to the motel. After cleaning and a call to Stef, I work on organizing my pack, planning what I will need for the next five or six days, then go to supper. They try, but the South just doesn't do good Chinese food. But that doesn't stop me from eating my fill at the buffet. Back to the motel a little after 8:00, and write today's journal.

Wednesday 6/11

Didn't sleep real well, but never seem to in town. I worked on getting my pack in order, went to breakfast, then set about my chores, but both the chiropractor and shoe shop were closed, so I headed to Wal-Mart. Nothing there but cheap footwear, and since I didn't feel like eating up a day going to Blacksburg, I got new insoles and a fleece blanket. It's too hot now for my sleeping bag, so I'm trading it in for a blanket. The trouble with my left foot started when I put new insoles in my boots in Damascus, so I figured maybe new insoles would take care of the problem. If not, an outfitter is only a week away. Back to the motel to get my mailing ready, then back to the food store, and back to the motel to put my pack together. OH, MY GAWD!!! My pack is some heavy! I don't know what I was thinking, but I've got a LOT of food. I hit the Dairy Queen on the way out of town.

The trail up out of town was a little steep and rocky for the first four miles, but then leveled out along a ridgeline for the last couple miles to the shelter. The day is hot and muggy, but it's a lot better than it has been for the past week and a half. The forecast for the next five days is for temperatures in the low 80s with a little chance for thunderstorms in the afternoon and evening. Tonight I'm camped at Rice Field Shelter. It's a beautiful spot tucked just inside the tree line from an extensive bald. It would be nice to cowboy camp on the bald, but the bugs would eat me alive. Of course, I can always pitch my tent. So far, I'm the only one here, and the only sounds are those of the gentle breeze, the crickets in the field, and the flies around the shelter. It is so peaceful! I enjoy the company of other hikers, but I prefer my solitude. Still, with nothing to distract a person, one's mind can become consumed with thought. It sure is interesting, this event called life. It being such a gorgeous evening, I pitched my tent on top of the bald, rather than staying in the shelter. I'm a little further away from water in the morning, but perhaps a little closer to God.

Thursday 6/12

Woke to a mediocre sunrise, not quite what I was expecting, as last night the sky became quite overcast. One thing about my tent is that it is very noisy in the wind, and it blew all night. Not much for sleep last night either. Good call on the fleece blanket; I was warm enough last night, I'd have been cold in just a sheet. Unfortunately, the blanket, which must have been returned, smells like stale cigarette smoke. It'll get washed as soon as I get the chance.

I was on the trail early, and the hiking is easy as the trail follows along a ridge line. The weather is cooler, and there is a nice breeze, making for good going. It's funny, sometimes you cover many miles without feeling it, and other times you hike for hours and never get anywhere. Today was one of the days that I didn't get anywhere. The first five or so miles went by easy, but the rest seemed to take forever. Most of the hiking was through hardwood forest which seemed rather thin, the trees widely spaced. It was through here that I saw my first rattlesnake.

I was walking along, daydreaming and gawking around when at the last second I saw it lying in the middle of the trail. I almost stepped right on it! I guess I need to pay attention. The snake lay there warming itself in the sun, and let me get a picture of it – it never even rattled at me. I wonder what the significance of a snake is... Eventually the trail dropped down through mixed forest, and a lot of laurel and rhododendron. I stopped at the next shelter to eat, and something happened, something in me changed.

I don't know why, but all of a sudden I got to feeling like a failure. This walk that was supposed to be so easy, is not; the folks I was walking with are all ten days ahead of me, and I feel like I'm struggling. In one of Stef's letters she asked me if I ever have bad days, or is this all so beautiful that I don't have any. My feet, ankles and knees were aching so bad I wondered why I was doing this. My pack will not stay in adjustment and ride on my hips, it hangs off my shoulders causing them, my back and my neck to stiffen up and become sore. This afternoon I felt like I wanted to quit – the constant ache and pain wasn't worth it. This journey is supposed to be fun, but this afternoon it was just miserable. The new insoles in the boots are a little better, but they're not cutting it. Still, I had to try, I had to do what I could, give it every effort before I gave up on them. Today I gave up on them. And the pack – it's not bad with a light load, but freighted like it is, it's torturous. There's an outfitter in Troutville seventy miles, five or six days away, and I see new equipment in my future. If I'm going to make this trip, I need equipment that will work for me. I'm all through trying to make something work that has ceased to work long ago. But I guess that's my personality, I keep trying as long as there's hope. This is where inadequate preparation and equipment get you.

When today was real bad, I sat on the trail alongside a stream and cried. I really felt like quitting. But I thought if I did quit, my life would go down the toilet, and everything I strived for and planned for would be gone. Yeah, today, this afternoon anyway, really sucked. I had hoped to be in Harper's Ferry by July 1st to meet Stef, but I'm not so sure that will happen – that's a long way away. And that has made me feel inferior, a loser, because I'm not hiking like everyone else seems to be. The real challenge to this hike is the mental game, and today I lost it in a big way.

The last mile today was an 1100' climb, and something happened on it – I just broke. That's it, the ego is dashed to pieces. Now that I've hit bottom, I've nowhere else to go but up. I'm going to get new gear as soon as I can, that will help with the physical pain and should improve my disposition. And if I can move better, maybe I can start adding a few more miles, and that should improve my disposition as well. I just know that I can't bring myself to quit because I'm wimping out. This has been my dream for so many years – I really want to see it through.

Friday 6/13

Up early, as usual, breakfast and packing done and I'm on my way – after the half mile walk for water. The air is heavy this morning, and there is not a breath of wind. The trail starts off very rocky, and I have to focus on my footing. Still, there is time to think. I had a good night's sleep, so I'm in a better mood after yesterday's burnout. As I walked, I thought about yesterday's visit with the snake, and what was the gift/message involved. It occurred to me that every year a snake sheds its skin, gets rid of that which no longer fits him, and starts anew. In thinking about that, I realized I needed to do the same. I hate to admit it, but I can be prone to having dark thoughts. I suppose we all can from time to time. At any rate, I knew that yesterday was one of those days, and if I chose to dwell on the foot discomfort and the ill-fitting pack, today would be also. Thoughts are energy, they create, but they are thoughts, and thoughts can be changed. This is elementary stuff I have known for years, but I guess I chose to forget.

So I'm sitting here after having walked five miles so far, today's destination is another ten miles distant. I'm taking a break and having a snack. The snack consists of an English muffin, beef jerky, macadamia nuts, banana chips, dried blueberries, a pineapple slice and a package of peanut butter crackers. Yeah, I pack a lot of food, it's heavy, but I eat well, and you need the nourishment when you're doing this kind of work.

Today's trail has been pretty easy, a little more up and down than the past few days, but not very taxing. That is except for the two miles of steady rocky trail from the ten mile mark of this fifteen mile day. The forest is quite open, and there is much more sun than shade. And then, just before the top of the last hill on the side of the trail is magic! An angel named Dave left sodas and candy. I had two orange sodas and three little candy bars. That goes a long way to improve a disposition. Much appreciated, Dave!

Just as I was getting back to the trail, it clouded in and opened up. The downpour lasted about fifteen minutes, and was quite refreshing. I had already decided that when I got to Laurel Creek Shelter I was going to bathe and do laundry, so I was in the pre-wash soak mode. The last couple miles to the shelter were rocky, and since I'd already hiked thirteen miles my feet were sore. Just when I figured I had another mile to go, I came to the blue blaze to the shelter. It's very pretty in here, and very peaceful. I am the only one here, probably will be. The first order of business is to get supper started, then to the creek for bathing and laundry. The day is warm, the bugs are few, so I lounge around naked and air dry. Clouds roll in and out, thunder rumbles all around, a few rain drops fall, and it is a most pleasant evening.

Saturday 6/14

A very dreamy night, didn't sleep as well as I would have liked; knowing that today's destination is a shelter just twelve miles away, I'm pretty slow getting started. My left foot is rather swollen and a little sore, which inclines me to move a little slower. Beyond a doubt, there is new footwear in the near future.

The morning is clear, but humid and without a breeze. I walk along through mature, mixed forest and talk with Spirit. Even though there has been a lot of pain on this journey, there has been much more beauty, and I'm grateful that Spirit has created this wonderful place for us, that I'm able to be here to enjoy it.

Before long I come to an abandoned house, nothing but the shell standing. I would guess the house was built in the early 1900s, but has been uninhabited for quite a while. It makes me wonder what the story is, how it had come to be, and what caused it to be vacated. In a mile or so, the trail is deposited onto lovely, lush fields of hundreds of acres. It would be easy to see why someone inclined to farm would want to do it here. This is beautiful, fertile-looking country.

After leaving the farmlands, I start the climb up to Sinking Creek Mt. Along the way I pass a HUGE oak tree, the limbs of which would be trees by themselves. Come to find out, it's the second largest oak tree on the AT. There is another, I'm told, that has a larger girth, but is not as tall or expansive. Huge old-growth trees like this are a rare and splendid sight. The climb up the ridge leading to Sinking Creek Mt. is fairly short, but steep. The day is pretty warm now, and the climb is strenuous. At the top I sit to eat and drink, but I still don't have a lot of steam. I attribute it to last night's restless sleep.

I'm in need of water, so I take the side trail to Sarver Hollow Shelter. I didn't really want to, it's about half a mile one way, but you've got to do what you've got to do. Down at the spring were the ruins of another old homestead. The old house was pretty much gone except for the fireplace and chimney, and a few collapsed skeletons of outbuildings stood nearby. It was pretty and interesting, and I wished I'd brought my camera. Another time. I got my fill of cool spring water, then headed back up the steep half mile to the trail.

Along the ridge are random piles of rocks, quite out of place. I was told they are there from the fellow who had the homestead years ago. This is where he had his orchard, and the rock piles are from his land clearing. From up on the mountain there is a great view of Sinking Creek Valley and the Blue Ridge Mts. behind. As the day has clouded in and is threatening rain, the view is not as nice as it could be.

My feet are quite sore by now as my boots have long since given me all the comfort they had to give. Four more days... I make it to Niday Shelter by 4:30. It seems too early to call it a day, but I've been twelve miles, and the next water source is ten miles away. Besides, I don't feel like torturing my feet anymore today. Why is it that as soon as you give something up, you want it? I just sent my wool socks home, they sure would have been a comfort to my blistered feet. And the weather is cooler again, my sleeping bag would be more comfortable than the blanket I now have. Oh well, make adjustments.

Sunday 6/15

The morning is mostly overcast and around 65° – a good day to hike. I left thinking I wanted to make sixteen miles today only on account of what my data book said there was for water.

I got going rather hurriedly, and about a half mile from camp I spooked a bear. He did not appear inclined for idle chit-chat as he made fast tracks for the next county. Animals are very sensitive and perceptive to energy – they need to be, that is how they survive. Had I not been rushing along anxiously and projecting such energy, perhaps brother bruin might have sat and taken tea with me. Message to self – there's no need to hurry, you're doing fine.

In another mile, I was in a low pine forest with a meandering stream, a very pretty spot, and jumped two deer. The second deer wasn't forty feet from me when she bolted – I was in a more relaxed frame of mind. She had run just a short distance and was still going when I whistled, and when I did she stopped, seemingly unalarmed, and turned to look at me. They often do that when you whistle at them. Just up around the bend in the trail sat a handsomely decorated turtle. He posed for a picture before withdrawing. In native lore, there is something about a turtle, but I don't recall what it is. In any case, a nice gift.

Today's trail took me through some of the prettiest country I've seen in Virginia. The last five or so miles were some of the hardest hiking I have done since Little and Big Hump in North Carolina. The last few miles ascended a high, rocky spine that had me clambering up, over and around jagged outcroppings. In reward, the views from Dragon's Tooth were incredible. Dragon's Tooth itself was quite spectacular with large, angled rock jutting straight up from the ridge, the effect was like a huge jawbone with large, serrated teeth. From these spectacular rock formations there was a great view of a peaceful, green valley laid out below and the long, lush mountain range behind.

The day started cloudy, but cleared by mid morning, and the air dried out a lot – much less humid. I did nearly eighteen miles today and I'm beat, but it's the best day of hiking I've had in a long time. It feels like something has really changed in my head because today, even though some stretches were tough, I thoroughly enjoyed the hike. When I get new, comfortable boots and pack, I'll feel like a new man.

Monday 6/16

What a miserable night's sleep. Maybe I was overtired, I don't know, but it felt like I didn't sleep a wink. I was up and going in good season anyway wanting to get sixteen miles in today. The trail is starting easy, it drops down and meanders along a stream, then cuts through a couple hayfields. Then it starts to climb, and I start to drag.

I say to myself, "This is tough, it must be because I'm tired because I didn't sleep well last night." I caught myself saying that a few times.

Then I think to myself, "Change your idea about it."

So I did, I thought, "You're doing just fine, you're going along good." And before I knew it, I was. The power of positive thinking!

So I got up, over and down the first mountain pretty well. I crossed the highway and started the climb up to McAfee's Knob. At the eight mile mark, I stopped for lunch and water at a pretty little shelter just off the trail. The day is sunny and breezy, a little warmer than the past few days. McAfee's Knob is 3200', up from 1800' down at the highway, but the trail is pretty easy. Once on top – boy oh boy – what a view! Mountain ridges and valleys stretching as far as you can see.

Yours truly at McAffee's Knob

The knob itself is a relatively flat area, one side of which drops precipitously to the valley below. There is one piece of overhanging ledge that might well be one of the most photographed spots on the trail. The view from the edge is fantastic – a great, wide valley dotted with homes and small farms all with lawns and fields of vibrant green, shouldered by long, continuous mountains. Directly below the edge is eternity; one wrong step and you're in for the fall of a lifetime – the last one – before striking unforgiving terra firma. I spend a good amount of time on the knob just taking in the view and the feeling of it before I move on.

Also at the knob was a man with his late-teenage son, and two of the son's friends. Being typical teenagers they were moving about excitedly. Before very long they were jumping around complaining about being stung by bees. In the midst of their commotion I quietly sat and ate a little, completely unmolested by the agitated bees. It all has to do with the type of energy you create.

A little further down the trail and I'm walking through the most gorgeous rock garden I have ever seen. The trail through here is only a few hundred yards long, but is simply enchanting. A fairly level, sandy, gravelly path winds around rock sentinels twelve feet or more high with dwarfed hard and soft woods, laurel and rhododendrons as the planted flowers. The handy work of the Master! I cannot help myself, nor do I want to, but I just sort of drift around in this area for some time absorbing the beauty of it all.

The trail drops a little and levels out, roughly, before rising up to the 3000' Tinker's Cliff. These cliffs are a continuation of the ridge, and are of the same structure as McAfee's Knob. However, this section is not as level. In one section the trail follows out along the precipitous cliff edge itself. The cliff here drops so that the face of it forms a veritable wall from the valley below. All about are more incredible views and rock formations. The beauty of this land goes beyond my limited vocabulary to describe. Ma sure would like to see this country, she always had a thing for rocks, as would Dad. Who knows, maybe they're walking along with me and enjoying it as well.

Along the way I'm talking to myself and I tell Stef that she needs to come here with me and see all this. Babe, I sure miss you, but I'm having a grand time doing what I'm doing. Though while I also miss D and Wasabi, the solitary time on the trail suits me fine. Yeah, I want to go up Katahdin before October 15, but I'm not concerned about it, I'll get there when I get there.

Tomorrow I'm going to Troutville for boots, pack and maybe a new camera. And while I'm there, a good steak with a salad and maybe dessert is in the works.

Tuesday 6/17

I've been getting up with the sun, but that's not as early here as it is in Maine. I was on the trail about 7:00 for a quiet, peaceful start to the day. The trail starts gently, but then climbs gradually to a long, rocky ridge. In Georgia, North Carolina, and Tennessee the trail pretty much went up the side of a mountain and back down again. Here, the trail runs more or less along the ridges. If the trail is fairly smooth, the going is great; if the trail is rocky, it's more difficult and slower. The forest around here is a very pretty, mature forest of mixed growth, and is very pleasant to behold. And I expect to see deer every day, which I have in the last bunch of days. This is very pretty country indeed, but there still isn't enough water for my liking. I guess I'll stay in Maine.

I make the eleven miles to Troutville in about five hours, and I didn't think I was moving that fast. I went directly to the outfitter for footwear and a new pack. I tried many pair of boots and shoes, a couple were pretty good, but I settled on a pair of hiking sandals which were comfortable and had good arch support. I hope they'll hold up well. If not, there's another outfitter in 150 miles. I threw big bucks for a nice pack. It got to where I was fighting so with the old one that I was cursing it quite regularly. I transferred my stuff to the new pack, and I didn't feel as though I had anywhere near the weight – it carries the load so much better. I think I'll be happy with it.

So, folks, if you're thinking about going on a long hike and don't have your gear yet, spend the money for good, properly fitting equipment! The investment is well worth it.

Wednesday 6/18

Had a great conversation with Stef in which we talked about the "You owe me big calendar." She's claiming that every day I'm on the trail, I owe her. No doubt that her support has made this adventure much easier and the help is greatly appreciated.

I got out of town about 12:30, but not before I picked up the last few grocery items, and being interviewed by a reporter from the Roanoke newspaper. He was doing a story on hikers, in particular about the body odor hikers cultivate while on the trail. A very friendly guy who asked me many questions about my hike and hikers in general. I told him of my experiences, and how I manage the trail, re-supplies and occasional cleanings. We had a nice visit, but it's time to get to the trail.

The day is beautiful, sunny, 75°, with dry air and a gentle breeze. I got a couple miles out when I took a break to eat an orange. Fresh fruit is something I miss on the trail; I would love to have more of it, but it's surprisingly heavy to carry. The only time I get some is when I'm in town, and my first day out I'll carry enough for the day or two. It was so peaceful that I stretched out across the trail and took a break – I might even have dozed a little. I'm so enjoying being here that I'm of two minds about it – I want to hike on, but it almost seems like hiking is an interference with just being here. Of course I will hike, but I really am quite content just to be on the trail and take it all in.

The new footwear is fantastic! The sandals are light, breathable, and take the jolt out of the trail. My left foot, which has been achy, feels much better tonight – even though I went nine miles this afternoon. I'm still figuring out the new pack, but it is a vast improvement over the old one. Even though I walked out with the pack weighing forty-three pounds, it carries the load so much better that I don't feel the weight near as much. So far, I'm very pleased with my purchases, and believe they will make the upcoming miles more pleasant. I didn't change gear sooner because it's my nature to make something work for as long as it can, even if it's not working well. If there's a hope or a chance,

I'll keep trying, so when the time comes to let something go, I can feel good about it.

Thursday 6/19

Today, the trail has been pretty easy all day, enough so that I make nineteen miles with a side trip. I came up on the Blue Ridge Parkway, a long scenic drive along the top of, you guessed it, the Blue Ridge Mountains. I understand the AT went through here first, and with America's love of automobiles and touring, they decided to build a road along here – mostly where the AT was. The trail crosses the parkway a number of times, and is often right beside it. When there's no traffic or you're out of sight of the road, you'd think you're on some remote mountain ridge. The biggest complaint from hikers about the parkway is that, since the trail had to be diverted to make way for the road, many of the best views are missed. But then, by virtue, hikers get to see so much more than those speeding by in their chariots.

The trail today is very gentle so that by 4:00 I have gone over sixteen miles. Down at the next road I met a woman who'd been out hiking. We talked a bit, and I told her I was heading for a campground about two miles away that had burgers and such. I hinted at getting a ride. She was a little leery at first, but I poured on the charm, or looked pathetic enough, that she gave me a ride there. Along the way the woman asked me about my hike, said it was a dream of hers to do it, and that I'm very fortunate to be living my dream.

I got to the store fifteen minutes before closing. I dined on two loaded bacon cheeseburgers, an ice-cream bar and chocolate milk. It was all much better than I would otherwise have had for supper. And the woman in the store was going past the trailhead on her way home, so she gave me a ride back. Providence.

A mile and a half later and here I am on a mountain top writing my journal and watching a lovely sunset. As I was taking my sponge bath tonight, a bear approached the camp. I never did get to see it because it took off for the nether regions when it saw or smelled me. Wild bears shy away from humans, as a rule, so you generally don't have to worry about them. Still, too bad I didn't get to see it. The sunset is getting prettier all the time with its glorious display of colors. I could have walked the two miles to the next shelter, but I probably would have had to share it with other hikers, and here I have the sunset all to myself.

Friday 6/20

Woke to a beautiful sunrise, had breakfast and on the trail in good season. It would have been an easy hike to the shelter last night as I got there quickly this morning, but I was glad I stayed where I did since there were seven hikers in residence. The next 4.5 miles were long, uphill ones, and I climbed over 2200' – the highest climb I've done in a while – over Floyd Mt. A half mile beyond was Cornelius Creek Shelter, and I got something to eat there.

The day is beautiful, warm, sunny and breezy. I wouldn't object if the weather could stay like this the rest of the way to Katahdin. The forest all around is predominantly mature hardwoods, though occasionally I'll go through a grove of rhododendron or laurel. The trail is pretty easy today, and I get to the next shelter, twelve miles from where I spent the night, a little after 3:00. I cook a dinner and am underway by 4:30. There are two spots ahead with water, one at three miles, the other just over six. Since I've got it in my head that I want to be in Harpers Ferry on July 4th, I set my sights on the further one. Yeah, I know, no more schedules...

I arrived at the first spring and found a great camping spot, and, not knowing if I had another three miles in me, decided to camp here. Just as well, I have chores to do and I'm feeling rather tired. It will be an early to bed night tonight.

Saturday 6/21

First day of summer – hike naked day. It's overcast and there has been light rain since daybreak. I'm feeling lazy, I'm still in bed at 8:00 or 8:30. I'll get up before long and get the day started. If I were to make it to Harpers Ferry on the 4th, I would have to do fifteen miles a day every day. It's not out of the question, but I don't like having to have a schedule. We'll see. But I'll have to get out of bed first. In a bit...

I couldn't seem to make any progress this morning. By 11:00 I had been only four miles! But the day is gorgeous and the hiking is great, so I give little attention to the distance. Today's trail had its ups and downs – literally. But, in general, hiking is like that. The trail, other than being hilly, is quite nice. Eventually I find myself walking along the James River, an easy, gentle trail. Here I cross the James River foot bridge, all 678' of it, the longest foot bridge on the AT. There are some teenagers jumping off the bridge to swim; I'm tempted to do the same, but don't seem to have the gumption.

I cross the highway, U.S. 501 & Virginia 130, then start a gradual climb along a beautiful stream. A mile or so along, and I decide to take a dip in that clear, inviting stream. So in I go, clothes and all, but not for long as the clothes come off pretty quickly. Ahh, a clean body and clothes! A couple of miles and I'm at Johns Hollow Shelter where I'd planned to spend the night. Problem is, so did a rather large boy scout troop. So I filled my water bottles, chatted a little, got a candy bar, and proceeded on. From there it was a rather steep climb three miles up to Big Rocky Row, an extensive ridge at 3000' overlooking the James River valley.

I guess I'm tired, I can't seem to think of anything else to write, I'm going to sleep.

Sunday 6/22

What a thunderstorm last night!!! I half thought of cowboy camping, but put the tent up to get away from the bugs. Just about the time I turned in, a breeze picked up which became a steady wind. At some point, I woke to a flash of lightning and a couple of raindrops. I scurried about to put the fly on the tent, and to get the pack and gear under cover. I don't know how long the storm took to reach me, but it came with a vengeance. At first there was just a lot of lightning and thunder, fairly loud as I'm camped on a high, exposed ridge, and little rain. And then the storm hit. When the rain came, it came as a hard, driving rain, thoroughly soaking earth and sky. I realized I had a puddle underneath the tent, the effect of which was rather like being on a water bed, and things inside were getting wet. But the storm, especially the lightning was just awesome! There were constant brilliant, flashes closely followed by deafeningly loud thunder. There were two occasions where the lightning was almost blinding (me being in my tent!), accompanied by – not followed by, but occurring simultaneously with – incredibly loud thunder which literally shook me. The storm was right on top of me, hitting the ridge where I was camped. On two occasions, I could feel the surge of electricity pass through my body, giving me a definite tingling sensation from my toes to my head. I thought "All I need is that little spark to make the connection, and I'm toast." I said a little prayer that I not be barbequed on this mountain top, and rolled over to try to sleep. The storm lasted three or four hours. It was fantastic – the best, wildest, most actively charged storm I had ever seen! I loved it!

Surprisingly, not a lot of sleep came last night – I may be dragging today. Once on the trail everything seemed to be working well, I was moving well – maybe the storm charged me up. A half mile from where I camped was a section of trail that made me stop and look and wonder for just a moment. In a low, fifteen foot section was something that didn't look quite right – the trail was covered a few inches deep in hail stones! That sure was some storm!

The day is beautiful, the trail is nice, and the forest... well, the forest is always beautiful. I'm walking a splendid trail while it hugs a rocky hillside providing splendid views of valleys and mountains distant, or as it slides through a low saddle saturated in all hues of green from the forest canopy and the lush fern growth on the floor all about. These are the times when hiking is magical.

I'm making pretty good time and mileage today, even thinking I'll do more than fifteen, but I run into Alaska and her dog, Buddy. I met Alaska when I was recuperating at Trent's. We sat and talked a bit, then walked on to Brown Mountain Creek Shelter. We got to a campsite at the shelter about 6:30 and decided to call it a night. After fifteen miles, my feet get sore, and I'm feeling last night's restlessness. I set up camp, have supper, good, light conversation with Alaska, and it's time for bed. There is some thunder rumbling in the distance; I hope it's not a re-play of last night's adventure – I'd like to get some good sleep.

Monday 6/23

I guess I slept well last night as dawn seemed to come all of a sudden. As forecast, thunderstorms again last night. Last night's storm was nothing compared to the magnificent one the night before. I'm glad the storms come at night; the rain is needed, and the day starts off nice and cool.

I had a very intense dream where I was flying, just myself, as natural as can be. I walked out of a house, set down what I was carrying, stretched out my arms and started soaring around the rooftops. One thing different about this flying dream is that I learned how to slow down and land; any other flying dream ended with me flying or not knowing how to, or being unable to land. A very interesting, fun dream.

But as comfortable as the bed is, it's time to get up and start the day.

This valley I'm in is very pretty, it's nice to see this much water. I'm walking along Brown Mountain Creek in a narrow little valley nestled between low hills, and there is vibrant growth hereabouts. The valley was settled in the early 1900s by freed slaves who sharecropped the land. One would suppose they couldn't make a go of it, else they'd still be here. Today, it's just a beautiful walk in the woods.

Once leaving the valley, the trail climbs to U.S. 60, and from there climbs and climbs to a mountain top, Bald Knob, at just over 4000'. The day is gorgeous and the hiking is grand. Three miles from Bald Knob, after dropping down into a gap, is Cold Mountain, again just over 4000', that is about a mile long of open fields affording awesome views to both sides. I love these high mountain meadows for the terrific views, and the fresh, sweet air. There are another couple easy descents and ascents, then the trail levels out pretty well making for very easy going. Along one of these stretches, I see plants that are growing to a height of eight feet. They look familiar, and upon closer inspection discover they are Queen Anne's Lace. Back home they grow to only two or three feet.

My initial plan was to camp pretty close to the road going into Montebello and hike in that morning, but then I figured that if I quickened the pace, I could be there tonight and go to the Dutch House B&B. So I got a wiggle on ("get a wiggle on" is a local expression meaning to get moving, to hustle), and as the last miles are easy road walking, I arrive in good season. The first order of business was a shower, then a delicious supper of salad, angel hair pasta with tomato sauce, chicken parmesan and bread. For dessert, ice cream with chocolate sauce over a cookie. An excellent meal. I made a few phone calls, and it's after 8:30, time for bed.

Tuesday 6/24

Happy Birthday To Me, Happy Birthday To Me –

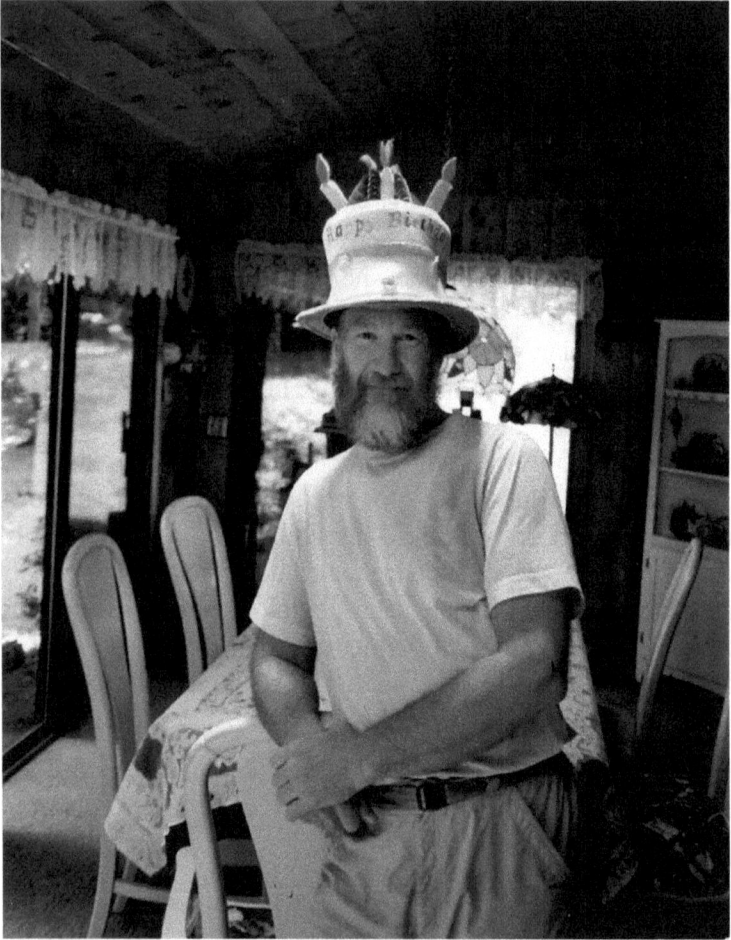

Gotta wear the hat—50th birthday

A rather restless night. The bed was a little small, my feet were aching from the previous day's hard run, and my roommate was up later than I, beyond what is comfortable for me, watching a movie. A delicious breakfast at 8:30 and off to the trail, via post office and store, about 9:30. Business finally taken care of and at the trailhead nearer 11:00. The Dutch House B&B does a free hiker lunch during May and June, and there were a couple hikers at the parking lot to take them up on the offer. So I figured I'd go back as well for another free meal; pasta with meatballs and sauce, bread, watermelon, and pineapple upside down cake for dessert. A nice birthday treat, but, whew, too full to hike.

Back to the trail 12:30ish, but it's slow going with such a full belly. A stop at Spy Rock for views, Priest Mt. Shelter for water, and an easy walk over the top of what is supposed to be a tough climb. It is so peaceful up here that halfway down the other side I decide to make camp. Last night's and today's interaction with so many people left me craving peace and quiet. Tonight I have it – a nice campsite off the beaten path, and no one else around.

I like people, I do, but sometimes they crowd my space too much. When I get back to the other world, I will have to make re-adjustments. I'm a quiet, private person anyway, but having this much time and quiet to myself has made the other world with all its people and commotion more taxing.

A young doe walked in to camp, apparently to figure out what the odd shapes were. She walked most of the way around the tent, and it appeared as though she couldn't make me out as she looked through the bug netting. I softly spoke to her and she didn't seem frightened at all. I unzipped the door so she could get a good look at me, and she approached within ten feet of me. I thought about stepping out of the tent, but I didn't want to scare her. What a wonderful gift on my birthday! She nosed around until her curiosity was satisfied, then moseyed off. This is becoming more my world every day.

Wednesday 6/25

Another deer visit during the night, perhaps the same animal. This one did the same – walked all around the tent, but took more time eating. She was close enough that I could easily hear her sniffing, nibbling and chewing. Even though I understand the etiquette with hunting, I'm not so sure I could kill one as easily as I have in the past, now that I've had more personal interaction with them. But then, I never was much of a hunter anyway.

The trail started downhill and was pretty easy with a lot of switchbacks. So many have talked about how tough the Priest is, and maybe north to south it is, but I thought it was easy. Crossed the Tye River, inviting enough for a swim, but it's early. The next few miles were a tough SOB of a climb – steep, rough and rocky. By and by I got there, only to start back down the other side. The AT used to follow a stream up the hill, but was diverted this way. Why, I don't know, because I sweat buckets coming up this way for lack of water when on the old way there would have been plenty. So it goes.

I stopped at the next shelter for another mid-day meal and water, then back at it. Today's hike is undoubtedly the toughest I've done in many miles of Virginia. All in all a good day's hike as I got twenty miles today. I just need to do twenty a day for the next nine days to make it to Harpers Ferry on the 4th. We'll see.

Thursday 6/26

Up and going early, but something's not right – too many demons, ghosts from the past. The hike was never supposed to be about a schedule, but a schedule is a method of testing myself. The ghost from the past is the old feeling of not doing enough, not being good enough. Old stuff from a life gone by that was brought into this one. And I know it has no place here, has no bearing on what I am doing now, but still, there it is.

The reality is that no matter what time I may finish, I'm out here living my dream; I know that, I fully understand it. But what to do when old demons come calling? I guess I just forgot the important stuff. Am I over it, will it come up again? I don't know. One thing I know for sure is that I came out here not just to hike, but with the understanding that I was looking for myself. And these demons are/were an aspect of myself. That being the case, this is something I need to confront, this feeling of inadequacy. Being able to hike the trail in the time frame I choose is me being able to measure myself and my ability/worth. And it's foolish because I know one has nothing to do with the other. Yet, there it is. It'll all figure out, work out, but in the meantime I'll have to deal with whatever issues arise.

I'm in Waynesboro tonight as it's time to re-supply. Getting cleaned up and going out for a good meal are always good things – things you take for granted when you're not living on the trail. Stef and I had a good air-clearing talk tonight that got a lot of stuff out in the open. The talk wasn't as chipper and upbeat as I would have liked, but it was necessary. She is so smart and wise, and puts things right into perspective – one of her many admirable qualities. I'm fortunate to have her as my gal. I appreciate everything she does/is for me.

Friday 6/27

The day started early enough, 5:30, as I was putting my pack together. Stef called just after 6:00, we spoke until 8:00. An emotional conversation, both of us having a lot on our minds. I sure miss her very much, as I know she does me. What does she see in me? It makes it hard to talk to her sometimes, I miss her so. I'm wanting to hike as fast as I can to get to Harpers Ferry on the 4th, but then I don't want to hurry the hike. Then again, sometimes I feel like just going home and really getting the relationship going. Of course, I'm not going to quit the trail, but I do feel pulled between hurry up and slow down. Why does what is supposed to be a carefree, enjoyable time become so complicated? Of course, it's only what I make it, but it's difficult being caught in between. This hike, this trail, is more than just a walk, it's a personal conquest. What and how I do on this journey will help me define me.

Directly after leaving Waynesboro, I entered Shenandoah National Park on a warm, sunny day. The trail is easy as it winds up and around low hills, across fields and through mature forest.

I'm sitting at the first shelter getting a bite to eat, and I think it's fixing to storm. I've made only seven miles today; I don't know whether to stay here tonight (it's mid-afternoon) where there's water nearby, or push on to the next shelter thirteen miles away – which is too far for me to make today. Plus, according to my data book, there's no water in between. Hmm… decisions… Well, not much for rain, a few drops, so at about 2:30 I move on.

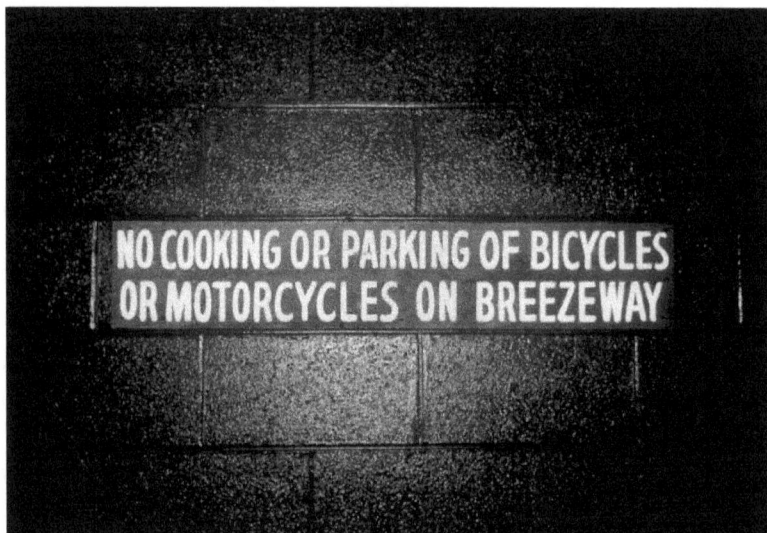

NO COOKING OR PARKING OF BICYCLES
OR MOTORCYCLES ON BREEZEWAY

Does that happen often?

The hiking is easy, the trails are good, so I make decent time. There is not much of a canopy on this section, so I'm feeling the effects of the sun. It's too warm to go too far on too little water; thirteen miles in between watering holes is just too far. But it is what it is, and you make adjustments. To my good fortune, there is a little spring a few miles down the trail that is not listed in my data book. I drank my fill and filled my bottles. What a welcome surprise. The forest here in Shenandoah is much more diverse than what I came through up on Blue Ridge Parkway. There are sections of all hardwood, mixed hard and soft, scrub and laurel ranging from open woods to very thick growth.

My resting place for the night is up on a long, level ridge in open hardwoods. There is a lovely breeze, and two young deer cruising around feeding. I saw two black bears today, both of them young, and both of them turned and ran when they saw me. Geez, I must look a fright!

So here's the thing – what's keeping me from proceeding better is that my left foot is paining me so. The back of my heel feels like it's forming a large blister under a very thick callous. The ball of my big toe feels inflamed as if from gout or arthritis. The heel started a couple days ago, the toe joint today. If it weren't for my sore foot, I could have made the five miles to the next shelter and water source. The question, of course, is what is going on in my head to be causing the pain in my foot? What is my mental state creating the blockage of energy? Well, let's see, the only two things in my life now are the hike and Stef. The hike and Stef, the hike and Stef... I don't know, I've got to think on it.

Saturday 6/28

The hike – not the euphoric event I had imagined. It is a lot of hard work, and you deal with aches and pains every day. Truthfully, I sometimes feel like I don't want to continue. But then, there is the beauty, simplicity and serenity while I'm out here following my dream. Upon waking this morning, I had quite a talk with myself about my condition and the cause. The gist of it was about my relationship with Stef. Basically, I'm in love with her, or perhaps, the idea of being in love with her – wanting to move ahead there, but also wanting to proceed very cautiously. I'm torn – at once wanting to go, and yet wanting to whoa. Conflicts, conflicts. They put a strain on both mind and body.

I've got to get my lazy butt up and get moving. No, that's not right, I'm not a lazy butt. However, there are times when it is good to lie, reflect, be, and times to move. So I'll move. In a few minutes. Probably.

The trail is fairly easy, so I go along pretty well. In a couple hours I meet up with a young guy out on vacation who's hiking what he can in two weeks. We walked to the next shelter as I needed water. I ate some, and we talked the while. A very nice guy, he runs a family bakery business in Florida. His young wife died of cancer, but before she went she wrote a book, *It's all in His name*, the proceeds of which go to helping people in Haiti and Africa. I suspect, like many of us, he's trying to make sense of his life, and a couple weeks in the woods are good therapy. I wished him well, moved on and never saw him again.

In another hour or so, I met Harvest and Scout, two friendly, attractive young ladies I met way back at Trent's when I was on the mend. I walked with them the rest of the day. It was fun walking with someone I know. Tonight I'm at Pinefield Hut in my tent. The gals are tenting nearby as the shelter is quite full with a group of guys. It was a good day of walking, something over seventeen miles, and that was enough. Harvest is a local gal, and she gave me the lowdown on Front Royal and Harpers Ferry. Since I'm no longer going to try to get mileage, it looks like Front Royal is where I'll be on the 4th. Besides, it's easier to get to Front Royal from I-81, and there is more to do in the area – so I'll meet Stef in Front Royal.

Sunday 6/29

Not a very good night's sleep last night, too much angle on the tent; I couldn't find a comfortable position. I tried something new for a pillow, but it was too big and hard. No matter, the body did rest even if I don't feel it had. Besides, now that I've quit pushing, or feeling the need to, and since I'm not trying for Harpers Ferry, I just don't have to do so much. I think I'm going to really enjoy this easy pace. I talked to a trail worker yesterday who said that he started the trail on April 10, 30 years ago, and when asked when he got done he said September 30. Yeah, well, I don't need to hurry it that much. I guess I'm not because I sure am slow getting going today. Also, I know I've got plenty of time to get through the Shenandoahs in time to meet up with Stef.

I'm first out of camp to a beautiful, quiet morning and trail. There is not much for scenery today as there are few open areas and the forest is fairly thick. Fairly early on the trail a fox comes trotting toward me. When he finally sees me for what I am he acts indifferent, but does not approach much closer before turning and running off.

Most of today's trails are long ups and downs with, it seems, more up than down. Even so, I make good time and distance doing about seventeen miles of trail, and a three mile round trip to a waterfall. In the three days I've been hiking in the park I'm almost half way through the 106 miles of it. And I'm not hiking that hard. Either I have to slow down and pace myself to get to Front Royal by Friday mid-morning, or go past it and hitch back to it. In the whole scheme of things, it doesn't make a whole lot of difference. And I have no anxiety about it one way or the other. So I guess I'll slow down and see the sights.

So tomorrow's Monday, five more days 'til I'm with my gal. It seemed like it would never get here, and now it's just around the corner. I am very excited about seeing her again – I miss her an awful lot.

It's evening, I'm turned in for the night, lying here in my tent writing. I'm camped ten feet off the trail under some pine trees. Out of the corner of my eye I catch a movement. Walking up the trail is a bear. He moseys along in typical bear fashion, but as he nears the tent he becomes cautious and eyes the tent suspiciously. As he's directly in front of me, maybe ten feet away, I move my writing pad and the noise startles him. As the old cartoon character, Snagglepuss, would say, "Exit, stage right," and he's gone in a flash. To be so close to one, what a gift!

Monday 6/30

Very lazy getting going this morning. Last night's bed was very comfortable and I was sleeping well, but then I started getting cool so I got up to put clothes on. I hadn't been back in my bed long enough to fall asleep when I noticed a couple flashes of lightning, and heard the thunder closer on the second. I got back up to put the fly on the tent, then crawled back in. And there was a good rain shower.

Today is cooler and the air drier than what it has been, a great day to hike – once I get going. Having only fifty-eight miles to do by Friday, I don't have to hurry, four more days 'til I'm together with Stef. How I look forward to that reunion. Yesterday I was having lunch with Harvest and Scout, and I told them about Stef and showed them her picture. Both of them said, "She's cuuute." Then I showed them the picture of me and the kids, and Scout wanted to know if Fuzz was taken, she said he was real cute. I told her he wasn't, she said she didn't understand why not.

As I'm writing this morning, there's a deer out there circling the tent trying to figure it out – maybe I've intruded too long. So I'm up and going.

My first stop is down by Pocsin Cabin for water. What a nice spot that would have been to camp. Had I known I was so close, I'd have camped there. Oh well, no matter. The trail today is very easy. There are some hills, but nothing very long or steep. As I walk along, I'm consumed with the idea of meeting Stef in four more days. I really miss her, and am very excited to see her again.

I had stopped at one of the visitor centers to make some calls. I called Stef to finalize plans to meet in Front Royal on the 4th. I stepped back outside and there were Harvest and Scout. They were on their way to the campground restaurant for blackberry shakes and a meal, so I joined them. The blackberry shakes are something of lore out here, and they live up to the reputation. And the food is good as well.

After the meal, I was ready to get back on the trail, but Harvest said she was going home, at least for a while, having too much trouble with her foot. Hugs, well wishes and goodbyes, and I'm on my way. So I get back to the trail and soon was walking past the end of the campground when the sky starts getting real dark. I got water and headed back up the trail a short way to a nice campsite. As I get there it starts to rain. I hoped it would hold off long enough for me to set up, but no luck. I got the tent set up and mostly dried, and a few minutes later the rain stops and the sun comes out. Had I known it'd be that way, I'd have hiked further.

Tuesday 7/1

I was lying in my tent writing when all at once I laid my pen and head down, and that was it for the night. I finished last night's journal this morning. I had to get up in the night to put on clothes as it got pretty cool since I was sleeping naked in just a bag liner and blanket. Early this morning the sky was all overcast and it was still quite cool, so I laid about. The sunlight is now pouring in, so it's time to get up and get going. The sun came, but it didn't remain.

Today is heavily overcast, breezy and cool. The thermometer at Rock Spring Cabin said it was 56°, a great day for hiking as you can walk right along and not break a sweat. But my mind is not on the trail today, it is on meeting up with Stef on Friday. I suppose there are nice views to be had, but I'm preoccupied. Of course there are nice views, there is lovely scenery all around. And I enjoy the deer that stand just beside the trail and gawk at you as you walk by. That doesn't happen in Maine.

About 1:30 I get to Sky Lodge and make reservations in Front Royal for the weekend, then call Stef to give her the lowdown. She thinks she will leave Thursday afternoon, drive 'til she's tired, take a motel room for the night, continue on in the morning and arrive in Front Royal before noon. I made some phone calls regarding the whereabouts and situation of my truck which was loaned to a supposed friend who was going to fix it in return for the use of it. Well, that didn't work out as it should, and I had to resort to police action in order to get the truck returned. After the calls, I went to eat – an order of turkey pot pie, then an order of chili; for dessert, a raspberry chocolate truffle brownie thing. Yum!

After leaving Sky Lodge, I got thinking about how I had been mistreated and lied to time and again about the deal with my truck. It really pissed me off; I thought I could trust the guy. So I hiked on this afternoon thinking all kinds of vicious thoughts about what I'd like to do to the guy, all the while knowing it wasn't doing any good – I was just creating negative energy. Eventually, I got it worked out.

I didn't get quite as far tonight as I planned – I'm less than a mile shy – but I'm in a picnic shelter that has a huge fireplace. There's nothing like a fire to warm you, body and soul. I gathered wood, and before long I have a nice fire going. I dragged the picnic table close to the fireplace, draped my tent parts over it to block the wind, laid my bed roll in front of the fireplace, and enjoyed a wonderful, warm bed. Only thirty-one miles to Front Royal and three days to get there. I'll be there before noon Friday, if not Thursday night.

Wednesday 7/2

I fell asleep in front of a great fire. I got up twice during the night, once to put more wood on the fire, again to put on more clothes when the fire lost its strength. Ahh… the best night's sleep in recent memory. I woke this morning to a beautiful, still, cloudless sky. Breakfast is now done, all I have to do is finish packing, then go walking in glorious sunshine and gentle breeze. Ohh, life is very good!

The start of the trail is rather rocky as I head up Pinnacle Mt. Once on top, and on top of the top, there is a tremendous 360° view of Shenandoah and surrounding Virginia. The trail down is just as rocky and rather slow going. What makes it even slower is that my head just is not on the trail. My mind is consumed with seeing Stef on Friday. And maybe it's because I've been in Virginia so long, and in the Shenandoahs for a while, that I feel I'm wanting a break from the trail. To get the pack off my back for a bit, and not have to trod uphill and down over rocks would feel good. Pretty soon.

After my late morning break I start to feel more at ease, back into the rhythm of the trail. The forest changes quite a bit on the afternoon stretch – sometimes dense, brushy growth, sometimes open, mature hardwoods, one stretch where the trees hardly had any leaves, other times mixed forest. Unless up high, there isn't much of a view – it's hard to see through trees.

A little after 3:00 I arrive at Elk Wallow Wayside, a stop I planned to make for just enough food for a day and a half to get me into Front Royal. While there, sitting outside eating my bacon cheeseburger, a couple of SoBo section hikers came in. There was the usual trail talk when all at once the woman asked me if I was Chris. I hadn't met them before, so I was a little surprised at the question. They met Wasabi in Front Royal yesterday, and he had given them a note to give to me. Unfortunately, they gave the note to another hiker who said he knew me and would probably see me before they would. So it goes. Many calls to try to get truck business taken care of – not sure that it was.

I left the wayside about 5:30 or 6:00 unsure of how far I would go. I came to Range View Cabin with a decent sheltered porch, a good spring very close, so I decide to stay here. I took a bath, with soap, and got some of the stink out of my clothes. Yeah, I know, Front Royal is less than a day and a half away, but I can stand just so much. Even if it is my own stink. Tomorrow I plan to get up and going in good season. We'll see.

Something large, a bear?, was just crashing around in the woods beside the cabin, and scared a rabbit that came running across the porch, stopped ever so briefly to check me out and continued on his way. Maybe I'll have a visitor tonight.

Thursday 7/3

Nope, no visitors, but kind of a restless night just the same. Got up a little groggy, but got going good anyway. Since I don't have too far to go, I feel as though I can ease into the day. Just one more day 'til I meet Stef in Front Royal. I'm nearly giddy at the thought of it. I'm really looking forward to spending a few days and quality time with my gal.

The trail today starts easy, I like to start the day that way, and before long I'm at the trail to a spring as I'm out of water. Half way to the spring, off to my right, I hear a snap and turn to see a bear. It's a young one, and he scampers off quickly. While I'm filling my bottles at the spring I hear a snap right behind me and know it is the bear. I turn around to see him about twenty feet away watching me. I'm sure he wants to drink at the spring. I keep talking to him, and he circles away and wanders off. I had asked earlier to see bears today as this would be my last day in Shenandoah National Park. Bottles filled, spirits high, I move on.

The trail is really nice, and before long I have gone five miles to the first shelter, time for a break and food. That being done, I'm back on the trail. Now the trail is not as easy and I'm heading up steeper and rockier slopes. Still, it's pretty good. In a few miles I round a bend and see another bear up ahead in the trail. He's an adult, two hundred or more pounds, feeding along the side of the trail. I said hello to him and he indifferently turns his head to look at me with an expression that says, "Yeah, what do you want?" I talk to him and get within about forty feet, but don't pressure him any – this one is not scared of me. In a few minutes he walks off the trail and I pass by within thirty feet of him, talking as I go. He seems almost annoyed at my presence, but with typical bear nonchalance goes about his business. Giving him space, I watch for a while then move on. Two bears on my last day in the park – such a gift!

The next few miles are two rocky hills, but nothing hard. Along this stretch I meet up with Slow and Steady, an older, retired fellow who is hiking north in a southerly direction. He leapfrogs his cars, moving the southerly car north of the other, then hikes south to the car he left behind. This way, he always moves north, but hikes south to do it. We share a fruit pie I had, talk a little bit, then go our separate ways. I decide to go to the last shelter before town, making for a very easy day tomorrow. I get to the shelter to find a half dozen young guys strewn all about. I make camp below the shelter, have my supper, then retire to my writing. Tomorrow I see my babe!!!

Friday 7/4, Saturday 7/5, Sunday 7/6

It was only three miles to the road into Front Royal, but it seemed like a long three miles to me – I suppose I'm anxious to see Stef. I got a hitch fairly quickly and got dropped at the shopping center where I went into the Goodwill store for nicer looking clothes. Got the clothes, got some milk and an apple from the grocery store next door, and headed for the hotel. I got there about 10:00, Stef arrived before noon. It was wonderful to see her, to wrap up in a hug. There was a little awkwardness, as if we had to rediscover each other again, but we managed just fine.

It doesn't really matter what we did that day, or any of the days we had together, it was simply wonderful that we were together. Some of the things we did do were going to the movies Friday night, Luray Cavern on Saturday, poking around a flea market on Sunday. I especially enjoyed touring the cavern. But just to spend the time with her…

Oh, when you've been wandering around in the woods for months, there is an adjustment period needed before you return to being a competent driver. I still wanted to gawk around as I had been doing, but now I was moving at a greatly increased rate of speed, and so were the other folks on the "trail." To say the least, my driving was interesting for those couple days…

Monday 7/7

A terrible night's sleep – a hard time getting to sleep, woke often. I think that maybe if I tried to ignore the fact that Stef would be leaving in the morning, that it wouldn't happen. Of course it had to, she needed to return to her world. She has been gone about an hour now, I feel empty. Crying over her leaving doesn't help, she is gone (for now) just the same. Just before she left the room, we embraced and cried. There's no way what we feel for each other isn't true, isn't genuine. The love I feel for her runs deep into the very core of my being. I don't know if I ever felt so torn – between wanting to go back to Maine with her, or return to the trail. Hiking the trail is seeing a dream come true, but then, so is the love of a very special woman and making a life with her. I suppose there's plenty of time for both. I want to call her and tell her to come back and get me, but I want to finish the hike.

In regard to the hike – as I walked Stef to the car I noticed my shin was sore; what is going on here? My ankle and foot have been hurting for some time as well; what am I telling myself?

Okay, here's the nitty gritty: If you asked me if I was enjoying the hike, I would have to reply, "Not as much as I thought I would." It's hard, it's punishing; it seems there are often more moments of "this is just hard work" compared to the moments of "this is really awesome." Sometimes I have to wonder if it isn't ego or stubbornness, more than desire, that keeps me out here. And maybe I'm just feeling the blues. I guess it happens a lot here in Virginia – having been so long on the trail and not feeling like progress has been made can leave folks feeling depressed. In a week or so, I will finish Virginia, go through West Virginia and Maryland, and get into Pennsylvania. I think the emotional boost of feeling such accomplishment will help greatly. Hmm, I'm on to something here – my shin, ankle, foot don't seem as sore as they did earlier.

I truly want to see this hike through, for a number of reasons, and the number of reasons to see it through is greater than the number to quit. There are lessons to be learned from most everything; I'm learning many along the way, but maybe I won't see the big picture until I'm done.

There is a recurring thought about quitting, and about how I may have been so quick to quit in the past (with my ex), and that if anything is truly worth it, you stick with it – no matter how difficult it may be at times. And it now occurred to me that it wasn't only in this life that I quit when things got difficult. In my last life I gave it all up when I felt it got to be too much to take. Is that the kind of legacy I want for my life – that I give up when things become too tough to want to deal with? Yes, this hike is difficult, in more ways than one, but I truly believe the reward for finishing it will be great.

As I was leaving town to get back on the trail, I stopped in to see a chiropractor. I got in to the chiropractor before 9:00, and out by 9:15. Carrier Chiropractic did a fantastic job of putting me in my place – I walked out with no pain in my ankle or foot. I needed that. I stopped at the store for a muffin, fruit, drink and a call to Stef. It had been only 4.5 hours since she left, but I was missing her something awful. After the call, I got a pretty easy hitch up to the trail, and I'm underway by 10:00.

Today is sunny, so it is quite warm out from under cover of the trees. The trail is pretty easy and the forest changes often. It is predominantly a hardwood forest, but there are sections where it is quite damp and the woods take on a jungle like appearance and the air is very heavy. And then I'd be in a section that would be rockier, drier and more open. This changing of the forest occurred throughout the day's travels.

Sometime early afternoon I stopped at a picnic table beside a stream to eat, then moved on to the next shelter two miles away. At Manassas Shelter I stopped for water and decided to make for the next shelter five miles further on. A quarter mile or so up the trail I realized I didn't have my data book. I knew I didn't look at it at the shelter, so it had to be back at the picnic table. I hollered and swore and yelled and swore and got upset. I didn't think I could rely on someone finding it and bringing it to me, so I left my pack at the shelter and beat feet the two miles back to get it. Sure enough, there it was. By the time I got through with that back-track, I had put an extra 4.5 miles on the day.

I got my pack, and with plenty of daylight made for Dick's Dome Shelter five miles away. I arrived in plenty of time to get set up, cleaned up, a little supper and write in my journal. So, backtrack included, I did almost twenty miles today. Not bad for not getting going until 10:00.

Tuesday 7/8

A very good night's sleep. Up and going early, the first one out. The trail is pretty easy, but I'm full of aches and pains, so it seems much harder. I obsessed on the difficulty of the trail and my aches and pains until I realized I was my own worst enemy. I know I can be a prisoner to having dark thoughts, something I'm working on changing, and I knew I needed to change my thoughts. It took some effort, but I got my head straightened out. Once that was done, the rest of the day went very nicely, especially when I reaffirmed with positive thought.

The first part of today's hike was easy, and I made nine miles by noon. My plan was to do fifteen, maybe eighteen, so I was at least half way done. At dinner I was talking with a couple of hikers who told me about Bear's Den Hostel, and the pizzas and ice cream that can be had there. That's all I needed to know, I was headed there. After dinner, I entered the renowned "roller coaster," so named because the trail goes up and down, up and down – ten hills in thirteen miles. Today was hot and I sweat buckets, soaking my clothes, as I trudged up and down the relentless hills.

I made it to the hostel just about 6:00. I got a cold drink, cooked a pizza, had a salad and ate with the hostel managers and fellow hikers. I felt so fat and happy I decided to stay the night. Bear's Den Hostel is a lovely, quaint stone and wood building in a splendid garden setting. Just a very short walk behind brings you to a cliff providing awesome sunset views over the valley below. It's one of those places that it feels good just to be there. A hot shower, laundry done, calls home, a pint of ice cream and I'm done for the night. Twenty miles to Harpers Ferry – I don't know if I'll do it tomorrow or not.

5

WEST VIRGINIA/MARYLAND

Wednesday 7/9

Up and going pretty good, before any sign of life in the hostel. I took a few minutes to admire the view from Bears Den Rocks, then finished up the roller coaster in a few miles. I had sweated so heavily and soaked my clothes so thoroughly yesterday that my inner thighs were chafed and sore. I was pretty sure there wouldn't be many hikers on this stretch of trail, so I slathered on the Bag Balm and hiked naked for a few hours. I ran into one young couple, but they didn't seem to be bothered by my naked appearance. Or if they were, they hid it well. Besides, that's why there are therapists.

Once over the roller coaster the trail leveled out pretty well and was quite easy walking. Seeing the Welcome to West Virginia sign really picked up my spirits. Finally, I was out of Virginia and making progress. From the state line, Harpers Ferry was seventeen miles away, Maryland 17.5. I was all set to make the twenty miles to Harpers Ferry. I walked along in good spirits, stopping to take a few breaks along the way.

Later in the afternoon my left shoulder was aching a little from the pack, so I figured it was time for a break. Afterward, I went to put my pack on and noticed that the hip belt didn't look right. Upon closer inspection I noticed it was broken. A $300, three week old pack shouldn't be broken, and it left me a little frustrated. I was all set to breeze on in to Maryland, but I guess I'll be delayed some while I get the pack squared away.

Harpers Ferry is quaint. That's an often over-used term to describe places, but it best describes this downtown section of town. The narrow little streets are lined up close with old stone, brick and wooden buildings set shoulder to shoulder. It's a very touristy downtown, though tonight it seems quite sleepy. This town is very proud of its heritage and its part in the civil war, as evidenced by the historic markers placed all about the downtown area. Along with the somewhat restored military garrison situated along the river, one almost has the feeling that it isn't yet over down here.

Tonight, I'm staying in a rather expensive hostel, $33 a night for a bunk, but the room I'm in has only two bunks and it looks as though I'll have the room to myself. Hopefully I'll be able to get my pack taken care of quickly and easily in the morning, and I'll be out of town no later than noon.

Thursday 7/10

Did not sleep well last night – so much noise! Up about 5:30 and trying to be quiet so as not to wake the others. Early call to Stef, then off to breakfast at the Country Café, "where the locals eat," and had a very good breakfast. Got some money, and picked up the few groceries I need for the next four days at 7-11 (really…). I then went to see about pack repair or replacement. I told them my situation and Laura, the owner, showed me a nice replacement pack, and set about making calls to Gregory and Outdoor Trails to see what was going to work best. The Gregory representative said he could have replacement hip belts shipped to me overnight, but that would mean another night's stay. Besides I was feeling leery that I could trust the new hip belt to hold up any better, so I opted for a new, quite comfortable Osprey pack. I finally had all the business work done by 3:00. Up the road for something to eat, one last call to Stef, a frozen custard and I'm on the trail just after 4:00. It's an easy, pleasant six miles to the Ed Garvey Shelter, the first few miles being flat trail alongside the river. I'm here by myself with plenty of light to write by – just what I wanted.

Friday 7/11

It's early morning, the sky is getting lighter, but the sun has not yet shown itself over the horizon. I slept okay, but not as well as I had hoped. I guess I went to bed rather emotional. I've been on the trail three months and a day. Sometimes it feels like I just started, other times it feels like I've been out here forever. It's funny, the dichotomy of it. At times I feel I could stay out here for a very long time, but then I'm anxious to get home. I miss Maine, I miss my kids, I miss family and friends, I miss all the things I could be doing. And I miss my gal. I dream of all the things I would be doing if I were back home with her. It won't be this summer, but there'll be others.

After breakfast and the nearly one mile round trip to the spring, I'm on my way. So far, I'm finding the trail through Maryland pretty easy. I'd heard it runs along a ridge, that much seems to be true, but I'd also heard it was quite rocky, so far that is not the case. Yes, there are rocky areas, but there is far more trail that is soil or gravel, much that is an old road bed.

The day is hot and muggy, but as long as I'm in the shade of the tree canopy it's not too bad. The forest is quite thin and open, most of it, with stretches of mature or young hardwood, and a few of pine. There are many patches of berries that are ripening nicely. One of which is the wine berry. It looks much the same as a red raspberry – a little larger, a little brighter in color, sort of sticky to the touch, but such a delicate, delicious flavor! I've eaten many handfuls today. Also, I've had blueberries and black raspberries. Such goodness that Spirit has provided for us. Thank You!

Today's trail has stayed easy all day, and I did 18.5 miles pretty easily, even with the heat and all. The new pack is pretty comfortable, the best yet. It was a good choice. Let's hope it holds up better than the last. I stopped at Pine Knob Shelter for supper. It's not very far from I-40, so it is much noisier than I'd like. 1.5 miles further on is Annapolis Rocks with camping and water. It's bound to be quieter, so that's where I head.

Along the way I had to step off the trail to answer a nature call. While finishing the paperwork, I noticed I had a visitor. In the roots of an overturned tree was a rock, maybe eight inches in diameter, that had a face profile etched into it. And there he was watching me. I'd made a new friend; he came with me.

I made it to the camping area, set up, got bathed and water, then went back for supper. It's a real pretty spot. Maybe three miles distant down in the valley is a drag strip, so I've had the pleasure of listening to many angrily screaming engines. Now that the sun has nearly set, they've pretty much stopped. Back at Pine Knob Shelter, I was reading the register and found that D had been there on the 3rd, and Wasabi on the 8th. It seems I'm gaining on them. It sure would be good to see them again.

Saturday 7/12

Slow getting going this morning. I was up with the sun and out of camp early, but just couldn't seem to get into the rhythm. I got the first five miles done sometime around 10:30. Taking a break to eat every five miles works pretty well for me, I'm usually hungry and ready to eat about then.

Today's trail starts easily (thankfully), but becomes a mixed bag of smooth, level road to rough, rocky ridgeline. Sometime around noon I come to the third or fourth road crossing and a stream. Off come the clothes and in I go – Ahh, refreshing! Unfortunately it doesn't last long as in less than a mile I'm huffing and puffing up a steep, rough hill on a section called the Devil's Racetrack. Once done with that, I decided I'm ready for more food. Besides, it has been another five miles. So back down another steep, rocky slope to the shelter. There I cook my big meal and take a good break. Not only have I been ten miles so far, but it is hot and muggy.

I have been toying with the idea of doing a flip-flop when I get through Pennsylvania, but I won't know until I get to the other end of the state. A flip-flop is when a hiker leaves the section of trail they are on to go to the other end and walk back to where they left off. There are pros and cons to doing a flip-flop, perhaps there are better arguments for the pros. That's a couple weeks and 220 miles away, no need to figure it out now.

The next five-mile mark put me at Pen-Mar State Park on the, you guessed it, Pennsylvania/Maryland state line. I walked up into the park to see about food or drink, but was told that the concession stand is closed until tomorrow. I plunked myself down on a bench with Bill, the park attendant, and had a pleasant chat. He suggested I could bum some food off a group of folks having a family re-union, but I said I didn't want to intrude. So he did it for me. Next thing I know, a woman comes over with a plate with a hamburger, hot dog, chips, melon, cashews and a cookie. Then she comes back with cold drinks, then with a plate of cheese and crackers. Before long I'm sitting on the bench feeling quite fat and happy. On her last trip by, I got up, gave her a hug, which she returned warmly, and thanked her again. Big score of magic from a true trail angel! Bill went on his way to do his chores, but not before wishing me good luck and a "God bless you." If ever I was a skeptic, meeting folks like them would certainly restore my faith in human nature.

Since there is a pay phone handy I called my gal. We had a pleasant talk, but she wasn't really with it, she was babysitting her niece. I told her of my thought of possibly flip-flopping, she said she'd support me either way. Maybe I thought she'd be more enthusiastic at the idea of me being around for a short bit this summer. But I'm sure she was just preoccupied with her niece, as well as being in a self-proclaimed funk.

After the call, I watered up and headed into Pennsylvania. I didn't go very far before I was down in a valley with a gurgling stream running through it. Perfect! I set up camp, bathe, do laundry and retire to my writing. The sun has been down maybe a half hour, and I'm using up the remaining light. It's time to make my bed and crawl into it. Good night.

Mama bear with cubs (barely visible behind tree)

6

PENNSYLVANIA

Sunday 7/13

A dream has left me feeling a little blue, it involved my ex. We were married, but at the end. She "found" some of my writings and learned something was amiss. She told me I had to leave, and then she said something to Ma about being sorry that she wouldn't be able to go or do whatever they had planned. It all seemed rather matter of fact, but there was still the emotion involved. Still feeling the emotion means that it is still raw, that it has not been all processed out. That is why I cannot fully commit to another relationship at this time. I still have stuff to work through.

I hit the trail fairly early, but I wasn't feeling just right. I drank a lot of water this morning, so by the time I'd been a couple miles I was feeling pretty good.

Just like all the other days, this one is starting hot and muggy. Once I make the first hill, the rest of the trail is pretty easy. Well, for the next six or so miles it is, then I go up for about a mile to a rocky top called Chimney Rocks. The forest along this stretch is quite thin, so there isn't much shade from the tree canopy to keep me cool. I'm sweating buckets. After I get over the rocky top, the trail levels out again and is pretty easy. As I approach Rt. 30, I drop down through mixed forest and I see a variety of trees that I have not seen in many miles. Along with all the hardwoods I am now walking through fir, hemlock and pine.

About three miles before Rt.30 I get caught in a thunderstorm. I covered my pack, but didn't wear my rain suit. I always used to enjoy walking in the rain, and I still do. And splashing in the puddles is just as fun as it always was. I make it to the road about

4:30, and though many cars speed by me, I had a pretty easy hitch into Fayetteville. I checked in at the motel, had a shower and got laundry done, had supper and back to the room to write and call home. It's still quite warm and muggy, but there is a window beside the bed and I'm hoping that will give me enough cool, fresh air. We'll see.

Monday 7/14
   I called Stef about 6:45 and we had a nice chat, though it had to be cut short. A walk to breakfast then to the post office for my care package, and some shopping for day food. Chores done, I make calls home. It's now 10:30, time to hit the trail. I got a hitch right away, thank you, and am on the trail by 11:00.
   A good hill climb from Caledonia State Park and I meet an older couple out hiking and seeing what's about. They think they would like to do the AT and ask me many questions; I regale them with stories of the trail. I wonder if I talked them into it, or out of it... The trail is wonderful today. There are only a couple rocky sections, the rest pretty smooth and lead through a very pretty forest of mainly hardwoods, sometimes softwoods, but all have undergrowth of rhododendron, fern, blueberries and many other low shrubby plants. It really is just a lovely place to walk, so beautiful and serene.
   The trail is so nice today that I make thirteen miles – not bad for not having started the hike until 11:00. I debated pushing another three miles to get to the shelter, but I opt for supper, start reading Stef's pages, and that's as far as I got. That's the way I like to do it best – stop earlier so I can eat, clean up, do laundry and retire to writing before dark. Yeah, I could do more miles a day if I hiked later into the evening, but that would cut into my writing time, and I'm not going to compromise that time. Another thing that made today's hiking easy is that the hot, humid weather broke. It was still quite warm – 85° or so – but the air is much drier and there is a lovely little breeze. Thank You very much!

The forecast is for temps in the fifties tonight. I don't doubt it will be, and I'm wearing long pants, long sleeved shirts and socks to bed. I am camped beside a small, gurgling spring that makes me think of a baby's gurgling and babbling; it's a happy, cheerful little brook. Ever since getting on the trail this morning, the whole day has been very pleasant and peaceful. Today I came back to the trail.

Tuesday 7/15
Well, that night flew right by. I guess I slept well, maybe because it was cool and dry. I'm glad I put on the clothes for warmth. Some disturbing dreams though. I don't remember much about the first except that in it my ex had died. I was sorrowful and crying and asking why the people in my life that I love had died. Stef, seemingly unaware of the death, was asking me if I was ready to go/do something. Then the chorus from the song ran over and over, "I still haven't found what I'm looking for." I went to bed thinking about the condition of my left foot, and what might be the cause of that – what thoughts or emotions that are creating the resistance to the flow of energy. I remember the dream from just a couple nights ago that involved my ex, and how the emotion is still raw; therefore, I feel unable to move too quickly into another relationship. I'm of two minds with this relationship business – the brain says go, the heart says whoa, or vice versa. This is the second time in as many days that this has come out, so there definitely is something to it. I was just thinking more about the relationship issue. It really doesn't have much to do with Stef, it's all my stuff to work through.

So I'm on the trail a little later than I would be if I hadn't written so much, but I had to write.

The trail starts out a little rocky, but easy. I stroll along at a good pace and think I'm making good time. The forest changes today, going from open hardwood to a lovely mix of hard and soft woods, all the while the undergrowth is mostly rhododendron.

There are some hills and rocky stretches today, but mostly the trail is good going.

Some time just before noon, I came to Pine Grove Furnace State Park. On a bridge crossing a stream I am besieged by a group of young guys on a walk being led by a park ranger. I answered a lot of questions about hiking the AT, and I move on. Just down the path is what they call a lake, though I'd consider it a small pond. In any case, the water is clear and inviting. I drop my pack, remove my shirt and footwear, and dive in. Ohhh... Nice! Whistler, another hiker, is there and we leave together. Shortly up the trail, we come to the half-way sign post. Hey!, we've done half the AT! We take pictures then move on. I take the lead after a bit as he is in pain and is slow due to shin splints. I sure can relate to that.

The forest is now back to open hardwoods, and I'm wishing there is more shade. Getting on towards late afternoon, and I start thinking about camping spots. There is a shelter coming up, but it's eight miles away, and I've already done fourteen. It's too early to stop, so I move on. After the third road crossing, I drop into a low land and in a half mile or so there is a camp site and a small stream. It would do, but I can do better. In less than a mile I come to a bottom land that has a nice stream flowing through it. At a bend in the trail and stream is an awesome camp spot. This is where I'm at tonight. I had the tent set up and was preparing supper when Whistler comes by. "Sweet spot" he says, chats briefly and continues on to the shelter maybe four miles away. I have a nice bath, with soap, do my laundry, have supper, then retire to my journal.

Just before getting to this spot, there was a lowland section of trail through a hardwood forest where I got a chill, then again and again. It wasn't a chill from cold as the day has been sunny and warm, but there definitely was an energy that made me tingle from the top of my head to my toes. An awful lot of the Civil War was fought in these parts, and I wondered if I walked through a battlefield and the old souls were still about. Whatever it was, the energy was strong.

So, yeah, I could have made it to the shelter and done a twenty-two miler, but the sun is just now dropping to the horizon, the light is gone from all but the tops of the trees, and my day is all done. Besides, eighteen miles is nothing to sneeze at. I like to end my day this way – easy, relaxed with plenty of time to set up camp, get supper, do chores and write.

At the halfway mark

Wednesday 7/16

I'm not too gung ho to move this morning, I'm not as well rested as I would like to be. It got cool down here last night, cool enough that I had to get up to put on clothes. Even still, I was chilly during the night. It's about twenty miles to Darlington Shelter; if the trail is easy that's where I'll be tonight. Probably.

After I get up and over the next rocky ridge, about four miles distant, I drop down to much farm land – fields of corn, wheat and alfalfa. It's very pretty country, but I prefer the woods as there is shade from the hot sun. At 11:30ish I come to a park, with the remnants of another blast furnace, in the town of Boiling Springs, Pennsylvania. Through the middle of town flows a small pond, maybe three hundred yards long by one hundred yards wide, appearing no more than three feet deep, but probably is. This is the out flowing from the boiling spring – a hole into the earth perhaps two feet by four feet from which a tremendous volume of cold spring water continually flows. I imagine this would have been a sacred place for the original natives.

While in town I have a delicious meal of a steak and cheese sandwich and house salad from an Italian restaurant just up from the spring. On the way back past the spring, a young fellow asks my trail name and I tell him, "Chris."

He says, "I heard about you. You're from Maine?"

"Yes, how did you hear about me?"

He said he met Wasabi some days ago, and that he spoke of me. "He spoke very highly of you," said the young fellow. He said Wasabi was maybe only a day ahead of me.

About 12:30 I head out of town, the day's destination uncertain. I marched on crossing roads, highways, fields, occasionally meandering through woods. I'm making good time, and think I can make the next shelter in good season. At the last road crossing, Pa. 944, there is a cooler – Trail Magic! I'm not a big soda drinker, but three cans of Mountain Dew go down pretty well. That with an apple, a big handful of wine berries and a Clif

Bar, I power up the two mile climb up to Darlington Shelter. My best day yet, 21.5 miles.

In reading the shelter register, I see that I'm two days behind Wasabi, and five days behind D; I'm gaining on both of them. I really would like to catch them before the end of Pennsylvania. So I place an order – give me strong, fast feet that I may catch my friends. Thank You.

While at the shelter, I met a young fellow hiking to New York. He's a writer and is working on a book, some sort of an inspirational book. As we talk I comment on some aspect of the trail. He asks something about the trail, and whether it was good or bad. I reply, "It is neither good nor bad, it just is."

He thought about that for a moment, then repeated it; "It's neither good nor bad, it just is." As he wrote it down he said, "I like that, I'm going to put that in my book."

Thursday 7/17

Did not sleep well last night. It was too warm and stuffy, and then the no-see-ums, very tiny, biting insects, found me. I knew I should have pitched my tent. I had wondered how good my foot was going to feel after the hard run yesterday, but it seems okay.

Today's trail goes down a rocky hill, crosses four large fields, meanders through some low woods for a bit, rises up a long, rocky trail to a high ridge which is mostly pretty rocky, and eventually descends a long, rocky hill to Duncannon.

My foot, which started out feeling pretty good, has been quite sore for the last half of the day's run. Occasionally I'd step on a rock just so and send a shooting pain right through my foot into my lower leg. And just for the fun of it, my right knee has become more sore to where it does not want to bend and support weight while stepping down. I know what this means, and I sit in the trail and cry. I have been debating the idea of a flip-flop, but now it seems it is more a decision of necessity – I have to get off the trail for a while to let my body heal. I don't like the idea at all, but it is what I must do, or I run a high risk of further damaging my knees, ankles, feet.

And so into town I go, get checked in at the Doyle Hotel, and get to the chiropractor. The chiropractor loosened the ankle up some, but most everything else was too tight to move. I got my laundry started, then headed up the hill to get my groceries. By the time I'd gotten to the store a little over a half mile away, I was limping and in pain – despite having taken four ibuprophen about an hour earlier. That pretty well confirmed what I already knew. I got the laundry done and taken back to the room along with my groceries, then went out to call Stef.

I got her on the second try and told her what was going on. She told me that she knew before she dropped me at the airport way back at the beginning that I was not going to do the whole trail in one shot. But I'm determined. I think that with a couple weeks of rest, I will go up to Katahdin and make my way south. And so what if I don't finish until October, or even November. So that's the plan. It's not my first choice, but it'll have to do.

Friday 7/18

Funny thing is, I slept better in this stuffy, noisy, run down, flea bag hotel last night than I did in the last shelter two nights ago. I have no idea what time it is, well, I have an idea – it's maybe 6:00 or 6:30. The umpteenth train has just shuffled through, and the street outside is getting busier with traffic. I'll go for breakfast, call Stef, then make my way to Harrisburg to catch a Greyhound bus home. I never ever thought it would go this way, but here it is. And this is the way it has to be right now. My foot is too badly hurt to continue hiking on it. I'm not happy about it, but I know this is the way it has to be, and I've come to terms with it. So a few weeks of R&R, get myself back in good shape, and I'll get back on the trail, Katahdin south.

You know, thinking back, I never was ready for the trail. I grossly under-rated what it would be like, I was too cocky and arrogant in my ability, and when the trail showed me what it was, it knocked me for a loop. I have been humbled. But I am not defeated. As soon as I am healed and ready for the remainder, I'll head out and finish this journey.

So I stood at the highway on-ramp hitching a ride and soon got one from a troubled young woman with three kids. She was teary eyed, obviously quite shook up, but didn't feel like talking about her problems. She took me close to the bus terminal, I got out, handed her $20, thanked her and wished her good luck.

The bus wasn't leaving until late afternoon, so I had time to kill in the busy downtown area of Harrisburg. I poked around, strolled by the river, got something to eat and poked around some more. Three young fellows making their way as best they could to some distant destination asked me for a handout. I'm a traveler myself, and I know what it is to want to get to your destination. I gave them $20 and wished them good luck, they were quite appreciative. Mostly, I just moped around while considering my situation as I waited for the bus.

A hot, stuffy, cramped bus ride, and I arrived in Augusta, Maine, about 9:00 the next morning. Stef met me at the terminal, and we went to breakfast. It was great to see her, but under the circumstances, I was not as jovial as I might otherwise have been. Now, I've got some healing work to do.

7

PAUSE

And that is how the first part of my hike went. Needless to say, I was severely down-hearted at the outcome of what was supposed to be the grandest adventure of my life. You could say the trail kicked my butt; in reality the trail did nothing, it simply laid there. I kicked my own butt.

I have said so many times that it is the mind game that makes or breaks you. Ultimately, I lost the mind game. Probably, that's what knocks everybody out of it. The thing is, if your mind is strong and healthy and focused, barring any debilitating physical injuries or other problems, you'll make the trip. When you're head's not together, nothing else will work. And the mind controls the body. Problems in the mind, mental/emotional problems, show up as ailments in the body. Clearly, I had plenty of emotional problems, and they caused a lot of physical trauma. Yeah, I lost the mind game in a big way.

A phenomenon of many hours, days and weeks of hiking is that the day's routine becomes so simple, though not necessarily easy, with few actions requiring direct attention. Because of this, the mind's focus becomes very narrow in dealing with the basic necessities of breakfast, packing up, hiking, stopping occasionally for water or food, making camp, supper and chores at day's end. And as a result of little that needs attention, the mind is free to wander where it may. This can be rewarding, but it can also have an adverse effect.

From the get-go, my head was not in the right place. I wasn't prepared for the trail, I pooh-poohed it as being a walk in the park – it is anything but. Mostly, my head was all screwed up by recent events in my life. The divorce in 2006 nearly devastated me, Mom's death in 2007 rocked me hard, and the relationship with Stef, which I was never ready for, had me so torn that I didn't know which way to jump. Mostly, I didn't know if I was on foot or horseback, coming or going. Also, I was plagued by old, old memories of a time long ago that I brought with me into this life. I have often suffered from a feeling of inadequacy, a mindset acquired from a hard, tough past life that left scars upon my psyche. It was no wonder I couldn't keep it together. I was just doing the best I could.

So, I'm back in Maine for rest and healing. I figured I'd be a couple weeks, a month tops, and I'd be back on the trail. But it wasn't as easy as that. Stef and I picked up where we left off – almost. Somewhere between the time Stef visited me in Virginia and I got back to Maine things had changed, our relationship was not what it was prior to my leaving. There was no one definitive moment or action that caused the change, more like a recognition that we weren't compatible as a couple. I'm sure we both tried to hold on to the magic that once was, but it was fading. Yet again, there was conflict and turmoil in my life. Would I ever get my head straight?

The following two entries are from when I was back in Maine trying to rest and heal:

Monday 7/21

Here I am at Stef's, she's off to a doctor's appointment. Just like so much lately, I'm both comfortable and out of place. I'm comfortable with Stef, out of place with myself. For all that I thought the hike would be it has not turned out the way I'd imagined. Come to think of it, many things in my life did not turn out the way I expected. Maybe there is something there for me to learn. Maybe?

It's the mental game that makes or breaks you, and this is especially true on the trail. I imagined the hike would be one way, I found it to be something different. And so I was rattled when presented with the reality of it.

The physical problems: According to Louise Hay's teachings, shins represent the standards of life and breaking down ideals; feet represent our understanding of life, ourselves, others; knees represent pride and ego. Shins – standards and ideals – what did I compromise? Are standards and ideals the same as expectations? If so, then having to adjust or change my belief of the trail in order to meet the reality of it could be in conflict with my idea of it. Feet – understanding life and ourselves. I thought I finally had figured myself out, but the trail really tested me, shook me up right to my core. Knees – pride and ego. Yeah, well, that sure got dashed to pieces. Okay, so now what? I have to heal my body, my self.

Monday 8/4

Very much out of sorts today. I'd planned on working on the car today, but I have absolutely no interest in it. Certainly I'm betwixt and between lately. Just exactly where I am I don't know. While on the trail, I was missing my life here, but here I am missing my life on the trail. It seems that no matter where I am, I'm missing my life.

Right now, I just don't seem to fit anywhere. I never did feel right staying at my brother's house and, although welcome, I don't feel like I belong here at Stef's. I am between. I am between the life I knew, and the one I want which is out there somewhere. Maybe I had too many expectations. Maybe it's not a matter of expectations, maybe it's a lack of a clear destination. And maybe it's not that, either.

I know what I want, where I want to be and what I want to be doing. I guess I'm feeling lost or out of place because I do not have anything I can call "mine," I don't have "my own place," a place where I'm comfortable, that I can call "home." Maybe I don't even have my self. So it seems the answer to this dilemma is to simply do what I want, and get what I want. However, there is more to this problem than the obvious.

What is going on in my head to cause the physical problems I encountered on the trail? I've pondered, thought about, and mulled this question over and over and have not come to any definite conclusions. The only thing that keeps coming back to me is that I'm ready for what I want. I want to, and I will, finish the trail – that is the realization of a dream. But I feel that before I can get back on the trail, I need to get my head straight. I need to correct my thought process in order to heal myself, and prevent any flare ups or other "injuries." What is going through my head? If only I knew…

The rest of the summer went on in the same manner. My body was improving, I was healing, but much slower than I had expected. Again, things were not as I'd imagined, hoped, believed. Nearing the end of August I was starting to feel like I was ready to get back on the trail. I was going to go up to Katahdin and walk south. I had plenty of time to do it this way – I had September, October and November to do it in, ending in Pennsylvania where I left off. Yes, it would be getting chilly then, but I would be much more southerly, and the climate warmer than in Maine at that time of year. It would work.

As I was gearing myself back up mentally, I got word that the old family home, which had been for sale since Mom's death, was sold and needed to be cleaned out by the first of October. I knew I was the only one of us seven kids that had the time and capacity to take on such a daunting task, it being a 13 room house with attached two story barn – all full of fifty-four years of living. Still, I wanted to get back on the trail and finish it. I talked to my sister and a couple brothers about this and they all said the same thing, "Hike the trail if that's what you want to do, we won't hold it against you; we'll manage getting the house cleaned out." But they all had so much going on in their lives…

I decided to take on the job of cleaning out the place, and getting the two brothers living there situated elsewhere. It was a big job, taking me until the first of October to do it. By then, I felt it was too late to get back on the trail that year. No matter, I'd get back to it next year. Still, I won't have done it in one season. And there's the ego talking again – more crap in my head.

In the meantime, the relationship with Stef went by the wayside. I was never ready for it in the first place, and we realized that we weren't truly compatible. It was tough, having "lost at love" again; at the same time, it was an issue that got resolved. Early on in our relationship we made a pact, we pinky swore, that we would always be open and honest in our communication – that we would always say what was on our minds and in our hearts. No matter how difficult it may be. We had a rocky stretch, not necessarily an easy flow, as we found that the boyfriend/girlfriend relationship was no longer working. So we ceased to be a couple, but because of our pact we worked through it. The good thing about it is that we still openly and honestly communicate with each other, that we share a love that remains today, and always will.

So there it was, the trail was done for this year.

What to do now? I needed a place to live, I needed to provide for myself. Where was I going to go, what was I going to do? My problem was answered in a few phone calls.

The local newspaper was running an ad from an outfit in Colorado looking for help – room and board provided. It seemed like this would work out well as all I needed to do was get there. Besides, all I was looking for was something for the winter as I would be getting back on the trail come spring. I'd always wanted to see the Rockies in the winter, so I inquired, applied for, and got hired working for Snow Mountain Ranch in Granby, Colorado.

It turned out to be a very good venture for me. The job I had was grooming cross-country ski trails, outside work in beautiful mountain country. The job and room and board worked out very well. I met, worked with, and became friends with great folks from this country, South America and Thailand. I had two consecutive days off, so with my camper on my truck, I traveled around the West and got to see some incredible countryside throughout Colorado, Wyoming and Montana. Rocky Mountain

National Park was an hour down the road, so I visited that often, snowshoeing many of the trails. While out there, I took a ten day vacation and toured up around Yellowstone National Park as much as I could, got to visit a friend in Montana, and got a good taste of the West in winter. A very memorable time – I loved it.

But most important, I was able to come to terms with, and let go of, much of the emotional baggage of my recent past life. Oh yes, we all have past lives. And future lives. Many of them. I saw the country the way it is today, while in my mind's eye I saw it the way it was all those years ago in another life with the native villages and bountiful herds of animals. I realized that, as a person, as a spiritual being, I was still alive and well, and the troubles from that distant time were all behind me. My mantra became, "That was then, this is now," and so I resolved to put my past behind me and focus on the present.

I left Colorado about mid-April to return to Maine, and to the Appalachian Trail. I did not get right on the trail, I had some work to do on vehicles that I needed to take care of, and I took my kids to Hawaii for ten days at the end of May. It wasn't until mid-June that I had all my ducks in a row, and was ready to continue with my hike.

Sunday 6/14/09

I leave tomorrow on the bus to Harrisburg, Pennsylvania, to continue my trail hike. I will arrive in Harrisburg Tuesday morning, and plan on meeting my friend and former co-worker, Adrienne, down there. It will be good to see her – I've always enjoyed her very much.

Funny, I'm not feeling great enthusiasm for getting back on the trail. Maybe it's the awareness of what can happen, problems, that could knock me down again. Maybe it's because I'm not quite 100% emotionally ready. On the other hand, I'm far better prepared for the journey this time than I was last year.

From the time I start until Baxter State Park closes for the season, I will have four months to complete the hike – plenty of time. I'm not starting this time with the arrogance I had before, that was a very humbling experience. This time, however, I am feeling somewhat apprehensive. Not sure why… Still, hiking the AT is something I've long waited to do, and so I will, and to the best of my ability. It will be whatever I make it, so I may as well enjoy it. Maybe it's like being thrown off a horse – pick yourself up, dust yourself off, and get back on. I've set my mind – Tuesday I'm back on.

8

PENNSYLVANIA

Monday 6/15

Some stuff to do this morning to finish getting ready: sharpen Jeff's knives, charged the calling card, wallet and check register into the pack, load the rest of my food, situate the truck, cover the camper, and some odds and ends. I still do not feel much excitement about this last leg of my journey.

Tom gets me to the bus terminal in plenty of time, so I pop into the Thai restaurant for a meal. I have enough left over for an evening meal. Once I am on the bus, my attitude changes, and I start to become excited about re-embarking on this journey. Instead of thinking about how it went for me last time, I am anticipating something special. I have no idea what it may be, and even though I'm fully aware of what can go bad, I believe my experience this time will be enjoyable, enlightening, magical, wondrous... I'm not sure of the proper adjectives, but I'm feeling it will be something special. Of course, it will be whatever I make it. Thank You, Spirit, for all the opportunities. Thank me, Chris, for daring to live my life as I want – without fear.

I don't care where I'm going, or what kind of schedule I have, I'm not taking a bus again. No sir, no how, no way. Although, I have experienced two things because of taking a bus: I've seen Times Square in New York City, and I got hustled. The hustler, who at first seemed like a decent guy, didn't get me for much, much less than he was hoping for. But that was the most expensive chicken sandwich and chocolate shake from Burger King I've ever had. Oh well, live and learn.

Tuesday 6/16

No Adrienne this morning. I was bummed, but not too surprised. I left the terminal just after 9:00, and started hitching a ride to Duncannon. I got back on the trail by noon.

My first thought about being back on the trail? Loneliness. I don't know why, but that was my first feeling. I was so tired from being up so long from the bus ride that I really didn't feel any emotions about the trail, I just went on autopilot and hiked.

The trail was pretty easy with some of the famous rocky stretches that Pennsylvania is noted for. I did okay getting to the first shelter, 4.5 miles in about 2.5 hours. I was getting sore and more tired, so I called it a day. Since I've been at this shelter, two gals and two guys dropped by, but all continued on the 6.8 miles to the next shelter. At one point I was thinking that if I averaged just twelve miles a day, it would take me three months to finish – should be an easily doable hike. But the first couple of days I'll ease into it as I'm out of shape and don't want to start off straining anything. I'm all alone in the shelter tonight, a lovely, quiet spot in a pretty, wooded area. It's nice to be back.

Wednesday 6/17

I slept great! I ate about 3:30 yesterday afternoon, cleaned up and turned in shortly thereafter. I woke between 6:00 and 6:30, brushed my teeth, thought about reading, but laid back down and fell asleep with the sun. I woke very well rested.

The day is overcast with a light breeze, maybe 50°. I start off on the trail and my unaccustomed muscles complain loudly. After a mile or so I warm up, limber up, and the complaining stops. The trail is very easy, fairly level and with very few rocks. Should the trail remain like this all the way, it would be a very easy hike. I follow along a ridge line through mature hardwood forest. The trail is so gentle that I'm not hiking, but strolling, I walk effortlessly. It's good to be back on the trail.

I rounded a bend in the trail to see a rabbit cross in front of me, and a deer stopped in the trail just up ahead. If I remember correctly, the rabbit represents abundance, and also represents fears, and the deer represents beauty and gentleness. I remembered there is an Indian prayer about walking in beauty, and that's the way I feel – I walk in beauty. The trail stays easy all day, but at ten or eleven miles I'm feeling tired. The sky is settling in low and heavy, the breeze is picking up, and light rain is starting to fall. After a bit the rain comes a little heavier, and I decide to make camp at the next water source. At just about twelve miles I come to a spring, and pitch my tent. I would liked to have hiked further as there is plenty of daylight left, but my tired body tells me to stop now. I have the opportunity for another good night's rest. I feel very good about the day's hike.

Thursday 6/18
Stayed in a little later waiting for the rain to stop. Got up, did my usual routine, and got underway. Within the first mile, trail magic! An orange, an apple, energy bar, peanut butter crackers, and a crème filled cookie. Excellent! Thank you, angel. The trail is a gradual, but steady uphill for four miles, then levels off. Very easy going through pretty country. I make seven miles easily, and twelve miles by early afternoon. With the recent rain, including today's, the trail is very wet and I walk in soaked boots all day.

I started the day with an 1100' climb, but otherwise have walked through low hills and rolling land, through hardwood ridges and softwood lowlands, crossing many streams as I head for the next shelter. Rausch Gap Shelter is in some very pretty country – a growth of mature hard and soft woods, a rushing stream just down the other side of the trail, a beautiful ever flowing spring right at the shelter – and I half think of staying, but there is too much daylight to quit now.

All day the trail has been easy and pretty. I'm enjoying the solitude. I was gifted today with a deer, two rabbits and a bear. The bear was a young one, walking down the ridge in my direction. He didn't alter his course, but body language said he was quite cautious. With my pack on, I'm over six feet tall and appear much larger than I am. To this young bear I must have appeared a rather formidable opponent, and he was ever so careful not to make eye contact with me. He carried on with his chosen course, passing me and heading off into the woods, but I could tell that he was ready to high-tail it if I made a move. It was very interesting to be able to study the bear, and to sense what he was thinking. I wonder if it would have made any difference if he knew that with his teeth, claws and strength, he could have easily done me in. I'm just as glad he didn't.

A few miles down the trail I ran into a mother and her young son. They are out for the summer hiking as much as they can in the time they have. She's carrying the bulk of the load as he is just a young lad and carries only his own food and clothing. I think that is just awesome! I hope the young fellow can appreciate what a special gift he is receiving.

I started thinking about how many days food I have, and what to schedule for a re-supply. So I go into Lickdale to pick up enough to last five days or so, and call Stef to place an order. I guess I sounded odd because she hung up on me. I called her back, got her answering machine and placed an order. I got a bite to eat, and went across the road to a campground for a shower, clothes washing and called it a night. It's late now, 9:30ish, and I'm beat. I need to re-learn trail smarts.

Friday 6/19

What a terrible night's sleep. But so it goes. I called Stef back to verify that she got my order, had a pleasant chat, and on the trail shortly thereafter. The first part of the trail was steadily uphill and was quite a chore, mostly due to inadequate rest, but I also did not drink enough water. Once on top of the hill, I follow a ridge line for miles, most of it pretty easy walking. Shortly on, I realized I left town with very little water – bonehead. That is so crucial – drinking enough water. The days I don't drink enough are the hardest, the days I drink a lot are the easiest. Oh well, I survived. Even though it felt like I was poking, I made the seven miles to the next shelter in good season. I ate and rested a while before moving on.

The next four miles to the 501 Shelter went easily, and since the shelter is right on the highway and it is before 3:00, I move on. The next five or so miles were a killer what with all the hilly country and rough rock, but I have to push on because I have to get to water.

By 6:00 I make it to the campsite, and I'm just whipped and sore. But all day has been pretty and provided me with occasional views from the ridges of lovely, lush farm country in the valleys below. Tonight I'm camped with Bonesy, a quiet young guy, and L-train, a lively, chatty, engaging young woman, the first time on this trip I've camped with anyone else.

Saturday 6/20

Woke with the birds as the sky lightened. The sky is overcast, but dry at present. Shortly down the trail I feel the first drops of rain – previews of coming attractions. The trail is very pretty, what can be seen of it. The forest is mature hardwood with much rhododendron and mountain laurel, mostly in bloom. The sky lies in heavy and the rain comes.

Stretches of the trail are pretty good, there are the rocky stretches, but mostly there is water and mud. There is no shortage of water on this stretch. With the sky so dark and the fog, it makes the woods appear gloomy and eerie. I make the nine miles to Eagle's Nest Shelter just after noon and call it a day. I had planned on going another six miles, but I gave up that notion as soon as I got into the shelter. I had gotten quite a chill, so I dried off, got into my sleeping bag and shortly dropped off for a nap. No point in wasting a rainy day by hiking.

In the shelter when I got there were Kentucky Hippo and Little Hippo, a couple in their forties, she out on her first backpacking adventure. She also had two terrific shiners.

"I didn't make his coffee right," she says with a smile. And, "What do you tell a woman with two black eyes? Nothing. You already told her – twice!" She enjoyed being able to tell the jokes.

He was uncomfortable with her telling the one about the coffee. "People will think I did that," he said.

Actually, she took a nasty fall, as many do, and went down face first acquiring the black eyes as a result.

The shelter filled up pretty fast and early today as hikers wanted a break from the weather. One of the hikers is a very pleasant, very attractive young lady going by the name of Egg, a great gal with bright, clear eyes, a warm, sincere smile and easy, open personality. Right away I liked her. We got around to the topic of feet, and seeing my blisters she gives me some Neosporin to apply to them. And in a few days, with the aid of Neosporin, my feet improve.

Sunday 6/21

Happy Father's Day, Dad. Happy First Day of Summer. Happy Naked Hiking Day.

Today started overcast and breezy, but I felt only a few sprinkles. But not a day for naked hiking. Brrr... First one out of camp this morning, and I find the trail drier than yesterday. The forest is unchanged in the past day or so – fairly open, mature hardwoods and the land laying fairly flat, or gently rolling with occasional hills. It is quite pretty. I seem pokey this morning, not making any distance. But then, my concept of time and distance is skewed today. It seems to be a day where not much thinking occurs as I just hike along. Sooner than I expected I come to a spring about half way to town. I guess I'm moving better than I thought.

I make the steep descent and arrive in Port Clinton about 11:30, making just over 8.5 miles before noon. Nowhere near a land speed record, but pretty good for me. I made a stop at the outfitter for new socks that hopefully will ease the torture to my feet. Every day my feet develop new blisters, and old ones worsen. A lot of the problem is that my socks are too thick, but mostly my socks and boots never dry out. Had I known I would be faced with this problem, I probably would have worn my sandals. After the outfitter, I get something to eat. A salad to start, then a huge hamburger with onion rings. I ate too much, even with giving half the onion rings to another hiker.

The trail out of town was agonizing due to being stuffed. But after the first couple miles of mostly uphill, the trail becomes pretty easy. Even still, I stop now and again to rest. The last couple miles of today's trail are like walking through a park – it is very pretty here. The sun has been out since a little before Port Clinton, so the hiking is splendid.

Shortly before getting to tonight's shelter I meet a woman on a bridge, and we strike up a conversation about the trail and hiking. A very pleasant woman and we talk for a half hour or more. She also stops other hikers to ask their names, where they're from and such. She is a trail worker and lives nearby, so she is able to give us much information about the trails in the area.

Just down the trail a few hundred yards is Windsor Furnace Shelter. My boots come off and my feet are a mess. Once through Pennsylvania I'm going back to wearing my sandals. Hopefully, the new, thinner, quicker drying socks will help out a lot. The forecast for the week is nice weather, maybe my boots will dry soon.

More of the grueling Pennsylvania rocks

Monday 6/22

Woke with the birds, got up to pee, but went back to bed for a little while longer, mostly because I didn't want to disturb the others still sleeping. But I had to get up, so I quietly practiced Tai Chi and before long the others stirred. I was the first one on the trail under clear and sunny skies.

The trail starts easy, but shortly makes a steep climb over rock to Pulpit Rock. Up there is a great view of the valley and farmlands below – all very lush and picturesque. The trail is a mix of easy, level stretches, or rough, rocky sections. It doesn't matter to me at all which it is, I'm enjoying the hike either way. It would have been nice if I had this mind set when I was hiking last year – I'm sure my experience on the trail then would have been much different. But it was what it was, and what it needed to be – I had important work to do.

When I get my trail legs and my feet heal, this hike will really become enjoyable. I feel a definite change in me over last year. On my first full day on the trail this year, I met a woman out day hiking, and was asked the usual questions. I told her I'm from Maine and that I'm walking back home. When we parted, I thought about that. I patted my chest over my heart and repeated to myself that I was walking home. That's what this journey is for me.

Today's trail was up and down a couple times, sometimes along a ridge or in a lowland. Sometimes the trail was tremendously easy, sometimes it was a scramble over rocks. But it was always enjoyable. The forest has not changed in the past few days – it is always pretty and serene, always inviting and welcoming.

About 5:00 I get to the shelter where I will spend the night. Today I hiked 16.5 miles at an easy pace, stopping to look over the overlooks, or to take a break when I felt the need. It's a little after 8:00 now, and this journal is the last thing I'm doing for the day. I'm tired from my day's good hike, so I shall bid you a good night. Oh, the new socks worked out as I had hoped – my feet were in much better shape by the end of the day.

Tuesday 6/23

Shelters are fine to sleep in when you have them all to yourself, but I'm some glad I slept in my tent last night – one of the fellows in the shelter was a real snorer. I was the second one up today, yet almost the last one on the trail.

The first six miles were easy, and I strolled along effortlessly. The forest now is a little more open, not as brushy, the trees younger and smaller. After the New Tripoli Campsite the trail runs along the ridge, and so becomes rocky. Still, it is not continuously rocky. And then I come to a high, jagged, narrow edge of ridge – the dreaded Knife Edge. It certainly is steep and narrow in places, a fall from it would be quite serious – even life threatening, but at something about two hundred yards in length, it's over before you have a chance to really enjoy it. I don't mean to offend Pennsylvania and its mountains in any way, but your Knife Edge pales in comparison to the Knife Edge up on Katahdin.

Just beyond the Knife Edge, on the other side of the trail, is a large, higher rock ridge that provides tremendous views of the surrounding countryside. The trail doesn't go up over this expansive rock pile, but it ought to – it's well worth the effort. Coming down off this formation, I spotted something shiny in amongst the rocks. It was a gold colored watch. I had been thinking about picking up a timepiece so that I could better plan the day's destinations, and here it was presented to me. Spirit always provides. And along came a young woman who I asked if she knew the time. She said 12:30. I asked her if it was more like 12:23, she said yes, it was. The watch was on time and working fine.

Just north of the Knife Edge, maybe sixty feet off the trail, was a very fine adult black bear, about three hundred pounds I'd guess. He did not stay around long and went crashing off through the woods. After all, being cautious is how the big ones got to be big ones. Thank You for another bear.

Maybe two miles from Knife Edge is Bake Oven Knob with expansive views to both sides. I was sitting there having a drink and a snack when quickly along comes Hotpants, slack-packing his way to Maine while his wife drives on ahead and sets up camp at designated spots. Seems like a pretty easy way to do it. His little daypack contained water, some food, a camera and what not. He's an energetic fellow who, when he was through chatting, left just as quickly as he arrived. And he never went the very short distance off the trail to take in the views!!

On to the next shelter for water and maybe the night. I dubbed around at the shelter about an hour as I debated staying or going. I started feeling lonely today, so I decided to walk it off. Walking is good therapy. Along the way I meet Yuki, a retired fellow from Tokyo who spoke English with kind of a British accent. His English teacher was Australian. We fumbled our way (the trail here not well marked) 2.5 miles to the next road where he made camp. I continued on for another couple miles and made camp up on a breezy ridge. Along the way, I was treated to ripe blueberries! Yum, yum, I love blueberries! As I stood in camp, twenty-five feet off the trail, along comes another hiker who never even saw me! How can you come to hike the AT and not lift your eyes off the trail to see what is around you?!

Wednesday 6/24

Happy Birthday To Me, Happy Birthday To Me…

A slow start, not too far to go today, I'm on the trail at 7:30. I don't go far when I stop for more blueberries. Along comes Yuki, and I introduce him to the fruit. He had never tasted blueberries, they don't have them in Japan, and he enjoyed them very much. As we gathered and ate berries, we talked about countries and cultures. He is an intelligent man who has traveled around, and so has a lot of insight to offer. We walk together to the next shelter for water. In less than a mile we're down at Pa. 873 in Lehigh

Gap, he goes one way, I go the other. I head into Slatington for my food drop, laundry and easy night in town. Except...

Fine Lodging, where I have a reservation for the night, is an old building on a crowded, busy main street. It is noisy and not air conditioned, so it is not a very comfortable place. So much for treating myself on my birthday. Well, at least I'm showered and my laundry is clean.

I get over town to the grocery store for my day food, then back for supper at 6:30. The pizza restaurant across the road had a great special, ziti, a big salad and bread for $7.40 – a delicious meal I certainly would not have had on the trail. Back to my room for a little TV, re-wash my hiking clothes, and re-assemble my pack. I'll have breakfast at the diner just down the street in the morning, and hopefully I'll be back on the trail by 8:00ish. I've had enough of this town, I'm anxious to get back on the trail.

Thursday 6/25

Surprisingly, I slept pretty good last night, perhaps because I could sprawl out. Got up about 6:00, showered, put my pack together and went to breakfast. Sometime about 7:30 I took a ride to the trailhead. At the trailhead at 8:00 and starting the trudge up the hill out of the gap. I was told by the outfitter in Port Clinton that this uphill out of the gap was pretty tough, that it would take an hour. Well, it was rather steep in sections, but I made it to the top in less than an hour – including the fifteen or so minutes I spent talking with a couple day hikers. I guess I didn't think it was that bad. Once on top the trail became pretty easy. Thankfully, as the day is fixing to be hot and humid.

As it has since Duncannon, for the most part, the trail follows the ridge line, so there is little up and down. The first portion of the trail, about four miles, was nearly void of trees due to industrial pollution from Palmerton Zinc, and is now a superfund cleanup site. There were blueberry bushes all over the place, the berries fully ripe, but I couldn't bring myself to eat any given the history of the area. For the remainder of the day, the forest is a mix of mature and young hardwoods, sometimes mixed with pines or scrubby trees and brush.

Quite early on in the journey, I was told that Pennsylvania was all rock, jutting up out of the trail in every imaginable shape, size and angle, that it was this way throughout the entire state. The fellow who told me that was a veteran hiker, so I assumed he was relating actual trail information. Naturally, hearing that, I was quite excitedly anticipating the prospect of hiking through the state. But the reportedly horrific Pennsylvania rocks still have not posed a problem. Yes, there are rocky sections, but they are not difficult, nor do they last long. You see, this is why it doesn't do a lot of good to ask folks how the trail is up ahead – they can only tell you how it was in their experience. In my experience, Pennsylvania, while it certainly does have its sections of rough rock, for the most part is pretty good going.

It must be some hot in the local towns because it's hot and humid in the woods. But the trail is easy, and I make it along pretty well. The only problem is, there is little water along this stretch of trail. I was relieved and delighted to finally make it to the night's shelter and water! Sixteen miles is too far to go in this heat on a half gallon of water. Tomorrow?, maybe fourteen miles to the next shelter, maybe the twenty miles into Delaware Water Gap. We'll see.

Friday 6/26

A brief rain before getting on the trail, though it looked as if it would rain all day. The first miles seemed hard today. My left ankle felt jammed up, and while not painful, it is not easy to walk on. I started thinking about what the cause of the problem is, and in just a moment the kids came to mind. Right away I knew this was something I didn't want to look at, but had to. When I thought more on it, I realized that I felt I failed my kids, as a father, that I wasn't there for them enough. This was quite painful for me, and it set the stage for me to walk with a heavy heart. Of course, I have no idea if that's how the kids feel, but I knew I had to write them a letter. And so I plodded along all day, watching the trail in front of me not only because you have to, but also because my mind was preoccupied.

The trail today is as it has been, some stretches rocky, some very rocky, some very nice and flat. I started this morning with only twenty miles left in Pennsylvania, but today's trail seemed to punish my feet, so I'm not going beyond the next, and last, shelter. The day has been sunny and hot, but a cold front has blown in and with it a very energetic thunderstorm. I'm glad I'm cozy and dry in the shelter. Boy! It's a wild one!

In the shelter with me tonight is Zoltan from either Romania or Hungary, I don't remember which. A very pleasant guy who started his AT hike up at Abol bridge in Maine in March. I laughed when he told me this. He said he got six, maybe eight, miles to where he camped the first night, but it darn near killed him – he said he almost froze to death. Even in March, northern Maine is still deep in winter. He walked back out the next day, went down to Georgia and resumed the trail, hiking north from there. Smart move.

9

NEW JERSEY/NEW YORK

Saturday 6/27

Woke at my usual time, but slow getting going – or so I thought. After breakfast, packing up, going for water and Tai Chi, I'm on the trail before 7:00. I've only about 6 miles until I get into New Jersey. In just a couple of minutes after leaving the shelter I stop to watch a bear, maybe sixty yards away. I didn't have long to watch him as he casually, in bear fashion, turned his head in my direction, and when he focused on me it was almost as if I could see his eyes bug out, and he wheeled around and bolted. It's always nice to see my friends, even if briefly.

The next four miles were pretty easy hiking, but I just wasn't into it. My right knee has been sore, so I started thinking on it. In Louise Hay's teachings, the knee represents pride and ego. I don't know why, but I started to wonder if indeed I wanted to do this hike, or was it my ego and "I hiked the AT" that kept me going on? And the conversation started. I remembered a conversation with Priyadarshi, my Tai Chi instructor, in which he told me I owed it to myself to hike the trail. And then I got thinking about being a quitter, and how so often in my life I quit something when it no longer worked for me. Maybe I'd even quit on my marriage too quickly. So I pondered being a quitter, but how I really want to do the trail since it has always been a dream to hike it. And then I just sort of let it all go.

And in a short while I was on Mt. Minsi about to drop down to Delaware Water Gap. For all the typical hardwood forest I'd been walking through, the descent was like walking through a garden what with all the rhododendrons, many still in bloom, that lined the trail. Very lush, very pretty in this short section. All at once I'm at the foot of the hill walking a paved street into Water Gap. There's a celebration in town today, Water Gap Day or something like that, and there are folks gathering all about taking in the festivities. I think I want to get out of town quickly.

The worst part of today's trail is the walk across the bridge over the Delaware River – all the noisy traffic! About 10:30 I'm in New Jersey. The trail in New Jersey starts in Worthington State Park, and is a very easy, gentle climb through lovely forest along a lively, cascading stream. There are many people on this part of the trail – I suppose because it's a lovely Saturday. About four miles up is Sunfish Pond, a 41-acre glacial creation, unusual for these parts. Such a pretty, tranquil pond set among low hills of mixed growth. For some odd reason, the pond is off limits to swimming! Someone said that if there is a stupid rule, New Jersey has it. After the pond, the trail rises gently for a mile and comes to a beautiful grassy ridge providing excellent views of the Delaware River valley to the west, and a large reservoir to the east. It's been some time since I've been on a high, grassy ridge, and I'm thoroughly enjoying it. D was absolutely right, New Jersey, at least what I've seen of it so far, is very pretty.

Tonight I'm staying at the Mohican Outdoor Center where I tent for free, get a hot shower for $3.00, and I can get supper leftovers (I'm told there's always plenty) for $5.00. As I'm going down for supper, I meet up with Hellbender, T-suds, OG and Track. They were debating paying for a meal, so I paid for all of them. Supper was awesome! An excellent salad, some creamy, cheesy broccoli noodle casserole, steamed mixed vegetables, milk, and pumpkin pie with whipped cream for dessert. I've died and gone to Hiker Heaven! And after supper, they had live entertainment in the form of a trio playing and singing older light rock songs. For as mopey as the day started, it turned out excellent! Thank You, Spirit!

Sunday 6/28

A little sluggish getting up this morning – I was up too late last night. Still, I was the first one on the trail. The day is clear and bright with a gentle breeze. I start off walking along a ridge that is very easy going with but a few rocky stretches.

I hike along on this beautiful morning and encounter five or six folks out on day or section hikes. One was a woman from Vermont who was quite chatty, and we talked for nearly a half hour. Even though I feel like I'm moving right along, I'm not making great time today. The scenery is very nice with ridges opening up for views, and the forest changing from mature hardwood to young scrubby growth to low hemlock and rhododendrons.

Today I re-learned a valuable lesson about drinking enough water. Even though I drank about 1.5 gallons, it wasn't enough. Towards the end of the day's hike the sun was beating on me pretty hard and I found that I had run right out of energy and collapsed into Brink Road Shelter totally beat. Drink often, drink lots.

Monday 6/29

Even though I was asleep early, I did not feel like getting up at the crack of dawn. Still, when all was done, I was on the trail before 7:00. I don't know if it was that the trail was easy, or if I was just moving good, but I made the 3.5 miles to U.S. 206, Branchville, New Jersey, in two hours. Just down from the trail is a coffee shop; yeah, I already had breakfast, but you can never eat too much out here. And I do enjoy eating. Into the shop I go for a donut and chocolate milk. Mmm, good. But there was something wrong with the donut... I went back into the shop to tell the owner of the defect with the donut – somehow, upon getting outside into a different atmosphere, the donut vaporized. Clearly, something was amiss. It was my duty to conduct a similar experiment on another donut, a different kind, to see if the same thing would happen. It did, but a little less quickly. Delicious, though defective, donuts. Such delights.

Back on the trail and an easy walk up the hill to a long ridge line. In two miles I come to Culver Fire Tower and an easy climb to the top for wonderful views. The day is mostly overcast and is much cooler, making for more comfortable walking. The going is easy, the scenery pretty, and I make nine miles by noon. On top of Sunrise Mt. is a grand pavilion of stone pillars, massive timber framed roof, patio stone floor, and benches along both sides for your sitting and viewing pleasure. Both sides of the ridge have wonderful, expansive vistas of the surrounding countryside. This is a great place to practice Tai Chi, take some food and drink, and relax for a spell.

Back on the trail with four gentle miles to the next shelter. There is no water at Mashipacong Shelter, but it is a good place to take a break and get some relief from the sun now shining brightly and hot. On I go for another three miles to the next shelter and water. Apparently there was a bad storm at one time as the trees along this last stretch are about eight feet tall mixed with old, broken trees.

About a half mile to the trail to Rutherford Shelter I encounter my first New Jersey bears. A mama with her cub – she sits quite contentedly and watches me pass by while junior beats feet for the brush. At the side trail to the shelter I debate continuing on, or going to the shelter. It's only 5:00, just two miles to the next road crossing and water, but I've already done sixteen miles. Even though I still have plenty of spunk I head for this shelter. I like to make camp and have everything done by 8:00. In camp tonight are Ironman, his girlfriend, and a retired teacher. We enjoy pleasant conversation around a campfire.

Unionville, New York

Tuesday 6/30

Trail stuff – yah, yah – uphill, downhill, trees, rocks, mud, a couple deer. I walked out of camp feeling fine, but after just a short while I realized I felt like I was attacking the trail. Where was my head? Thinking on it, I realized that I was lonely. Thinking about that, I wondered if that wasn't a recurring theme in my lives. It seems to be now, it was in the last one, and in at least one other. And I thought about "I'm hiking home." I cried often, my heart was so heavy, and on I walked. Later in the day I thought again about if I even wanted to finish this walk – what is my real motive?

"Why am I doing this?"

"It's something I've always wanted to do."

"Am I really loving the hike?"

"Aspects of it, yes."

"Do I want to finish it because I really want to do the hike, or is it my ego that wants to say I've hiked the Appalachian Trail?"

And my head isn't on the trail so much.

I missed the road to Unionville, New York, where my next re-supply is waiting. Fortunately, only a little while later I run into Egg; she gets me straightened out, and we walk together back to Unionville. A quick stop at the store, picked up my parcel at the post office, and off to the Mayor's House for the evening. The Mayor's House, now known as the Outhouse, is the private home of Dick Ludwick who, along with the help of his cohorts Butch and Bill, takes in hikers, feeds them delicious meals, and gives them a place to sleep, clean and do laundry. Terrific folks, and I have a new outlook on the trail.

Wednesday 7/1

After a great breakfast, again, many thanks to Dick and crew, a quick ride to the trail and I'm under way. I don't know what happened to the new outlook, but I haven't gone far before I'm feeling like I'm not wanting to do this, and an argument with myself begins. And the mosquitoes are chewing me up. So I'm just in a bad mood feeling like I could chuck my pack off a cliff. What happens is that I'm hoofing right along doing almost three miles an hour. But it works for me as the exertion burns up all the negative energy. By 11:00 I'm at the road to Glenwood, New Jersey, and I'm feeling good – I've done nine miles in three hours. The rest of the day's hike went really well and my mood is much improved. When all is said and done, I'd hiked sixteen miles in eight hours.

Just before Wawayanda State Park I meet up with a couple hikers doing a slack pack and then going back to the Mayor's House (The Outhouse). After little deliberation, I decide to go back as well, get a shower, another terrific supper and breakfast, then get a ride back here in the morning to pick up where I left off. Same number of miles, much better accommodations. Tomorrow I'll officially be in New York.

Sometimes you know right where you are

Thursday 7/2

Another great breakfast then a ride to the trail and the hike gets started about 8:00. The day is heavily overcast, but is not raining. However, it has rained so hard lately that the trail is very wet. Right around the NJ/NY border the land changes dramatically. All of a sudden it is hilly, rocky, and the forest is very thick with mixed growth.

At the first ridge I encounter Carpenter who believes that someone is playing a joke on us, that another set of blazes were placed upon the trees to throw us off the trail.

"No, this is the trail," I said. "You didn't see any other trail off this trail, did you?"

"No, that's true," says Carpenter, "but this trail just disappears."

"It has to be there, let's go look," I reply.

I point out the white blazes as I see them, proving that we are still on the AT; however, down at the foot of the hill, the trail does seem to disappear under water. Upon closer inspection I notice the defined edges of the trail under the water.

"This is the trail," I said, "it's just under water." Into the eight-inch deep water we go, and very soon I point out the next white blaze dead ahead.

"See the blaze on that tree? This is it."

Now sure of where he's going, Carpenter rapidly moves on and I never see him again.

The trail follows a ridge for the most part, is frequently up and down, often an exposed rock ledge, and is covered or surrounded by short pines, scrub oak and mixed growth. At one point the trail is a stream – literally – there is so much water everywhere! I gave up long ago trying to keep my feet dry, and slosh through the puddles rather than try to skip around them. This goes on for about four miles. Then, as abruptly as the trail got rocky, it smoothed out and was nice walking. And the day has cleared pretty well, becoming mostly sunny.

Down at NY 17A is an ice cream stand with delicious homemade ice cream. You can never eat too much ice cream while on the trail. After my treat I continue on and in a couple miles I come to a narrow, rocky ridge – Cat Rocks – and very nice views of low forested mountains. In just a short bit I'm at Wildcat Shelter for the night. Also there for the night are Mr. Ed and Lightweight, L-train, Hellbender, Hulk and a couple others.

Most of the day my right shin has been bothering me, quite painful in fact. I have a knotted, swollen area just above the outside ankle. I can't think of anything drastic that happened to it, but something is sure bothering. Then as I walked along the last couple miles it occurred to me that I had not been walking naturally on my right foot since that foot blistered then got infected. I suspect that by walking on it in such an awkward manner I put more strain on it than I normally would have. So I figured that if I resume walking naturally, it ought to mend itself. I'm hoping it works out that way, but tonight it is quite sore. I'll nurse it along and pay attention to it.

Friday 7/3

First one up and out. The trail is drier this morning, though still quite wet in places. The first couple miles of the trail are pretty easy, but then I spend the next eight or so miles scrambling up, over and down rocky ridges around Mombasha High Point, Buchanan and Arden Mts. It seems the easy trails of Eastern Pennsylvania and New Jersey, where you run along ridges for miles, are long gone. Since entering New York, the trail runs across the ridges, so there is a lot of up and down again. The good news is that the hills aren't large, so the ups and downs aren't too laborious.

Just as I'm coming to Harriman State Park there is an angel doing magic. He's an avid hiker somehow affiliated with outdoor gear stores; he is offering new socks, which I don't need, also drinks and snacks. I have a root beer soda, an orange and three small candy bars. Excellent! Thank you very much!

Harriman State Park is very lovely. The forest is open, mature hardwood, and there are many large, open grassy areas, mainly on hilltops, that are so serene and inviting. Along the way I had a lot of fun going through the Lemon Squeezer, a very narrow pass through vertical rock ledges, and up over the rock knob just beyond. Unfortunately, it is over about as quick as it began. I've seen five deer in the park in the short time I've been here. By late afternoon I arrive at Fingerboard Shelter, and rather than stay in the shelter, I set up my tent. I went for a bath and returned to the shelter for supper, but not before a thunderstorm hit. It was over pretty quickly, but I got fairly wet in its brief visit. In the shelter were Mr. Ed and Lightweight for the night, L-train, Hulk and another who hiked on after the storm.

Saturday 7/4

I woke this morning wishing I had a woman to make love with. So it goes.

Breakfast, packed and on the trail by 6:30. The swelling in my right leg is greatly diminished, but I don't go very far before I realize it's going to be a long day – with each step the pain in my leg becomes more intense. I think there is no way I'm going to make the sixteen miles I want to make today, so I resign myself that I'll do what I can do. I made three attempts to fashion a cane, but each time I tossed it. I know what I need to do.

I start to think on the pain and wonder why I want to cause that pain in my body. For a while, nothing came to me, but I kept at it. Before long I was feeling quite lonely, and I started to cry. I thought more on it and what came to me was that I had never let anyone get close – get inside me. The sobbing became bawling, and I sat on a tree and cried and rocked. I felt like I'd had my heart broken so many times – not just in this life – that I always guarded myself and never let anyone get too close. I cried and I cried until I felt better, then I moved on.

I said I was sorry to my ex – she never stood a chance. Then I thought about how I never really opened my heart to my kids, and how that not only hurt me, but them as well. And I bawled. I was walking through beautiful forests, but the tears in my eyes made it difficult to see beyond the trail. I thought more on the pain and found myself saying in disbelief, "No, no, no," and I started to wail. Strangely, even though my belief is strong, I realized I hadn't let God into my heart. And I lost it completely. I thought about how, "That was then, this is now." I said I was sorry to all I may have offended, and I forgave all who I felt offended me. And the leg pretty much stopped hurting, but I knew I still had more work to do.

Somehow, with all the pain and stopping to cry, I was still making good time and miles. About 11:30 I was sitting on Black Mt. having a bite to eat when along comes Stretch, Tin Man and L-train. L-train said she'd be meeting her folks a little later on and that there'd be magic – strawberry shortcake – and we were invited. So the four of us sort of leap-frogged down Black Mt., up and down the next (a steep one), up Bear Mt. with a little break to climb the tower and take in the view, then down the other side. Those younger folks walk much faster than me, but I keep a steadier pace, and I'm down the mountain before they are.

The north side of Bear Mt. is a park alongside a small lake that was jammed full of people and families enjoying a beautiful Saturday 4th of July. The smells of all the barbeques and grilling food sure made my mouth water! L-train caught up with me about half way through the park. We both commented on what a zoo it was there (figuratively as well as literally), and how tough it was to find the trail through there. Along here, this being Trailside Museum and Zoo, is where the lowest section of the trail is, by the bear den. We never did see the bear den for all the people. But L-train and I found our way through the park, across the bridge over the Hudson River, and shortly found her Mom and Dad.

I was treated to a couple root beers, a couple hot dogs, chips, watermelon and strawberry shortcake. We had a pleasant conversation, mostly about the trail. L-train has very nice folks, and I thanked them often for their generosity and kindness. As I still had 1.5 miles to go to my camp for the night, I bowed out as Stretch and Tin Man arrived.

Heading up the last hill I encountered a woman out on a day hike who was coming down. I offered her a dollar to carry my pack up the hill. Oddly, she declined the offer.

"Why are you carrying that pack?" she asks me.

"Why am I carrying this pack?!"

"Yeah."

"Because it won't walk by itself."

Not sure what she mumbled...

So I did well today, 16.5 miles on a bum leg. Tonight it is very swollen, red and hot. I've got more work to do.

Sunday 7/5

Fireworks and trains last night, not as quiet as I like. A little slow getting going this morning, on the trail about 7:15. The day dawns clear and bright, promising to be a nice one. After an early little uphill, I'm treated to much easy, level walking – the first I've seen since getting into New York.

In a short while I'm at U.S. Rt. 9 and find a convenience store right there, so I stop for milk and a donut. I'd have called home, but there was no pay phone. Across the road and a few hundred yards through the woods I come to the Friar's Hermitage. I read the sign indicating the trail through there, but I misread it, and didn't see the AT blaze across the road, so I went on a wild goose chase to locate the trail. Finally, I walked back to where I walked in, and found the trail. That little foray took about thirty minutes, and rather annoyed me.

The next three miles were pretty rocky and steep in places, and I missed a turn in the trail at the top of one of the hills. I didn't go a hundred yards before I realized my mistake, turned around and got back on the trail. A little more annoyance – need to pay closer attention. I'd been feeling a little off this morning, and I guess it affected my concentration or something. I stopped for dinner at noon and saw that I had done seven miles – not bad, but could have been better.

Another mile and OH MY GOD MY LEG IS HURTING! I rested on a rock wall and massaged and stretched it, then went a little further until I came to a stream where I soaked it while filling my water bottles. I went on with it still hurting, so I started breathing energy into it. The lower right leg, just above my outside ankle swells up, gets red and warm, so I imagined a ball of cool, blue energy surrounding it. It took me a short while to focus my concentration on it, and that's when I realized I hadn't become at ease yet with the trail.

By now I'd seen my fourth deer, and I remembered some bit of an Indian prayer about walking in beauty. I made up my own little prayer and repeated it a number of times. With the energy breathing and the prayer my leg is soon feeling pretty good, and I make the next, and last, three miles of the day pretty well.

I arrive at a state park with camping and fresh water right here. It is about 4:15 when I arrive, I have done twelve miles. I debated going on, maybe taking a different trail that goes by some ponds, but as it was by then nearing 5:00 I called it close enough. I set up camp, took a bath and rinsed my clothes in the brook, then got supper. A little before 7:00 I crawled into the tent to do my journal for the day. It is now 7:45, the sun is below the horizon and I'm ready to call it a day.

Monday 7/6

Slept chilly last night – very unusual for me; woke chilly and started hiking with my long clothes on. More and more I'm thinking Lyme disease. Back in Pennsylvania I had dug a deer tick out of the back of my right leg in my lower calf, pretty close to the area that the swelling and pain originates. Though the swelling in my right leg is down and it is much less painful, I walk and ask for help getting me to my next destination. Before long I warm up, change into my hiking clothes and start laying down tracks.

New York has some very pretty hiking – the trail running up rocky hills, through open woods crisscrossed with old stone walls, along little streams, sometimes through old mature hardwoods, sometimes through mixed growth, sometimes scrubby hardwoods, on hilltops with nice views, or meandering through lowlands.

I certainly must have received the help I asked for as I'm covering miles today – eleven by noontime. The next shelter is nine miles away, which would make a twenty miler for me today. After my dinner, about 1:00, I head off figuring I'll go as far as I can, and stop by 6:00. Well, I'm still moving pretty good and cover those nine miles to Morgan Stewart Shelter, arriving by 5:30. 19.6 miles in about ten hours, for me that is pretty good. But I arrive feeling beat and my feet aching – the miles aren't worth the punishment. From here it is about 17.5 miles to Connecticut. We'll see how it goes in town tomorrow.

Tuesday 7/7

A quick three mile walk to the road and a quick ride into Poughquag. My re-supply had not arrived at the post office; Stef numbed it and never got the package mailed out, so I went shopping for groceries.

Just for the heck of it, I went to the pharmacy to ask about medication for Lyme disease. I was told about a walk-in health care place down in the next town, and another customer offered me a ride there. It'll probably eat up most of my day, but I've got to get this taken care of. On I go to the clinic. The fellow who gave me the ride told me that this area is the Lyme disease capital of the country, that it is a common occurrence for folks to get it, and prescriptions are handed out with almost no questions asked.

The doc wasn't convinced it was Lyme disease, but then, he didn't seem to have an opinion about anything. No matter if he agrees or not, it is what it is, and I'll soon be on the mend. I left the doc just after noon with a prescription for Dexocycline. A tough time getting a hitch back to Poughquag, but I arrive about

2:00. Picked up my meds, chatted with the ladies in the store, got a real good meal of Chinese food at the restaurant next door for $5.41 – paid for with money I found today, thank You very much – left town about 3:00, got a hitch from a nice young fellow in a mile or so, and back on the trail about 3:45. Four miles to go to tonight's shelter.

I walk along Nuclear Lake, so named because of nuclear experimentation a while back, not because of contamination in the lake. Or so we're told. It is a very pretty, picturesque lake surrounded by lush forests and some fields. The four mile trail is up and down, twists and turns, eventually rising over a low mountain.

Shortly down the other side of the mountain is the spur leading to Telephone Pioneers Shelter where L-train, Hellbender, Leon with his dog, and Will and Way are camped. I bathe, rinse my laundry, enjoy an orange by the fire, then set up camp and retire to my journal. L-train asked me if I was going to publish my journal as I write so much. We'll see what happens.

10

CONNECTICUT/MASSACHUSETTS

Wednesday 7/8

My tent no longer keeps the water out, last night's thunderstorm dampened my sleeping bag. I'm thinking I'll try treating the tent with silicone. The clothes I hung out to dry last night weren't. No matter, they dry or get wet pretty quickly anyway.

Lovely farmland in Connecticut

I am on the trail about 6:45, the sky is dark, but it's just a low, heavy fog. The trail is easy going and very pretty, despite the boggy areas. After the first three miles, I cross the Metro-North Railroad at NY Rt. 22, and stroll through beautiful farmland. I climb up to a ridge which I follow for about four miles through lovely, scenic forest. I got to Wiley Shelter about 11:30 having made 8.5 miles so far this morning. At this point, it is just over a mile to the Connecticut state line.

By now the day is sunny and warm, the hiking is pretty easy. I feel elation crossing into Connecticut as I'm back in New England. In four days I'll be in Massachusetts, and it'll really seem like I'm getting close to home. At this point, I'm feeling very confident that I'll make the rest of the journey to Katahdin.

Thursday 7/9

Woke pretty early, got going and on the trail by 6:00. The day is starting clear and bright, and I start the day's travel with a pleasant walk along Ten Mile River. For the first time in a long, long time I walk through a forest of predominantly softwoods – hemlock and pine. For more miles than I could remember, the forest has been of hardwoods. This is a pleasant change, though short lived. After a mile or so I'm at the foot of Schaghticoke Mt., and the forest is again mostly hardwood.

The trail up the mountain is gradual at first, but becomes steep and rocky. The uphills wear me down what with the Lyme disease – I fatigue easily. By and by, I make it to the top, and I can breathe easy on the flats. This hill seems to go on and on for miles. Once over the top it starts to drop, but then turns into an up and down rock scramble for what seems like a very long time. Eventually, I come down to Ct. Rt. 341, nearly nine miles from last night's shelter, and it's just 10:30. The intention is to make good mileage today, so I can be sure to get into Salisbury by Saturday morning. At this point, I'm doing well. A break to eat a bit, and I move on.

At noon I'm on Caleb's Peak, having done twelve miles, and meet Egg. We chat for a brief time, then hike on together. An easy go for a couple miles, then down some steep rock for maybe a mile, and we come to a river. For the next four miles, we are blessed with an easy, level, scenic walk along the river. Such a blessing indeed! My intention was to stop at Silver Hill campsite, nineteen miles from where I started, but when I got there I found I still had good legs, so I went on for another 3.4 miles to the next campsite. At the next road Egg leaves me to go into the town of Cornwall Bridge. Too bad to see her go, I very much enjoy her company.

About 6:00 I arrive at Caesar Brook campsite to find two very lovely ladies there, Karen and Jackie – Jackie from Scarborough, but now living and teaching in Connecticut. Not much time for talk as I've got camp to set up, washing to do, supper to prepare, then retire to write. Because I did extra miles today – my biggest day yet, 22.3 miles – I don't have to get right out and get hard at it tomorrow. I've got a fifteen miler planned, which will leave a six miler into Salisbury on Saturday morning. I'm hoping my re-supply package will be there waiting for me.

Friday 7/10

Didn't sleep as well as I'd hoped. My legs and feet were quite sore from the trek and kind of kept me up. I rolled out at 6:00 and was on the trail by 7:00. This part of Connecticut has a lot of ups and downs, but they're fairly low and easy.

After the first three miles I climb up onto a ridge and am blessed with an enchanting, peaceful walk – the only sounds are the songs of birds and the scurrying about of little animals. I certainly enjoy walking through the forest when it is this serene – you feel as though it is all placed here just for your enjoyment.

About seven miles along the trail winds down hill and I take my dinner at a spring. It is about 11:30 and I've done eight miles since starting. Down on the highway the AT is detoured due to bridge construction up in Falls Village, and I walk roads for about three miles. I feel like it is taking me out of the way, like it's a lot longer than it would be normally, but it's probably not that much longer – maybe even quicker.

Back on the real trail and I have only 3.5 miles to my destination. I get to the side trail to Limestone Spring Lean-to at

3:00, but decide to go the four miles into town. I move right along and make it to town by 4:30. Four miles in 1.5 hours – very fast for me!

My package is at the post office – surprise! – a trip to the bank, then across the street to a house where the homeowner takes in hikers. Got a room, all to myself, got a shower, then out to supper. Roots, also staying at the house, accompanies me to supper. We asked a lady we met about a place to eat. There aren't many options in Salisbury, and she offers us a ride to the next town if we wanted. We declined saying we'd rather not travel too far, and the woman, perhaps really wanting to help, gave me $5.00 to help pay for a meal. I told her I didn't need it, but she insisted – thank you very much. Gotta love those trail angels! We went to the Whitehouse Inn just down Main Street. It's a little pricey, but I got the delicious prime rib and strawberry/rhubarb pie I'd been craving. After days of trail food, it is enjoyable to eat delicious food that someone else cooks. Back to the house to do my chores, then off to bed.

Saturday 7/11

Up at 5:00, but back to bed. No chance I'll get back to sleep, but no reason to be up. Just down the Main Street from the house is a clock in what may be the town square. I never did see it, but I heard it – all night long. The damn thing would chime once for every fifteen minutes, that means that on the half hour it would chime twice, at quarter till it would chime three times, and on the hour it would bong out the hours. Why in the world would anyone need to know the time that often? And why in the world would anyone want to put up with such annoyance?! I need to get back to the trail.

A little after 6:00 I got up to get my pack squared away, called Stef to chat and place an order. We talked for about forty-five minutes, having a lovely conversation. Afterward, I went to breakfast and did my grocery shopping. I returned to the house to put my pack together, get my things ready for mailing, cut my

hair and make a couple phone calls. Everything done, I head to
the post office about 11:20 and meet Mr. Ed there. He and
Lightweight are going to spend the night in the same house. A
quick trip to the store for chocolate milk and I see Egg. We chat
for a while, I go buy fly dope, and we head out of town together.

We walk up the road gabbing and having great fun, and walk
right past the trail head. We went about a mile too far before we
turned around, but right away got a ride from a trail worker. Egg
and I hiked the rest of the day talking and having a good time.
Our first climb was up Lion's Head which someone had said was
a pretty tough climb. I'd been up a lot worse. Then there was the
higher Bear Mt. with a rock pile where it looks like an old fire
tower used to stand. From the tops of both these hills are very
nice views of the rolling countryside. Very shortly we arrive at
the Connecticut/Massachusetts state line and had to observe the
celebratory rituals of crossing a state line with congratulations
and pictures. She teased me about my old-school camera. She's a
great gal, and great company. If I were a younger man...

Our destination is Laurel Ridge Shelter in Massachusetts, and
we arrive there about 6:00. We waste no time setting up our tents
and getting supper as it is threatening rain. Only a few sprinkles
come, and we beat those. A good night to retire early.

Today's trail has been very pretty with a climb up two
mountains, the tops providing terrific views of surrounding
countryside. The last couple miles were along a beautiful, clear,
cascading stream as it cut its way down through a ravine. I kept
seeing pools that looked like they'd be great trout fishing. This is
very pretty country reminding me of home.

Sunday 7/12

Well, the rain did come – thunderstorms that seemed to last
most of the night with much lightning and periods of heavy rain.
The tent was rather damp inside, quite wet outside. A nice sunrise
this morning promising a lovely day. I'm on the trail about 6:30,
but stop pretty soon as I find a good place on a ridge to practice

Tai Chi. Not sure what it is about this morning, but my pack feels like it weighs fifty pounds, and I don't feel like carrying it. The Tai Chi helps to ground me, and I walk on a little easier.

In a little while I'm up on Race Mt. I have no view as it is foggy/cloudy, but the mountain itself is very pretty with abundant blueberries, dense scrub oaks, but mostly covered with what look like huge bonsai pine trees and one lone laurel bush still in bloom. A very enchanting place. Down the rocky north side and I know why I didn't feel so much like walking – these steep, rocky descents are killers on my feet, knees and legs. I guess I'll have to toughen up to it as there will be a lot more of it coming up.

In another few miles is another steep, rocky ascent and descent on Everett Mt. The view and landscape on Everett are much the same as it was on Race. It would be nice to have a view, but there's still wonderful scenery right in front of me. Down at the foot of Everett I'm in a little picnic area, so I stop for a bite to eat. So far today I've done eight miles.

After these mountains the trail levels out pretty quickly and wanders through marshy lowlands, softwood forests and fields for about five miles. I make good time here as the walking is easy, and slowing down means getting swarmed with mosquitoes. No one wants to miss out on any part of the AT experience, but after you've participated in the third or fourth swarming of blood-thirsty mosquitoes, you've got a pretty good idea what it's all about, and no longer feel the need for any more experience. As fun as it is.

Finally through the flatlands and I start up East Mt. I was thinking I might try for the next shelter until I see a sign informing me it is five miles away. In a mile or so I come to a spring and just beyond is a level spot to make camp. I've gone about fifteen miles today, my body is sore, so I make it an early day. I could have made it to the shelter as I still had a couple hours of daylight, but no sense in pushing the body that hard. Besides, the mosquitoes here look hungry.

Monday 7/13

I slept great last night having retired early. I was up early and just as well as the mosquitoes haven't become very active yet, but by the time I was finishing packing they were coming around. I was on the trail about 6:15 with a sunny, cool start to the day.

I was feeling a little agitated this morning with no idea why I ought to be. At the first hill climb I found myself annoyed that the trail planners had run the trail seemingly out of the way just to have it descend a steep, rocky hillside only to turn back in the direction I came from to scramble up another steep, rocky hillside and wind up pretty much where I started all that. Then I found myself wondering why I was even doing this hike.

DANGER, WILL ROBINSON!

When I caught myself thinking this way, I knew I had to change my mind, and so I did. It wasn't long before my attitude changed and, you know, the mosquitoes didn't seem to be pestering me nearly as much.

After what seemed like a long four miles I arrived at the next shelter for water. Egg was there, as well as Roots and four others I did not know. I got my water, exchanged pleasantries, and on my way. Egg caught up to me just before the road she was going to take to her destination. We had a short, pleasant visit. Had I known that would be the last time I'd see Egg, I'd have visited longer.

The day is now sunny and quite pleasant, and the trail pretty easy with some gentle ups and downs. At one point I walked along the edge of a small pond, and the smell of the water and the sound of the waves gently lapping the shore made me think of Maine. Again I said to myself, "I'm walking home." That phrase has come to mean a lot to me.

I stopped to eat about 11:30 and Stretch, Tin Man and a few others pass me by. I hadn't seen Stretch and Tin Man for about a week and assumed they had sped on past me. But that's how it goes out here – the AT leap frog. In just a very short distance I meet up again with all those folks as they are strewn about at a trail intersection taking their dinners. There was the usual chatter about the weather and destinations, and one of the fellows commented on how he was a little leery about the weather, what with the gathering clouds and all.

"Fair weather clouds," I said, looking up at the sky, "nothing to worry about."

"This, from our resident meteorologist," he remarked, unconvinced.

And so it is, the day is gorgeous – mid to high seventies with a cool, dry breeze.

Eventually, the easy, meandering trail starts to make a descent, and does so for a long while it seems, starting to drop towards Tyringham. As the trail approaches town, it leads through some gorgeous farm country of beautiful fields surrounded by rolling hills. After winding around in the low grasslands for a few miles, I cross the road into town and start to climb again.

My destination for the night is a mountain road, rather, near the road, at the next water source. Just down the trail is a nice little spring and a good spot for the tent. I have walked about nineteen miles today, so all I do is set up camp, get supper, and retire to my writing.

Tuesday 7/14

A little sluggish to get up this morning, but up and going and on the trail by 7:00. Another clear, cool morning. Just up the trail I realize I'm feeling slightly agitated with hiking. I figure I've got to change my mind, do so, and the trail becomes so easy that I'm really enjoying today's hike. In four miles I come to Goose Pond, a tranquil, inviting pond in a very pretty, forested setting; makes me think of home. There were a couple fishermen out plying the water, and when asked how the fishing was their reply was, "We got a couple, but it doesn't matter if we don't get any." Yup, just to be out on a day like this is reward enough.

I did something new today. As I started the trail, I cut a couple small trees for hiking poles. As the day wore on, I noticed that my knees are not at all as sore as they would normally have been. So far, I'd have to say that I'm going to continue hiking with them.

I stepped over or around a lot of blow-down today. Up on Beckett Mt., the whole top, most of which is beech, is a broken, shattered mess! I'm told it was due to last winter's ice storm. Down over the other side, past a small pond, I'm gifted with the most glorious scent of balsam fir. Balsam fir is beyond a doubt my most favorite scent. I rub the needles, stick my face right in, and deeply inhale that most pleasing of aromas. Sometimes I'll find a blister on a tree, pop it, and rub pitch on my pack straps and carry that wonderful scent right with me. Ohh, heavenly. More and more it's looking, and now smelling, like the north woods of home.

Before long I'm at October Mountain Lean-to for the night. It's a quiet place when I arrive, only two other guys, and I debated setting up my tent, or putting up in the shelter. Shelters are noisy, but easy. Tomorrow I'll be in town anyway, so for the ease I'll put up in the shelter. In the lean-to are Caribou, a retired judge from Maine, and Philadelphia, a fellow my age, from Florida. And a little later L-train and five others I do not know come into camp. It's getting to be noisy.

Wednesday 7/15

I'm not a good shelter dweller. I'm ready for sleep by 8:00, the younger hikers are up until 9:00, 10:00 or later, and their conversations and camp noise pester me. In the morning I'm up by 5:00 or 6:00 while they are still sleeping, so I try not to make any noise as I get breakfast and load my pack. It doesn't work out well on either end, so I need to camp away from the others.

I was on the trail a little past 6:00 to a clear, cool morning. The start is very nice, even going and I make the first road crossing, about two miles, in a short time. Pretty soon, off in the distance, I hear a loon, not long afterward I flush a partridge, then there's a red-winged blackbird singing by a marsh, finally the scent of balsam fir. All this makes me long for home.

This is an emotional morning – I'm feeling sentimental, lonesome, longing, weepy. I also realize I still haven't fully embraced this hike for the sake of the hike, rather only because I've always wanted to do it. Again I found myself sort of attacking the trail. Realizing my frame of mind, I set to change it. And the day is gorgeous with bright, blue skies and a lovely breeze – just a wonderful day to be hiking.

The forest changes a few times today from dense thickets of mixed growth to areas of open hardwood to a fern-covered hilltop, and back and forth a few more times. A few miles before the town of Dalton, I pause to admire the beauty of the land and reflect on my journey. Indeed I am blessed.

Just before town I meet up with L-train, and we walk into town together. I make a stop at a lumber yard for a piece of Tyvek to make a ground cloth. L-train and I then go to dinner about 1:00. A great tossed salad, loaded cheeseburger, strawberry milkshake and a chocolate chip/pecan cookie. Mmm, it hits the spot! Down to the post office for my parcel, a few calls home, a little day food and chocolate milk, and I'm headed back for the trail.

Having rested and fueled so well in town, I fly the five miles – mostly uphill – to Crystal Mountain Campsite for the night. I arrive at 5:00 giving me plenty of time to wash up and do my laundry in the small stream. No need for supper, so I settle right down to my writing. I'm expecting a good night's sleep tonight.

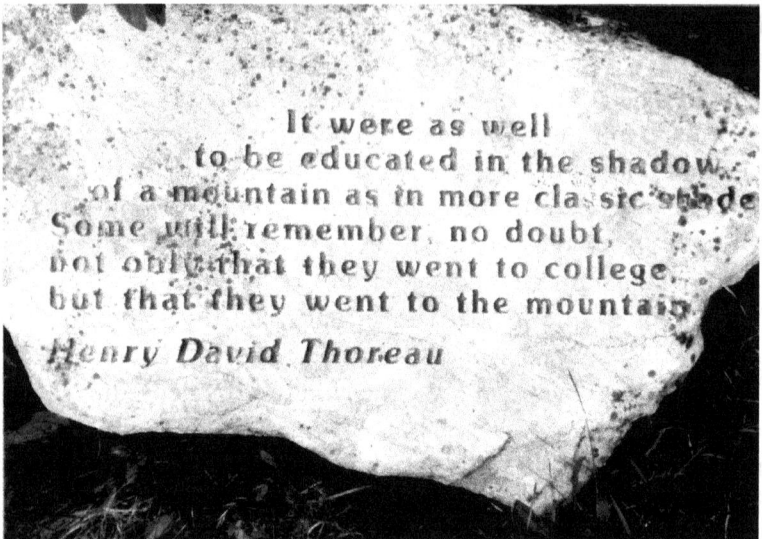

It were as well
to be educated in the shadow
of a mountain as in more classic shade
Some will remember, no doubt,
not only that they went to college,
but that they went to the mountain.
Henry David Thoreau

Mt. Graylock, Massachusetts

Thursday 7/16

Up at my usual hour after a dreamy night, and on the trail about 6:30. A rather uneventful 4.6 mile walk to town, arriving in town about 9:00. Dropped off a post card, then went to a convenience store for an orange juice. And a donut. Then another donut, and then a chocolate milk. It all tasted very good, especially the donuts – best I've had – but when I got started up the trail to Mt. Greylock, it didn't feel as good.

Mt. Greylock is about 3500', the highest climb since Virginia. It was a long uphill from the road, almost eight miles from the highway to the summit, but pretty gradual most of the way, so fairly easy going. Up nearer the top it was like hiking in Maine, the forest looking so similar. And the balsam fir! The most wonderful aroma there is. It's absolutely delightful to hike through this area. The last half mile before the top the trail climbed steeply, and then I'm on top and it is gorgeous. Had it not been a hazy day, the views would have been stunning. Instead, I had to settle for terrific.

At the top is Bascom Lodge, built in 1937 as a get-away for the well-to-do. It is a beautiful fieldstone structure overlooking an extensive range of mountains. They put up guests, do fancy suppers, and have a snack bar. When open. Today they are closed as they have been refinishing floors. At the very summit of the mountain is a tower dedicated to men killed in battles. Nice to have the tower, but wouldn't it be better to still have the men? The observation room in the top of this tower provides a tremendous 360° view of all surrounding countryside. After a snack and poking around for a while, I move on.

It is a little over three miles to the next lean-to, much of this section of the trail steep and rocky. As I approach Mt. Williams, another NoBo hiker I'd camped with recently (I'm terrible with names) comes down the trail in my direction. Upon seeing me he acts quite surprised.

"Chris!" he exclaims.

"You're going the wrong way, fella," I tell him.

"You sure?" he asks, rather dumbfounded.

"Yup, you're heading back to Greylock."

In his confusion, he mutters to himself, wondering how he managed to get turned around, but he puts the pieces together, wheels around and makes tracks, this time heading the right way. I never did see him again.

Soon I arrive at the junction of Mt. Williams trail and an overlook. I went for the view, a pretty valley flanked by low mountains, and when I get back to the junction I see where he made his wrong turn. I didn't make the same mistake, and proceed onward. Being tired from having done about fifteen miles at this point, this section of the trail is quite punishing as it is steep and rocky. Fortunately it doesn't last long. Finally I'm down to the road, and it's less than a half mile to the Wilbur Clearing Lean-to.

I arrive at the lean-to and have it all to myself. Unfortunately it doesn't last long as four young hikers come in later. Hopefully it won't be very noisy tonight. D, as me, did not finish the trail in

'08 and returned this year to complete it, stayed in this shelter on 6/14; that puts him just over a month ahead of me. I imagine he's in Maine by now. Unless he decides to hang around some place for a while, I don't suppose I'll see him on this trip. But one never knows.

11

VERMONT

Friday 7/17

Slept well last night despite four others in the lean-to, I must have been tired. Up about 5:30 and since it's only three miles to North Adams I figured I'd have breakfast there. Shortly down the trail I come to an exposed ridge with a great view of the valley below and mountains ahead. I can see nothing of the valley as it is completely blanketed in a thick fog. All that can be seen is the clear early morning sky, tops of the distant mountains, and the heavy cloud laying in the valley. It is all very tranquil. Much of the walk to town was steep downhill except for the last mile or so.

It's about 8:00 when I hit town, and it's still fairly quiet. I went to Friendly's for breakfast and had a western omelet, home fries and toast, and it was some good! I enjoy the cereal I carry for my breakfast, but after a steady diet of it, it gets boring – this morning's meal really hit the spot. I did a little grocery shopping, then made a call to Stef to make sure she got my last message. She had, and the package is on its way. It was then about 10:00 and I headed back for the trail. Sitting in his dead car in a parking lot was Caribou. We talked a little bit until the wrecker arrived, then I got back underway.

The trail goes uphill pretty steadily for about three miles, the first mile or so along a rushing little stream, and an easy 1.3 miles to the Massachusetts/Vermont state line. I'm in Vermont!!! I'm ecstatic about crossing into Vermont, do a little dance, and thank Spirit for making all this possible. I sat and ate some, and three other hikers stopped for pictures and a bite to eat. I was soon back under way, my day's destination unsure.

The next shelter is three miles away, the one beyond that another eight miles further. I didn't feel like stopping so early for the first one, but didn't think I wanted to go another eight miles to the second one. In between is something called Roaring Branch which I figured to be a stream I could camp alongside. I guessed it would be 5:30 when I arrived there, which is just about the right time for me to call it a day.

I arrive at what I thought might be the place, though it is not roaring as beavers have dammed up the stream. It has just started sprinkling, so I hustle to set up the tent and get in. Inside I look at my watch to see that it is only 4:45. If I had gone on, I'd have made the next shelter by 6:30 or 7:00. Then I took a look at my data book and realized I underestimated the distance between towns and re-supplies, and how I probably don't have enough day food. Then all hell broke loose.

From somewhere deep in my psyche came the awful, crippling ages-old feeling of being a failure, and I started bawling. And I cried and cried, saying over and over, "I'm not a failure." And I rocked and wailed. I didn't know I had any of that old programming left in me, I thought I had gotten all that stuff out, but there it was.

It's now 6:20 and I'm drained. I haven't washed up or rinsed my clothes, let alone got supper, and I'm not so sure I'll get to any of that, though I really ought to. Maybe I'll just spend the rest of the night talking with Spirit.

And something felt squishy, so I checked under the sleeping pad only to find a puddle of rain water that was funneled underneath the tent via the ground cloth. It had the same effect as confirming that I was a failure. That did it, whatever composure I had was gone, and I fell apart. At that point I just cried and wailed. I think I fell asleep crying because when I came to it was dark. Oddly, or maybe because of the release of all that old emotional baggage, I slept pretty well that night.

Saturday 7/18

I was still feeling out of sorts as I tore down camp, but I was underway at 6:00 and feeling better for walking. At 7:00 I stopped for breakfast and my demeanor was continuing to improve. But then I came to a large, rushing stream and I doubted my location last night, and I started to doubt myself all over again. Then in a very short time I came to the next shelter, which, according to my data book, was almost five miles from Roaring Brook, and I knew where I was and where I had been. It – I – was okay.

From there it was a pretty easy uphill to Harmon Hill, then a steep, rough downhill to the highway that goes to Bennington, Vermont. I've done eight miles by 10:00. My goal is a shelter about nineteen miles from where I started, so I'm moving right along. Most of the trail is uphill, with just a few level or downhill sections. There isn't much for views as the forest is now very thick and is often like walking within close walls.

I keep moving right along and come upon another hiker dressed in rain suit and hat. As I drew nearer he turned and I saw it was Yuki. The last time I saw him was on my birthday when I turned to go into Slatington, Pennsylvania, and he kept on the trail. I didn't expect to see him again figuring he was a day or more ahead of me. We didn't stand and talk long as we were both headed for Goddard shelter. As I was moving faster than Yuki I got ahead of him and hiked by myself, encountering a few SoBos and one other NoBo along the way.

I arrived at the shelter before 4:00 to clearing skies, the sun being warm when out. There were three section hikers at the shelter when I arrived, Yuki came in about thirty minutes after me, and six others arrived later on. I had laid out my tent, sleeping pad and sleeping bag to dry. I had plenty of time to bathe, wash laundry and get supper. Within a couple hours everything is dry and I'm sitting around feeling pretty good. I did 18.6 miles in a little over nine hours. This fellow is no failure!

Sunday 7/19

It was chilly overnight, and the wind had blown in clouds and rattled my tent fly all night. The day starts overcast and chilly; I need my rain jacket to keep me warm. I wasn't figuring on going far today, maybe thirteen miles, so I kind of laid about instead of getting right up and going. I got on the trail just after 7:00. I ought to have gone up to the tower, 1/4 mile away, last night when the sky was clear because there sure isn't any view this morning. That's the way it goes.

In about twenty minutes I meet up with Yuki who had left a little before me. We sort of hiked together today. I'm faster than he is, but when I'd stop for a water break or something, he'd catch right up. It was pretty much that way all day. I stopped once to point out a small swamp to tell him that that would be the kind of place to look for a moose. I also showed him a pile of moose poop so he'd be able to tell if any had been around. He was very interested in all this information.

Today's trail is pretty easy, not many hills, but as the forest is quite thick there isn't much for views. Yuki and I ate dinner at Story Spring shelter about noon. He tells me he is always hungry and runs out of energy in the afternoon. His diet seems very basic and maybe doesn't supply him with much nutrition. I gave him a half of a bagel with honey, chunks of cheese and pepperoni, then some chopped dates and dried fruit. He enjoyed all of it and said he was full. My guess is he'll hike better this afternoon.

Aside from a couple little ups and downs, the afternoon trail is quite easy. The day broke off sunny about 11:00, and we now have lovely blue skies and a light breeze. At 3:00 we came to a road just before the three-mile climb up Stratton Mt., elevation 3936'. It is just over six miles to the next shelter. There had been no definite plan about a place to camp for the night, and I figure that if I hump it I'd get to the shelter at 6:00 or 7:00. Yuki said he was not going to go that far, but that's his choice.

I pushed it and got to the top by 5:00 and climbed the tower for tremendous views all around. I didn't dilly-dally as I worked up quite a sweat on the way up, and it is breezy and cool on top. I continued on, and just over the top walk through heavenly balsam firs, so I decide to try to find a place to camp amongst the firs. No good camping spots in the firs, but I got a good one about a half mile down. There's nothing here but me and the trees. It is very quiet and peaceful, a good place to sleep.

Monday 7/20

Some animal, it sounded like it might be a fox, cruised by the tent a few times during the night – one time quite close. Curiosity, I suppose. I get up later than I supposed I'd be, but going just after 7:00. The day is clear and bright, promising a fine day.

The trail is easy this morning, as level as I've seen it for a while. In less than an hour I'm at the next shelter and Stratton Pond – a smaller, pretty, peaceful, mirror-smooth pond ringed by low hills. This would have been a great place to arrive in the afternoon. On I go, headed for Manchester Center and my re-supply. The trail is still very easy and leads through beautiful forests of dense softwoods and large hardwoods. It's nice to see trees grow to their full potential, and I admire the size and beauty of them.

Before long I come to an old county road leading by Prospect Rocks with great views of the near valley and distant mountains. It seems that, since Virginia, the land, as viewed from the overlooks, is basically laid out the same – long, narrow valleys shouldered by a range of mountains of relatively even height that stretch on into the distance. And yet, even though there is similar construction, they are all uniquely attractive. Much like humans.

Shortly back down the road and a turn to the right and I'm headed up towards Spruce Peak, the road to town just five miles away. Three miles of this trail are easy, gently rising and falling through a predominantly softwood forest, but the last two seem to be sort of a roller coaster that send me up and down for no apparent reason. It seemed like the longest two miles I'd ever walked.

I got down to the road just before 2:00, and pretty quickly got a ride to the post office. I picked up my parcel, then stopped at EMS to see about new boots. I look at a few pair and talk with their salesman about my boots and getting replacements. Their boot guy told me that Garmont would probably go good for new boots considering the young age and terrible condition of my boots. But I decide nothing as there is another outfitter just down the road to check out. I look at a few pair there, but they're not so anxious to help me until I clean up. I can't say that I blame them. I get a room at Sutton's place, a shower and I'm off to do laundry. As I'm heading to do laundry I meet Yuki, also staying at Sutton's place. We agree to go to supper when I'm done with my chores. Laundry going and phone calls to the kids, both doing great. I go back to EMS to get Garmont's phone number so I can call about my boots.

Chores done, back to Sutton's place to get Yuki and go to supper. The Sirloin Saloon it is, and it is very good – a terrific prime rib, a great salad and tasty dessert! Back to my room at 9:00 and straight to bed. I'll have some chores to do in the morning before I get back on the trail.

Tuesday 7/21

I tried to sleep in some, but no good. When it's light, I'm awake. Eventually I got up and started putting my food together to figure out what I had, what I needed and what I could forward. Yuki and I went to breakfast, then I went to the post office and on to EMS. Finally got it figured out how to get replacement boots, I'll have them in a couple days. Off to get remaining groceries, then back to Sutton's place to finish putting the pack together. Everything done and I'm heading out about 11:30. I was hoping to leave by 10:00, but guess I had too much to do.

A real quick hitch to the trail head and I'm hiking before 12:30. It has started raining, so I'm in for a wet hike. I start right off with a hill, though a fairly gradual one. Before I reach the top I meet up with Yuki. I make a quick stop at a hut, chat a little with Misha and Gutsy Rabbit, but I don't want to get too comfortable and have to go back into the rain. On I go, down Bromley Mt. Then I go up Styles Peak and down only to go up Peru Peak and down once more to Peru Peak Shelter. Three ascents and descents in ten miles, about 4000' elevation gain and loss, all in about 4.5 hours. I was moving right along to stay warm as I was thoroughly wet from the chilly rain.

At the shelter are two young women section hiking, and Hulk. The first thing to do is dry off and change clothes. Hulk leaves after a while and I teach the ladies, who were playing cards, the wonderful game of cribbage. It was great fun, even though I lost to Mudboots. Beginner's luck. Yuki and four others arrive, so we have a full house, but we're all dry. Supper, journal and to bed by 8:00. I'm the last one up. Unusual.

Wednesday 7/22

Still overcast and misty this morning, so I slept in a little later. Up about 6:15 and on the trail a little after 7:00. There's a lot of water dripping from the trees, but no rain. Less than a mile out of the shelter is Griffith Lake, a small, shallow and pretty pond set in a thick forest.

The first mile of the trail is easy, then there's the climb over Baker Peak which is fairly steep right near the top. If it were clear, I'm sure there'd be excellent views, but nothing this morning. After Baker Peak the trail becomes pretty level for maybe ten miles. I've planned on going just 14.5 miles today, so I take my time. Fifteen miles a day is plenty, is easily doable, and I can walk at such a pace as to be able to enjoy my surroundings.

The forest spreads out, sometimes mature hardwood, sometimes young softwood, but rarely is there a view on account of the thickness of it. Back at Goddard Shelter, one of the hikers there commented on how the trail in Vermont is referred to as The Green Wall due to the density of the forest. Yeah, it's pretty much like that. I know they're around, but I haven't seen an animal in some time, and maybe won't.

On today's trek I cross over a couple small rivers that look like they'd be very good for trout fishing. And me without a pole. I'm really enjoying walking at this relaxed pace, I can see and hear and smell my surroundings, I can feel the earth. I'm seeing more and more SoBos now, most of them having started in Maine around the first of June. They've got the hardest part done now, but they're also walking into the heat, and they're welcome to it. But after all the gloomy, sodden reports I'd heard about this past spring in Maine, they may not mind.

After many miles I come to Little Rock Pond, an inviting gem of a pond nestled in low, green hills. If it were a warmer day, I'd have dropped my pack and taken a swim. The pond appears to be a great place for trout, and I imagine paddling my canoe along the rocky shore trolling a worm, lure or fly. Again, I think of home.

In a couple miles I make my last climb of the day, but it's not much of a climb. Over the top it becomes a forest of mature fir and spruce. It is very pretty and so easy to walk through. In a little bit I come to a stack of rocks, then many stacks of rocks – built up from the forest floor, from exposed ledge, from trees – some small, some large all perfectly placed. Evidently folks have been adding to this monument for some time. I thought it really quite fun, though another hiker kind of grumbled about it. I guess he might have thought it out of place, but he took a couple pictures just the same.

Cairnville

A little beyond is the side trail to White Rocks overlook with great views of the near valley shouldered by beautiful, high, lush green mountains. A half mile beyond White Rocks is the trail to tonight's shelter. The first one there, I bathe, get supper started and build a fire when Yuki and two SoBos arrive. It is a soft, pleasant evening, the two SoBos enjoying the fire before retiring to their camp early, and it's just Yuki and I in the shelter. Soon my day is done and it's time to turn in for the night.

Thursday 7/23
    Woke to fairly clear skies; it looks like, weather wise, it'll be a good day to hike. I still didn't feel like getting right out of bed, I turned in too late last night. Since I'll be going to town today for new boots I take off and get going at it. Not much for hills, just one – Bear Mt. – so the going is pretty easy. Even Bear Mt. was good going, and I get up and over it pretty quickly. One side of the mountain was open woods and dry, the other was dense and

wet. It's obvious which side gets the weather. Once over the top I'm cruising right along.

As always, the forest is very pretty, and it's quite enjoyable to walk through it. I meet a few couples out day hiking, otherwise all is quiet. Basically, I'm walking a ridge until the descent to Clarendon Gorge and Mill River. Here the river cuts through bedrock, exposing the many layers of geologic time as it churns its way through the forest. So much like many rivers in Maine. The closer I get to home, the more anxious I become.

Pretty quick I'm at Vt. Rt.103 to North Clarendon to Rutland for new boots. I make a stop at a little store to see if I can connect with a gal who works at EMS, but it's a no go, so it looks like I'm hitching the four miles to get to EMS. Fortunately, I got a ride right away from a guy who thru-hiked in '97, and he took me right to the mall. There was some confusion at the store as the fellow in charge didn't know what arrangements had been made, but all was cleared up soon enough. I caught a hitch for three of the four miles back, picked up my pack and headed for the trail.

In the parking lot at the trail head, Tim and Mike are doing magic – ice cream with cream soda, chips, cookies, and candy. Just the ice cream and soda for me, some chit-chat, and on the trail by 2:00. I'd hoped I'd be back on the trail sooner, but so it goes. I've got seven miles to do, so I get a wiggle on as I want to make camp by 6:00. This portion of the day's trail starts hillier with a couple higher, steep sections, but then becomes more level as it parallels a meandering stream through a lush forest.

In four or so miles I meet Yuki, and we're both headed for the same shelter. I arrive at the Governor Clement Shelter, an old, stone shelter with built-in fireplace, at 5:45 and start gathering firewood. Yuki comes in a few minutes later, it's just he and I here tonight. A night's worth of wood gathered, a warm, cheery fire going, bath and laundry done, supper, relaxing to my journal, then to bed. As I get into bed, I have the thought, "Oh, what a beautiful life. Thank You ever so much, Spirit."

Friday 7/24

A cool, lightly rainy start to the day. Up at 5:30, but don't feel like moving yet, so back to bed for a short while. A sluggish start, but on the trail by 7:00. Just out of the shelter there is a steady uphill, a couple times steep, up Mt. Killington. This section is about four miles, and would provide excellent views were it not for the clouds rolling through. Since the trail is wet and slippery, my view does not change much anyway as I need to watch my footing. Except for the occasion when I stop to drink or look around, the trail at my feet and directly in front of me is my view. There is a short side trail to the very peak, but as I'm in clouds there would be no view, and I am wet and chilly so I pass it up. If it was a clear day, that would be another story. A quick stop at the mountain top shelter for a bite. Apparently another hiker packed more food than needed, so left it behind for anyone who wanted it. I help myself to some of it, then I move on.

Now starts the long descent. About half way down is one of the prettiest pieces of woods I have seen. There are acres and acres of beautiful birch trees, and a forest floor of ferns making a lush, green carpet throughout. Even in the dim light, the birches shimmer and glow white and golden, and the ferns radiate deep greens. Some places are pretty, some are spectacular, but this morning this forest is magical. My spirit soars as I stroll through this enchanted forest.

And walking along the trial, I get the feeling that someone is behind me, I turn around and see no one. This has happened many times on my hike. Then I felt Dad's presence and realized he has been hiking with me. And so he was again today. And whenever I would get the feeling again, I would say hello, and have a conversation, though one-sided, with my Dad. And it happened with Mom, too, though I didn't get the feeling so often that she was hiking with me. Oh, how I miss my folks.

Nearing the bottom of the mountain is another roller coaster – down a rocky section to go up another only to go down then back up some more. I know that sometimes the trail has to go where it does, and that the land is what it is, but I also believe that the trail planners had to have had days when they were feeling a little feisty and decided to give you an extra workout. Whatever. It's all good.

Eventually I'm at the highway into Killington and get a quick hitch to the store and post office for my re-supply. A call to Stef for a re-supply order and a pleasant conversation, and a call to family to inform them of my location and condition. A quick hitch back to the trail head – courtesy of the local bus – and I'm going again. It's hard to believe that such a short trip ate up at least 2 hours. I ask a number of hikers if they'd seen Yuki, but none had. We had planned on staying at a particular shelter, but when I arrived there were already five hikers in a shelter with only four bunks, so I continued on. Little did I know that when I left our shelter that morning, it would be the last time I'd see Yuki.

In two miles I come to Gifford's Woods State Park where I hosey (local expression meaning to claim or take, as in "I hosey the front seat," or "he hoseyed the last piece of pie") a camping spot a little bit in the woods not far off the trail. I imagine I'll be on my way out of the park before most of the campers are up, so I figure I'm good. Camp set up, my bath, supper and at 8:15 all is done and I'm going to bed.

Enchanted forest south of Killington

Saturday 7/25

I went to bed without the fly on the tent as the sky had cleared pretty well. You'd think I'd have learned by now. At some point during the night I heard the first few spatters of rain, so I scurried and hurried to get the fly on the tent and gear under cover before everything got wet. A little rain got in the tent, but not too bad. This morning I found that the tent still leaks, even after I treated it, and there was a slight puddle under the foot of the sleeping pad. That discovery rather soured my mood for the first few hours. Eventually I let that go and set my mind on the hike as I plan to go almost seventeen miles today.

The first few miles were pretty easy as they led me along Kent Pond, through easy woods, and on a boardwalk across a marsh, but then I came to a hill that seemed to go up and up without stopping. That set the pace for the next twelve miles as the trail was up and down, up and down, up and down… It was the toughest day of hiking I'd seen in quite some time. The uphills were physically demanding, and the downhills were tough on the feet and knees. Still, one foot in front of the other and keep on plugging.

By 10:00ish the day had cleared out pretty well, and by noon there was bright sunshine with an occasional puffy cloud, the nicest day in quite a few. By mid-afternoon I'd come fourteen miles and arrived at a side trail that led to an overlook, and since the day is so nice I go to have a look. At the hilltop is a small cabin, homey though neglected, with a ladder up the roof to a platform from which there is a tremendous 360 degree view of all surrounding countryside. It's too bad the cabin has been so neglected, it's in such a spectacular setting; it's in desperate need of a new roof, consequently the inside is starting to rot. But what a peaceful spot and terrific view from this high, open hilltop.

The last 2.5 miles of the trail are good going, and I'm at Wintturi Shelter before 5:00. I set about hanging tent parts and sleeping bag to dry, bathe and do my laundry, and prepare my supper. While I'm waiting for supper, I set up my now dry tent. After supper it's journal time. It is now 7:30 and all I have left to do is brush my teeth. Finally, I will be turned in by 8:00!

Sunday 7/26

Just a little rain this morning, mostly dripping from the trees from last night's little shower. I wiped down the tent as best I could, but I still packed it away damp. I hadn't planned to go far today, but I'm on the trail at 6:45 just the same.

I'm loving the trail this morning, it is easy, rolling and open, I can see a hundred yards into the woods. It's a beautiful trail, rather gentle compared to yesterday's steep roller coaster. I get to the first road crossing, about four miles, in an hour and a half – and I'm not pushing it! At the road there's a billboard and a sign telling about the On The Edge Farm selling ice cream, baked goods, snacks and drinks. But they won't be open for another hour and a half. I sure could have enjoyed some fresh baked goods... So it goes. Instead, I eat a couple delicious and appreciated pears that someone had left at the billboard. I always love the magic.

After that road, the terrain gets a little higher and steeper, but nothing like yesterday's trail. And the sun comes out today! It has other days as well, but today it came out early. As I'm walking today, I'm reminded to take my time and experience the world around me. This adventure is not as much a hike as it is a journey, so slow down and enjoy it. I cross a number of roads, and at each crossing it's always the same, you walk down to the road, and up from it. Yet the trail stays gentle.

About noon I come to Cloudland Road, and just up the road is Cloudland Farm with a store selling organic ice cream, baked goods and such. Closed most Sundays. I'd heard the store was closed today, so I didn't bother to go up. Later in the afternoon I learned that they were doing magic in the big house as their son is hiking the trail, and they're throwing a big hiker party. Oh well, missed that one also.

I get to Thistle Hill Shelter, where I was thinking of staying, just after 2:00 and have a bite to eat. I debate staying or moving on, and then a SoBo hiker comes in and tells me about the General Store in town and how there is camping in the area, so at 3:30 I decide to go another five miles. But just as I get back on the trail something stops me and tells me to go back to the shelter for the night. Why I should, I have no idea, but I heed the inner voice and go back. A very relaxed, quiet evening, just me and two other hikers here. I know there's some reason I came back – something about cosmic timing and planetary alignment...

Monday 7/27

A nice night, a good start to the day, and I'm on the trail by 6:30. A very nice trail this morning, gentle and mostly downhill. This section of Vermont is quite easy hiking and very scenic. The trail is easy enough that, even though I'm walking right along, I can gawk around. The woods are so pretty – open enough that you can see into them for a distance, and the high meadows provide nice views.

In a few hours I'm in West Hartford and make a quick stop at the store for milk and a pastry. The day is sunny and is getting quite warm. A little bit of road walking and I'm glad to be back in the shade of the forest. A few hills, but nothing hard, and by 11:30 I'm at Happy Hill Shelter for food and a break. This is the last, or first, depending on direction, shelter in Vermont; a newer, pretty stone structure.

I've now done nine of today's fifteen miles in five hours. Six more miles to go to town. The woods are pretty, the trail is gentle and rolling, a great way to end in Vermont. The last few miles are road walking. It is along the first piece of road that I see the only deer I've seen in all of Vermont. It was in someone's back yard. Very soon I'm on the bridge over the Connecticut River – the border of Vermont and New Hampshire. I'm in New Hampshire! Just like the song from Grand Funk Railroad (c'mon, you know...) "I'm getting closer to my home..."

Into Hanover by 2:00 and straight to the post office. Package there, but no replacement socks. Next, it's off to the outfitter for alcohol, then to the restaurant offering a free piece of pizza to hikers, then off to find a chiropractor. I found one local – on vacation as of today. It wasn't really needed, but would have felt good. Back to Main Street for a great meal of Thai food, waterproofing from the hardware store, ice cream, then catch the bus to the motel. This evening's chores – tent treated, a shower, laundry, sort out the pack, and calls home. Finally all done – thankfully – as it is 10:00. Time for this little hiker to call it a day.

12

NEW HAMPSHIRE

Tuesday 7/28

Up about 6:00. I didn't sleep real well, kind of a warm, stuffy room, but I'm rested. Made calls to home, filled up at the complimentary breakfast, and into town about 9:30. I got the needed film and glucosamine at CVS, film and journal pages mailed home, and re-supply at the well-stocked Co-op. It was about 11:00 when I got on the trail.

It was a gentle up, then easy ups and downs for most of today's miles. It was getting hot in town, but it's much more pleasant in the woods. So far, the first eleven miles of New Hampshire are good going. I make it to Moose Mt. Shelter about 4:15 and debate going another two miles to the foot of the hill to camp near a brook. I didn't get a good answer about a place to camp near the brook, and feeling like I want to get into a more relaxed hiking mode, I stay put. A full house in the shelter tonight, and there is much lively conversation.

For the next few days I'm planning on twelve to fourteen miles a day, a pace I'd like to maintain. But, if the day is going good and I make more mileage without pushing, I'll do it. If I feel like it. This shelter sure is in a pretty spot, sitting on top of a hill with a long view of distant mountains. This is why I'm not hurrying.

Wednesday 7/29

Woke early this morning to a rose red sky. I wonder if the old adage "Red sky in the morning, sailor take warning; red sky at night, sailor's delight" will come to pass... While getting breakfast and putting together my pack, I move about as quietly as possible so as to not disturb the others, but soon they are stirring as well. I am on the trail at 5:50.

It's easy going this morning and I'm just poking along enjoying the morning. I'm planning on going just twelve miles today, so there's no need to hurry. I'm really enjoying this pace, it's easier on me and I experience more of the trail. Three of the young guys from the shelter have already passed me, I guess they have more urgent business to attend to. When I arrive at the next shelter, nearly six miles away, I run into Misha, who I last saw a week ago. In about three miles we get to the Lyme/Dorchester road and meet the three young fellows who had hurried on ahead. Nearby there lives an older man who does magic at his house, ice cream bars, popsicles, inexpensive sodas, and the five of us go to find him. We find the house, but no one is home – no magic this time around.

The trail stays easy most of the morning, and is quite pretty with gentle, rolling hills, small hay fields, and healthy forests of mixed growth. And then starts the climb up to Smarts Mt. The trail goes up rocky ridges, and up some more, and when you think you're at the top, you look off into the distance to see the tower on the mountain you're headed for. It's only a mile or so to the destination, but it appears to be a lot further. Along the way I meet with day hikers out enjoying the beautiful day and scenery.

The day has gotten quite warm and I'm sweating heavily as I climb. Near the top of Smarts Mt. the trail becomes rather steep, but before long you reach the summit. There is a fire tower on top of the mountain providing excellent views. The country is becoming more mountainous now. Misha and the three other hikers are there, but they are moving on to Hexacuba Shelter, 5.5 miles away. It's mid-afternoon, only 3:00, I think about moving on. I start to, getting maybe a mile further, but I change my mind and head back to the old fire ranger's cabin.

It's near 4:00 when I get there and have it all to myself. I get my water, take a little bath, and go back to the shelter to start my supper. Shortly, six other hikers arrive, the three Smith brothers,

Couscous and his girlfriend, and one other. Couscous and gal, and the lone fellow decide to tent, so there's just four of us in the old cabin. About 5:00 it starts to rain – that "red sky in the morning…" thing. I'm glad I'm set for the night.

Thursday 7/30

Boy, did it rain hard last night! But I was dry and cozy in the cabin. The morning is still dark and overcast, so I sleep in 'til about 6:00. I'm on the trail about 6:45, slogging through water and mud. At one point on the way down the mountain, I broke out of the low firs and drop under the branches of beech trees. It is quite dusky under the dense canopy, and it takes a few moments for my eyes to adjust. The gloominess isn't as bothersome as is all the water and mud in the trail. But that's the way it goes.

Four miles down from the cabin I come to the south fork of Jacob's Brook. I look for the blaze on the other side of the brook because it doesn't seem possible that the crossing is where it is, but there it is. There are steep banks on both sides, which, in itself, is no big deal, but the stream, which typically would be an easy crossing, is a deep, wild, rushing torrent after last night's heavy rainfall. I look up and down the stream, but see no other place that looks any better to cross. I went down stream a couple hundred yards to where the stream becomes wider, shallower and less threatening to make my crossing. It was still knee deep and rather forceful, but by facing upstream, side-stepping with short steps and paying very close attention to my footing, I make an easy crossing. But my boots are thoroughly soaked.

Then there's the three mile walk and a climb up to Mt. Cube and on top is an awesome view – of clouds. There were a couple small, random patches of blue sky, but nothing affording a view. I eat my dinner and move on. Down at the foot of this mountain I have to ford my third brook of the day. Again, it would have been an easy crossing were it not for last night's deluge. Before long I'm at NH Rt. 25A, and I have 2.4 miles to the next shelter. A muddy slog up to Ore Hill Shelter and I'm tired. I've done 12.6

miles today, but it feels like a lot more. I've lamed up my right knee, I'm ready to call it quits for the day.

I'm at the shelter about 3:30 and I'm whipped. Eventually I get around to bathing and laundry, and just have some day food for supper. I plan my meals and re-supply, and do my journal. A few more simple things to take care of, and it'll be an early evening. There are just three of us in the shelter tonight, myself, Grommet and one of the three speedy hikers from yesterday morning. Grommet said rain is forecast for the evening, but we can do without. It'll be a quiet evening as we all are turned in by 8:00.

Friday 7/31

I'm up and on the trail by 6:30, the sky getting heavier as I go. The trail is still very wet, probably will be for some time, given the amount of rain of late. Even with everything so wet, I get along pretty well and make it to the road into Warren, where I will re-supply, around 7:30.

I didn't have to wait long before I got a ride right to the post office, and then to the store. The timing was perfect for my package as it had only just arrived. There's a pretty nice little store in town, they had what I wanted. I place a quick call to Stef to order my next re-supply, finish arranging my pack, then head back out. It had started raining a little bit ago, so I'm in for a wet walk again. In a few minutes, the same fellow that brought me into town took me back to the trail; a genuine nice guy. Thank you.

I have six miles to go to the next shelter, probably my destination for the night, so I don't hurry any. An easy couple miles up to Mt. Mist, certainly living up to its name today, and three more down to the road. A few miles up this road is a hiker hostel that reportedly has very nice accommodations. I briefly consider going there, but I really don't want to be in a noisy, crowded environment. Across the road is another stream crossing, this one also very swollen and fast from the recent rains. A hundred or so yards down the road I spy what looks like a road heading into the woods. If so, there would have to be a bridge. It was and there was, so I had an easy, dry stream crossing.

It's a mile, mostly gradually uphill, to Jeffers Brook Shelter. It is still lightly raining, but I couldn't care less as I'm now in a fine, dry shelter in a very pretty spot among stately pine trees. I arrived at 12:30 and could have pushed on to the next shelter, but that would be five tough miles up Mt. Moosilauke, and two more to the shelter. Better to make that trip tomorrow when the weather may be nicer. Besides, if I move too fast, I will arrive in the next town well ahead of my re-supply.

So, I get my water, change into my dry clothes, hang my wet stuff, put out my sleeping pad and bag, and settle in. A bite to eat and it's nap time. I wake at 4:00 and write in my journal.

One thing I noticed this morning as I slogged along the muddy trail was that I was feeling agitated. I wasn't sure why, I had no reason to be, yet I was. Maybe it was just the weather. And I started thinking about my attitude, and the more I thought I realized I was feeling lonely. The past few days I'd been feeling it more and more, and I'd begun imagining meeting a woman along the way. But what I thought would be the best thing would be finding the place in my heart and soul where I wouldn't be lonely without someone else. And I'm pretty sure such a state exists, but I'm not familiar with it.

When I got to this shelter, I had it all to myself. All right, I thought, peace and quiet. Then the thought came to me that if I was looking for a woman, I ought to go where the people are. There surely would have been people at the hostel, perhaps an available woman, but I so prefer the quiet. Besides, the woman I would be looking for, like me, would not be in the hostel, but would be in a shelter. Well, it's now 6:10 and there's no woman. I'm not going to fret over it, I will meet her when the time is right. But, Spirit, just so You know, I'm feeling ready again.

A little later in the evening, Stretch, Tin Man, the gal who's been hiking with them whose name I can never remember, and two other fellows come to the shelter. Stretch, Tin Man, what's-her-name and one of the fellows set up tents, the other fellow shares the shelter with me. A very relaxed, quiet evening.

Saturday 8/1

It's 6:30 and I'm still in my bag. Today will be a short day, so no need to hurry.

As I lie here, I'm feeling antsy, like I must get up and get moving. Then the thought comes to me, "This is where you learn to slow and settle down, you've always lived your life frantically." I wouldn't have thought of myself as living frantically, but I guess I've always been on the move – often doing, always looking. I suppose what I've needed all along was to take the time to look inside. It appears that now is the time. I still have more walking to do on my way home.

The day is still foggy as I leave camp around 7:30, but it looks as though it will clear off. The first mile or so of the trail is very easy as it crosses a gravel road, follows a paved road for a short bit, and re-enters the forest on an old woods road. After that, the trail climbs for about three miles, steep and rocky towards the top, to the summit of Mt. Moosilauke, the longest continuous climb since the big hills way down south.

Yes indeed, the day is clearing off. The climb is nice and easy, a little steeper and rockier nearer the top, and I give no thought to the time or distance – I hike along at an easy pace. Before long I'm at a trail junction and a sign post indicating 0.8 mile to the summit. Half of this distance is a nearly level trail through a corridor of six to eight-foot tall balsam fir trees. Oh, the loveliest scent on earth. I stroll along easily, then break out of the tree line to make the last little rise to the summit.

At the top – my oh my – what a view!! Spreading out all around are majestic mountains, one stacked upon the other, seeming to stretch to eternity. What spectacular country this is! And the day is clear with a few passing clouds and a light breeze. Just a perfect morning to climb this 4802' mountain. I stayed on the top for about two hours losing myself in the view, soaking up the sun and good earth energy, and chatting with the other hikers. The crown of Moosilauke is all rock, but you only have to drop a few feet in elevation before there are a few singular trees, then clusters of them until you get back into the dense forest. About 1:00 I started poking my way down with Solo, a 52-year old guy – though he doesn't look it – from Milwaukee, originally from the Dominican Republic. He's a very friendly, chatty guy, and I'm enjoying his company.

A day hiker I talked with had said the north side was steep, and he wasn't exaggerating. Along with being steep it is also quite rocky, so the descent was much slower than the ascent was. Again, the mountain seems best approached from the south. It's a gorgeous day and I don't have far to go, so I'm very content to poke my way down. In two miles we come to the side trail to Beaver Brook Shelter where I thought I might stay the night. At the shelter I get the water I need, Solo stops for a food break, and I continue my descent.

The trail now is quite steep and rocky, but I would rather do it now than in the morning. Just about all the way down the trail follows a waterfall – nearly two miles! The trail becomes so steep that in places there are wooden steps secured to the exposed ledge, and steps of rock are constructed where they need and can be. I'm glad I'm going down rather than up.

At the foot of the mountain near the road I leave the trail to find a place to camp for the night. Camping alongside the trail is prohibited, but I get far enough away that no one could see me unless they walk in to where I am, and I always practice leaving no trace. In fact, I often leave a site looking better than I found it, as in tonight's case, by picking up some trash left behind by someone else. I locate a fairly level spot close to a small, clear brook. A great place except for the road noise – primarily Harley Davidson motorcycles – but they'll probably stop after nightfall.

What's-her-name (Wisp?) had mentioned a hostel in a town that has a movie theater. I thought about going, it would be fun to see a movie, but I didn't want to stay in a noisy hostel. So here I am in my tent in the woods writing in my journal. It's now 7:00 and will be getting dark in an hour or so. It's quite peaceful here; I'm anticipating a very restful night.

Sunday 8/2

I woke early, but didn't feel like getting right out. I'm finally up about 6:00, the day is clouding in. All done and underway at 7:00ish.

In no time I cross the highway at Kinsman Notch, and the trail immediately climbs. I'm climbing up Mt. Wolf, elevation 3478', and I find it is a tougher climb than going up Moosilauke at 4800'. I think New Hampshire is now showing me what it is. This trail is rocky, rooted and muddy. It is also steep, narrow and slippery – it is beautifully raw. I'm planning on doing only 11.5 miles today, so I don't have to push any.

Sometimes the sky will be completely clouded in and threatening rain, and then it will clear for a few minutes. It does this for most of the morning. At the top of Mt. Wolf there are some views of nearby mountains, when the sky clears enough to allow, but it is nothing like the clear skies and endless views of yesterday. And so I continue on.

Heading down the other side, I notice something in the trail. I stop and pick up a Croc shoe, thinking I will find the owner, or I'll dispose of it more properly. As I'm walking down the trail, I recognize I'm stumbling, and in thinking about it realize that I haven't drank enough water, that I'm dehydrated. It's easy to do when the days are cloudy and cool, you don't feel as thirsty, so you don't think about drinking. I finish off what water I have and hope I will find some more soon. If nothing else, the shelter is only a couple miles away.

Well, there was no water until I got to Eliza Brook Shelter, but here is a beautiful, clear brook. I drank my fill, and filled my bottles. I went up to the shelter for a bite to eat and found that Solo was still there – at 12:30! He hadn't made any great time or distance by hiking a longer day yesterday. I'd stopped earlier, but here we were at the same place and time today. We talked as I ate and he told me he was upset because he had lost one of his Crocs.

"Like this one?" I asked, and I handed him the shoe I found on the trail – his lost shoe.

"Oh thank you; you made my day!" he exclaimed, delighted to have it returned to him.

We left the shelter together to climb up Kinsman. This is another steep, rough trail, but we are going only four miles to the next shelter, so there's no need to hurry. By the time we get near the top, the somewhat sunny day has clouded in and started to rain. On the top, it was windy, rainy and chilly. There is not a view to see, and the weather sends us on our way. Down through a saddle the weather is more tolerable, and then we come up to the north peak, maybe a mile away. Just like at the south peak, the weather is rough and there are no views. We don't dilly dally and keep moving down to the shelter.

We arrive at Kinsman Pond Shelter at 4:00 to find a family of three there, a father with son and daughter out for a few days. Wet clothes changed for dry, supper is underway and more hikers come trickling in. There is now a full house as folks are quitting early due to the rain. Tomorrow I go into town for my re-supply – hopefully my package will be there.

Monday 8/3

I got up during the night and found that the sky had cleared and stars shone brightly. I finally got up around 7:00 when everyone else started stirring. The clouds are again rolling through this morning; even so, there is enough blue tint to the sky to hint to it becoming a nice day.

The descent off Kinsmen is not nearly as steep as the ascent, but the trail is very wet – many little streams are crossing and flowing down the trail. Even though the walking is easier, it is still slow going. In a couple miles I get to Lonesome Lake Hut, and stop to check it out. And get a piece of cake. The hut wasn't so fascinating, but the view was terrific across serene Lonesome Lake up to picturesque Mt. Lafayette. The day is now clear, so the view is grand. On down the trail I go to Franconia Notch.

The forest is fir and hemlock up high, but as I get lower in elevation turns to beech, maple and birch. The trail follows a lively, clear stream, so there is plenty of water. Soon I'm crossing under I-93 and get on the bike path to the Flume Visitor Center. Even though it is Monday morning, there are quite a few folks here taking in the sights. I grab a quick bite to eat from my pack, but forego the $3.00 root beer offered inside.

A little after noon I start walking/hitching to town and the post office; I got a ride most of the way there with a local fellow. I comment on how the place looks familiar, but I don't recall so much development. Then I notice Clark's Trading Post and ask if they have bears there. He confirmed that they do have trained bears there. I knew I had been there before, but it was maybe twenty-four years ago. How things change.

I waited around until 1:30 for the post office to open, got my package and am off to Lincoln, just a mile away. I get in town about 2:00, get my shopping done and mail some food ahead to Mt. Washington, about four days away. I was told about a hostel in town that is pretty nice, so that's where I go for the night. I get a shower, laundry going and my journal started before I go to supper at a restaurant just on the edge of town – an excellent, reasonably priced steak supper.

The day has been sunny and warm, it would have been an excellent day up on Franconia Ridge had I continued on. I suppose it will be tomorrow as well. The plan is to get up and going early, stop for breakfast, and get on the trail as soon as possible.

Tuesday 8/4

Up and out at 5:40, headed for a diner for breakfast. The earliest any one of them is open is 7:00, so I have an hour to kill. It took a while, but I finally found a pay phone and called Stef.

After the call I got a very good breakfast then headed for the trail. I'm on the trail at 9:00, not as early as I'd hoped, but not bad.

The first mile or two of the trail is easy, but then it becomes steeper and I have to climb. A stop for water at Liberty Spring, another mile or more of up to Little Haystack Mt., and I'm on a ridge; a pleasant walk through spruce and fir. In another mile or so I break out of the tree line and, OH MY GOD! the views are spectacular!

Franconia Ridge

For about four miles the trail runs up over two mountain tops and all along the way are continuous awesome vistas of this magnificent mountain country. Walking up here is fantastic, heavenly, a hiker's paradise. After Mt. Lafayette I drop down into the trees for a mile or so, then the last climb up to Mt. Garfield, the fourth mountain peak I'll climb today. The trail to here is steep and rocky, but as bad as I'd heard it was, I didn't think it was too tough. Going down the north side of it was steeper, but most all seem to be that way – more gradual on the south side, steeper on the north. For this reason, I suspect it's easier hiking the trail south to north.

About 5:00 I arrive at Garfield Ridge Campsite, and after some confusion about a campsite, finally got set up. Thankfully, as I'm tired and getting grumpy. A hurried supper and finishing up, I retire to my journal. It's nearing 9:00 and I've got to hit the hay. All I need to say about the day is that the hiking was very good, and the views nothing short of spectacular. As long as the weather stays nice, and it's supposed to for the next few days, hiking through here will be terrific.

Wednesday 8/5

Awake early, and under way about 6:30. The sky is cloudy, but it doesn't look like rain.

A very steep trail to start; in fact, not far out of camp I looked down at the trail and said, "Are you kidding me, that's the trail?!" This short section is very steep and very rocky as the trail descends with a stream as it tumbles over and around rock of nearly all shapes and sizes. Well, it is what it is, so I proceed with caution. Obviously it was doable as I'm still alive and well to write about it. I woke tired this morning as I didn't sleep well last night, and I don't have a lot of energy or enthusiasm for this rough, tough trail. Some days are like that. Energy or not, I move along as best I can.

I'm planning on doing 14.5 miles today, so I'm making quick miles as long as it's easy. After the steep down it's pretty good going for a mile or so, and then a moderate up to Galehead Hut, still not as bad as foretold. After the hut it's a steep mile up, and then the trail turns and runs side hill. Aside from a couple gentle ups and downs, the trail is the most level I have seen for quite some miles – and I'm enjoying it.

Before long I'm on Mt. Guyot and looking eastward down a long, deep valley flanked on the south by Franconia Ridge. Mountain after mountain roll away into the distance. Such breathtaking country this is. On the windward side of Guyot, the fir trees are about a foot high and growing very close together giving the appearance of a thick carpet. On the leeward side, the trees resume normal growth, size and shape.

It's a gentle trail to Zeacliff with rock overhangs exposing a long view of the valley below, the AT being at the foot of the mountains on the other side of the valley. From Zeacliff it's a steep downhill to New Zealand Hut. I arrive at the hut about 1:30 and my body is hurting – my knees ache with every step. At the hut, four other hikers and I stop for dinner. I got a candy bar and a $2.00 bowl of chicken noodle soup. The cook also brought over a bowl of mixed vegetables, leftovers from the night's meal preparation, and I kept mixing them in with my soup; I got about four bowls of chicken noodle/mixed vegetable soup out of the deal. Some of the day/section hikers were leaving, so they brought us their excess food of granola bars, trail mix, candy bars. With the soup, candy bar and magic, I'm good to go.

It's five miles to my destination with most of the trail being pretty easy – the easiest five miles in the White mountains – but I am getting so tired that I stumble and fall three times along the way. I thought about taking the side trail to another pond to camp for the night, but I don't feel like doing the extra mileage. Finally, I am so relieved and glad to be at the Ethan Pond Shelter. After taking a little while to relax and settle in, I go to the pond for water and to bathe and do laundry. At the shelter tonight is Zoltan, who I haven't seen for quite some time. When I finish with this journal, I'll cook my supper, eat and turn in. It's been a long day and I'm beat.

Thursday 8/6

Slept well, packed up and on the trail by 6:30. Three miles of trail to the road at Crawford Notch are mostly pretty easy, but a little steep down to the road. Down at the trailhead parking lot is a former thru-hiker doing magic. I got a soda, some grapes and pleasant conversation.

After crossing the highway I start a gradual climb up to Mt. Webster, which becomes fairly steep near the top. The day is mostly sunny with a light breeze and the hiking is wonderful. Up on Webster there are great views of Crawford Notch and surrounding mountains. Leaving Webster I start to walk along the ridge line. I'm in the Presidential Range, a very pleasant walk with terrific, stunning views all around. This section of trail goes over Mts. Jackson, Pierce and Franklin on its way to Mt. Washington. I wondered what the early Native Americans had called this stretch of mountains. Most of the trail is above tree line, and the seemingly never ending views are spectacular. The day is in and out with moderate temps making for very comfortable hiking.

At one stretch after Webster, I came upon a sort of a swamp up in a saddle. There was a boardwalk through this high mountain marsh, fortunately, for if there hadn't been you wouldn't have walked through there. From the boardwalk, I stuck my hiking pole into the quagmire to have it penetrate three feet of black muck. Interesting, oddly pretty, but you don't want to walk in it.

The final destination of the day is Lake of the Clouds Hut, 1.5 miles from Mt. Washington. There is a program at the huts where the first couple hikers, four hikers at Lake of the Clouds, in for the night get to work for supper, a place to sleep and breakfast the next morning. Since I'm going to Mt. Washington in the morning for my re-supply, this is a good place to spend the night. Also in for the night are Zoltan, Monte, and a couple whose names I either don't know or don't remember. I'll know better in the morning if this work for stay arrangement is a good deal.

Friday 8/7

Well, it was a good idea in that it was really the only place to sleep up on this barren land, but as far as it being a good night's sleep, it wasn't so good. Yeah, I got fed a good, hot supper and had a bed out of the weather – for that I'm very grateful – but I couldn't make my bed until 9:30 at the earliest, and it was quite noisy. By now you know that I like to turn in early and have it dead quiet. Still, I was warm and dry. Breakfast was cold, stiff oatmeal and some egg dish. The egg dish was pretty good, and along with fruit, toast and juice breakfast was good. I guess it was all worth the price of the two hours of dishwashing.

About 8:30 I'm packed and headed for the summit of Mt. Washington, the day is cloudy and breezy. Although the forecast says no, it sure looks like rain. I make it to the top and the visitor's center before 9:30, but have to wait until 10:00 when the postman comes up on the train so I can get my packages. In the meantime, I made calls home to let folks know my location, and to order my next re-supply. I sat around a while putting my pack together and drinking hot chocolate, hoping the weather would improve before continuing on. But the weather does not improve – actually it gets worse.

In leaving the comfort of the visitor center, I am enshrouded in clouds and battered by gusty winds. But I can't sit around on account of some nasty weather. After all, I'm an AT hiker. I bundle up and head for Madison Hut, six miles away. Often the winds and clouds are bad, but occasionally the sky opens just enough for a nice, though brief, view of the valley below. About a couple miles on the sky closes right in, and the rain starts to come. It's not heavy or steady, but uncomfortable with the cool temperatures and gusty winds. A few times I am rewarded with hail as I trudge along this wet, cold trail. And that's the way it is to the hut. I count off the miles when I get to signposts at the trail junctions, and that helps encourage me, brightens my spirits.

Nearing 6:00 I arrive at Madison Hut, and, inquiring about work for stay, am told that they'd find something for me to do as they wouldn't turn me away in this weather. I'm very glad to hear that. The place was small, crowded due to the weather, but I'm indoors. I'm still chilled, and this old building is very drafty and chilly. Six of us hikers take up what free space there is, which isn't much; mostly I stand around shivering.

After the guests eat, it is the hikers turn. It's plentiful and delicious. I have my assigned work done by 9:00, and wait for lights out at 9:30 so I can go to bed. Finally in my sleeping bag on a table top and I'm drifting away to sleep as the wind and rain outside carry on in earnest.

Saturday 8/8

Another noisy night what with a mid-night invasion of workers from another hut, and one of the hikers here being up and rustling about at a very early hour; but I slept better than the night before, I guess I must have been tired. I was up, packed and out before breakfast was served. I think I've had too much noise and commotion.

The morning is clear and bright, but there remains a gusty wind. From the hut I climb up to Mt. Madison, the last of the 5000+ footers until Katahdin. The wind is pretty strong, and with the extra surface area of my pack, I'm easily pushed around; I have to pay close attention to my footing. On top of Madison I'm blessed with tremendous views in all directions. I get to see what I walked over yesterday that I couldn't see then.

After the summit of Madison, I start a long descent along a ridge line, all the way being pretty steep, before eventually coming into the trees. After having been above tree line for a day, it seems funny to be crowded in by close trees. Though it's a comfortable feeling. Yup, the Presidentials have been pretty easy hiking, and the views, when available, have been awesome. I could come back here to hike some more.

The trail continues down until I come to Osgood Tent Site. I met up with some hikers who stayed at that tent site and said they had the pleasure of having a bear in camp last night that was trying to get to their food, but their big black dog chased it away. From the junction to the tent site, the trail turns, runs side hill, and, though far from smooth, is more level.

I'm at a much lower elevation now – the trees are much larger, more diverse. There is now a lot of fresh water, and I cross a beautiful, crystal clear brook, and shortly the noisy, rushing, clear West Branch of the Peabody River. I've met a lot of folks out on the trail this morning, but no wonder as it's a gorgeous

Saturday morning. The trail is still rough and up and down in places as it winds through a lovely forest of mature mixed growth.

By and by I cross the auto road that goes up Mt. Washington, and I'm somewhat taken aback by all the traffic. It is quite a shock to step from the peaceful mountains and woods directly onto a road with so many cars speeding their way up to Mt. Washington; it's a startling thing to encounter all of a sudden. After crossing the road, it's an easy mile and a half walk through a very pleasant forest and I'm at the Pinkham Notch Visitor Center.

I walk in to the visitor center thinking I might get a bite to eat, and Gutsy Rabbit calls to me. She's a very pleasant young woman whose company I've not shared since some time in Vermont. I sit with her as she eats a sandwich, and we talk about the trail. While we're there, another hiker comes by to share his overload of food. Both of us grabbed the best stuff, and let the rest go to whoever wants it. I call Stef to give her a heads up about clothing I'll need, then Gutsy Rabbit and I hit the trail.

After Pinkham Notch there is an easy walk for maybe a mile that leads along a small pond on delightfully easy trails. In the course, Gutsy Rabbit tells me she is thinking about going on to the next hut, six miles away, but I'm thinking I'll find a nice spot to camp sooner than that. In just over a mile I find a nice spot, but there's still a lot of road noise, and since it's only 3:00, I keep going.

I'm starting to climb Wildcat, so it's getting steeper and good sites are harder to find. At about two miles in, I climb up to where the land levels off some and I find a good site just off the trail. I have to build up a tent pad, but there's not much better to sleep on than fir boughs. Yesterday's journaling, supper, and today's journal being completed, I'll be in bed by 8:00. Yeah, baby!

Sunday 8/9

A terrific night's sleep on my bed of fir boughs; so welcome after the past two nights. The day is starting clear and sunny with a gentle breeze.

The trail up Wildcat is up and up, and is fairly rough. I'd heard that this section of trail, the Wildcat/Moriah range, was quite difficult. Well, it is what it is. But I plod along and take breaks to catch my breath when needed. After a lot of climbing, you come to a level spot with some nice views and you think you might be at the top, but it's just a tease – the real summit is still a mile away with more climbing. Once on top of Wildcat, the trail follows along the summit more, so the climbs are fewer, less high or steep. The day is very clear, so when there is an opening, there is a great view to behold.

After Wildcat's second peak, the trail starts to drop, but then goes through a few steep ups and downs. Eventually I come to a quite steep, quite rough descent to the Carter Notch Hut. There, I got my water bottles filled, and when I inquired about any leftovers, I was asked if I was hungry. No, I wasn't really that hungry, but after I devoured the delicious, big cut of pumpkin cake, I wished I'd said I was – I could have enjoyed more.

I leave the hut and get right into yet another steep climb up to Carter Dome. But it's only a mile and a half, and only the first half is steep. On top of the dome I expected to have a view, but there's none, just a wall of fir and spruce all around. However, it is only a mile to Mt. Height. The AT doesn't go over the top, though it ought to, but a side trail takes you to the top on which is an awesome view in every direction. I really enjoy hiking above tree line where the views are so awesome. The Presidential Range dominates the skyline, the beautiful New Hampshire countryside sprawls out all around, but most spectacular of all is the first best view of home – the mountains of western Maine. The feeling of being so close to home is comforting, exciting, and elating.

First view of home

From Mt. Height it's about five miles to tonight's destination. The trail here is not so up and down, and I walk along easily. I arrive on North Carter to more great views, though the day is clouding in. After North Carter the trail drops, seemingly for quite a long distance, and in places is quite steep. This stretch of mountains – the Wildcat/Carter/ Moriah Range – is the toughest hiking I've done in New Hampshire; it's about fifteen miles of steep and rough ups and downs. But it is also terrifically scenic.

I'm at the side trail to Imp Shelter by 4:00. A quick bath in the cold mountain stream, I get supper going, then crawl into my sleeping bag to warm up. The caretaker arrives and we have a very pleasant conversation. Four SoBos come in as I'm having my supper, and there is much chatter. Time got away from me and it's 8:00 before I start my journal. When it's done, I am too. Time to turn in.

Monday 8/10

Feeling a little lazy when I woke this morning, but I was packed and on the trail at 6:45. The day is starting sunny, but it is quite humid – it feels like it will be hot and sticky.

A couple miles of fairly steady, relatively easy climbing, and I'm on top of Mt. Moriah, the highest point I will climb today. On the way up, I'm feeling fatigued, and I have some tightness in my chest. I'm sure it's nothing serious, but I need to think about it. Yesterday when I was sitting on Mt. Height, I saw a hawk circling overhead. I commented to a couple I was chatting with that hawks are messengers, or rather, foretellers of messages, either receiving or giving. So this morning when I had the experience I did, I took it as a message to me. Again, the message was to relax and enjoy this journey. Not that I haven't been enjoying it – I certainly have – but to always see the beauty of it, and to not get caught up with or dwell on the less appealing aspects of the trail. I know I can be that way, a little negative if you will, so the reminders are a good thing for me. It behooves me to notice what and how I'm thinking, and to correct myself should my thoughts go astray.

After leaving the mountain top the trail descends steeply downhill, but only for maybe a mile before leveling out. But, you know, I've sort of given up caring about the condition of the trail. It is what it is, I will hike it no matter what, so whether it's up or down, rocky or smooth, it becomes like the weather – something you exist with. And it doesn't bother.

After three miles or so, I'm in an entirely different world than what I have been for most of the past few days. The trail is now relatively flat and covered with softwood needles. Some contrast to walking over rock. Along the trail are large hemlocks and more diverse hardwoods.

I'm walking along Rattle River, more of a large stream than a river, that is crystal clear and boisterous as it tumbles over rocks on its way down the mountain. Another thing I notice at this lower elevation, along with the increased temperature and humidity, is the increase in the number of flies. Up on the ridges the air is cooler, and there is nearly always a breeze to keep away what few flies there are.

I arrive at the trailhead sometime before noon, and see Stretch, Tin Man and Hotsauce (that's what's-her-name's name!) getting ready to get back on the trail. I talked with them for a bit, then caught a ride into town from the woman who brought them to the trailhead. Little did I know that that would be the last time I'd see those three hikers again. I'd enjoyed their infrequent, brief company since I met them in Pennsylvania. But that's the way it goes.

In town I got my package at the post office, sent stuff back, and got laundry going. Now, I don't know if it's because I'd been in the woods for a while, or if it's just me, but I was in Rite-Aid picking up a new notebook and what-not, and after I made my purchases I was standing off to the side putting things into my pack. I was mumbling to myself as I often do, and soon noticed that the two ladies working there had stopped talking and were sort of staring at me.

I looked up, surprised by their expressions, and asked, "Was I talking to myself that loudly?"

"Yeah," came the reply, "We didn't know if you were talking to us, yourself, or who."

I just laughed and said, "Yeah, I do that often."

Still, they eyed me suspiciously.

When laundry was done, I then got a motel room. After a shower, I went to supper at a Chinese buffet, then went shopping for what I needed for the next few days. Back to the motel for calls to home, my journal, and I'm ready for bed at 8:30.

Tuesday 8/11

Up at 5:15, too early, but I can't get back to sleep. I look at my food supplies and figure out what I will need for re-supply and assemble my pack. I call Stef, have a pleasant chat and place my order. Rather than go out to breakfast, I eat out of my pack. I leave the motel about 8:00.

On the way out of town, I stopped to call brother Bill. He informed me that sister Kath was having a cookout coming right up. I called Kath and got the details. Yes, they're having one, but it's not this weekend coming, but the one after – the 22nd. I'll be there for it. I never pass up an opportunity to gather with family and friends for merriment and feast. I called the kids so they could plan on getting the day off. I left a message for Beck, but was able to talk with Fuzz.

All business done and I'm hitching to the trailhead about 9:00. I got a ride pretty quickly, so I'm on the trail at 9:30. I didn't have a definite destination for the day, but decided I'd head for Gentian Shelter, twelve miles away. I'm starting about three hours later than usual, so I get myself motivated.

I make seven miles by 1:00, and run into Solo. We have dinner together, and wait out a brief thunderstorm under an outhouse compost drying rack. It didn't smell bad, was as clean as any piece of ground, and was dry underneath the tarp. It worked for us. We're back on the trail just after 2:00 for the last five miles. Quite a varied trail today: steep and rough in places, level and easy in others, with occasional balds providing great views.

About 6:00 we arrive at the shelter. Supper prepared, a bath, a lot of chatter with Solo and a very attractive, young female SoBo, writing in my journal, and I'm ready for bed.

13

MAINE

Wednesday 8/12

Awoke at 5:30, up at 6:00, packed and on the trail at 6:40. A cloudy start to the day, and a trail that starts right off with a climb.

I'm not feeling real good this morning, my guts are doing flip-flops, and I've got the trots. It's bad enough having diarrhea at home, but here in the back country doing what I'm doing, it's just plain miserable. I've felt it coming on for a few days, and today it is enough of a problem that I don't eat any breakfast – eating only aggravates the diarrhea. The more I walk, the more peaked I feel. I figure if this keeps up, I'll have to get off the trail as soon as I can – the next road crossing will be tomorrow – until I can get straightened out. I don't want to have to, but if I need to I will.

As the morning goes on I feel weaker – not bad, but not good. To make matters worse, I come to a steep, rocky downhill ledge that looks quite slippery. "I'll have to watch where I walk," I think out loud to myself. I plan my route, but instantly lose my footing and am in a fifteen-foot tumbling face-plant. I end up in a heap at the bottom having banged up my right leg, bumped my face, and landing with the root of an overturned tree jabbing me in my lower back. Oh, that was fun. Nothing is badly hurt, fortunately, but I am sore. I really need to stay focused and pay closer attention to the trail.

The whole day the trail will be hilly, very often steep, generally muddy. I plod along over more rough, steep, slippery, hilly countryside when I round a bend and spy a sign – two, actually. One is the official New Hampshire/Maine State line trail sign, the other says "Welcome to Maine, the way life should be."

I dance a little jig on a flat rock and say my thanks as I celebrate being back in my home state.

However, living up to its reputation, the trail here is even harder and more difficult. At lower elevations the sun is doing its best to shine, but up on the mountains the sun's appearance is a rare occurrence. Once in a while the clouds blow out providing a view of gorgeous valleys, while the high mountains remain enshrouded in clouds.

This high mountain country is unusual, a rather inhospitable place with many low, flat areas where the land seems to be afloat. In many sections the mud under the boardwalks is one to two feet deep. Best to mind your footing well.

Eventually I cross over the last mountain of the day and start my rough descent to Full Goose Shelter where I'll spend the night. I arrive at the shelter where there are two other hikers taking a break before heading on. It is now 3:30 and I have walked ten miles today. If the next shelter were closer, and I didn't have to go through Mahoosuc Notch or over Mahoosuc Arm to get to it, I might continue on, but I really don't feel like going any farther.

It's now 7:30, I'd been the only one here since shortly after my arrival. I'd prepared a supper, but decided not to eat as it would only aggravate the diarrhea. Pretty soon in comes Solo. I offer him my meal and he welcomes it, delighted that he doesn't have to bother to fix his own. It's a chilly night as the woods are permeated by a light fog. This would be a great time to have a woodstove in the shelter to drive out the chill. I'm hoping tomorrow clears out and is sunny.

Thursday 8/13

I woke still feeling punky, skipped breakfast, packed up and on the trail by 6:30. The morning is foggy and overcast, but there is a hint of blue in the sky which might bring sunny skies later on.

The first mile or two of the trail are fairly decent going, and I make it along pretty well. I'm glad the trail is as good as it is since I'm feeling weak. Huh, imagine that. Before very long, almost as if it snuck up on me, I enter the renowned, often dreaded, Mahoosuc Notch.

I'm not sure what I was expecting, if anything, but what I encountered was not the hell-hole of folk lore. Nestled deep in a crevice between steep, unyielding mountains, the notch is undoubtedly a scramble over, under, around and through a great jumble of boulders and rock; but the hardest aspect of hiking through there is simply figuring out which way to go.

About half way through the notch I encountered two young fellows headed south. After greetings, I was asked if I was Chris Cribbage. Taken aback, I raised my arms as if in triumph and exclaimed, "Yes, I'm famous."

"Your reputation precedes you," says the young man, "I would like to challenge you to a game of cribbage."

Of course, why not; what else would you expect to do in the middle of Mahoosuc Notch?!

So the young fellow produces a deck of cards, I get out my note book and pen for score keeping, and the great Mahoosuc Notch cribbage tournament commences. We had a wonderful time, this young fellow from Edgecomb and I, as we played and chatted. Eventually, I proved to him that I was indeed Chris Cribbage by skunking the lad. We parted with handshakes agreeing that it was a very enjoyable time, not soon to be forgotten, and wished each other well.

His friend, who up to this point had not said boo, passes by and says, "Thanks for screwing my friend."

I replied, "You know, there aren't many times when you can say that and it's okay."

I continued on my way through the notch arriving at the other end without any ado. Whatever other folks' experiences with the notch are, I found it to be magnificently wild and beautiful; I had fun and thoroughly enjoyed my "walk" through it. For the record, cribbage game included, it took me only about an hour to get through the notch, and I never had to remove my pack.

After the notch was Mahoosuc Arm, which seemed to climb on relentlessly. It was only a 1500' gain in a mile and a half, but the arm kicked my butt. Many sections were quite steep, or slippery, or both. And it was one of those hills that, when you think you're at the top, you're not – you've still got more to go. I've no doubt that my struggle with it was in part due to my weakened condition. Finally at the top and I'm sure there would be a great view – if I could see it. The clouds come and go, but they're here at the moment. The top is open for the most part being covered with moss and low bushes, with stunted fir and spruce trees growing in clusters.

Given my condition of the past couple days, I'd already decided I would head off the trail when I got to Grafton Notch so I could take care of my intestinal ailment. Up on the hilltop I met Yak, doing a flip-flop, and asked if he had a cell phone, and if he did, could I use it. He did, and so I did. I made a call to a brother, and arranged a pick-up. I proceeded on to Old Speck Pond and Campsite. I took a break there to rest and drink a bottle of Gatorade. In comes Annie, a SoBo thru-hiker, and we chat for a bit before she decides to go for a swim.

I started on the last five miles of the day up over Old Speck Mt. The hike up was easier than I expected, a gradual climb up through mixed forest until it becomes predominantly softwood. There is no view at the top due to the weather, so I continue on. The hike down is much longer than I remembered it from a previous hike. I hiked down with a couple of young ladies with three dogs. It was nice to have the company to take my mind off my complaining body.

I was tired upon reaching the trailhead parking lot, and discouraged that my ride was not there. I waited a while talking with a park ranger who offered me a soda and cheese crackers. I wasn't sure if I ought to eat and drink anything of the sort, but guessed I'd be okay. Then along comes Hellbender, and the three of us stand around chatting some. Hellbender had arranged a ride to Bethel, and since my ride had not arrived I caught a ride with those nice folks down to the highway.

At the junction of Rts. 26 and 2 is a small store where I used a phone to see if I could learn about my ride. I had no luck, I couldn't get in touch with anybody. I waited at the store a while watching for my ride until I figured something must have gone wrong. I described my brother and his buggy to the gal in the store asking that, if he showed up, she tell him I was hitching a ride home.

Onto Rt. 2 heading east towards Rumford. This is a heavily traveled road, so I figured I had a good chance getting a quick ride. But not for a little while ...and just as well. As I was walking and hitching, I felt the urge to fart, and let it go. It went alright, but it wasn't just a fart. What a great time for the diarrhea to kick in! Geez, as if things weren't bad enough already! But there is Providence in all things. Imagine if I had already gotten a ride when that happened... Fortunately, I was right in front of a boat launch on the Androscoggin River. I went to the river, dropped my pack and shorts, took off my boots, and stepped in to clean myself and shorts as best as possible, then I continue to hitch a ride home.

I hadn't been trying long when I got a speedy ride to Mexico. A short walk across the bridge, and I continue hitching east on Rt.2 toward home. I made a very brief stop at a small car show, and continued on. Very shortly thereafter, I got a ride from a guy who was at the same show. A real nice guy, heading home to Farmington, and he went miles out of his way to bring me to the end of my driveway. Thank you, angels! My brother, my arranged ride, arrived about fifteen minutes after I did. All's well.

Friday 8/14

I got to the doctor at 9:45, and after a brief examination and discussion of my recent activities, I'm being treated for giardia. Three pills a day for a week – I should see improvement in a few days.

So there you have it, my ego – cockiness and arrogance – got the better of me again. Early on the trail this year was so much fresh water that, in an effort to reduce weight, I sent my water purification filter home, rationalizing that I had always drunk right from streams without any problems. And I was doing good until I drank right out of Kinsman Pond. Well, it caught up with me, and I paid the price. I am, yet again, humbled by my thoughts and actions.

Folks, take it from one who knows first hand, it's always advisable to treat your water.

So now I've got a little time for recuperation. Earlier in the hike, perhaps in Vermont, I got thinking that I might be getting to Maine, Andover in particular, about the middle of August. I started figuring the mileage and time, and called my buddies, Stan and Jim, to set up a tentative plan to meet in Andover so we could get together for the last of brook fishing. Fishing for brook trout is something we absolutely love, and I have been missing out on it as I've been on the trail. Well, I've got plenty of time to go now.

Saturday the 15th, the last day of the season, we headed up country on our brook fishing outing. I hadn't realized how depleted I had become on account of the giardia, accompanying diarrhea, and hiking for two days with nothing to eat and very little to drink. I didn't last long walking the brook and fishing. After the first short foray, I was spent and went back to the truck. It took me about a week to get feeling good again and get some strength back.

And my sister's outing never came to be as it was postponed due to the weather, then cancelled altogether the following weekend, again due to weather. So it goes. At least I'm getting rested and my strength restored. At the time I came off the trail, I had withered to a very lean 173 pounds. Inside of the few weeks I was lounging at home, I'd gotten back to near 190 and feeling strong. It's time to get back to the trail.

Monday 8/31

My brother, Tom, gave me a ride to Rt. 2 on the other side of Rumford. I put on my pack, grabbed my poles, gave him a hug, walked to the side of the road, stuck out my thumb at the first vehicle coming along, and got a ride to Rt. 26. Within a half hour I got a ride to the trailhead, and was underway about 9:30. I smiled happily when I saw the first white blaze of the trail – I felt like I was back home.

The day is bright and sunny, but cool and breezy. The trail up Baldpate was easier than I remembered it as it wound up through a forest of mature mixed growth, occasionally following or crossing a stream. In a short while I'm at the first lean-to, two miles from the road. I stopped briefly for water, read the log in an effort to see when other hikers I knew came through, then got back underway.

On top of Baldpate the views were stunning in the clear air. Maine's western mountains, the Rangeley lakes, and the Whites of New Hampshire stood out boldly for anyone and everyone to behold. Oh, it's good to be back. As well as being clear, it was also windy and chilly on the top, so I didn't dilly dally as I was dressed lightly in just my shorts and t-shirt. I met three SoBo hikers on Baldpate, a couple and a lone guy, all dressed in jackets and hats. The lone fellow commented about my being dressed so lightly. "You must be tough," he says. "That, or numb," I reply. Just down over the hilltop, inside the tree line, I stopped and ate my dinner. Down in the trees again I'm out of the wind and become quite comfortable as I hike.

The trail between Baldpate and Dunn's Notch is quite pretty, varied hiking, and, though there are a couple steep places, rather easy going. I get to the Frye Notch Lean-to just past 1:00, stop briefly to read the register, then move on. The forest through here is very pretty being mostly hardwood and very remote feeling. A little climb up a low mountain, then it's an easy trail past Dunn's Notch to the road.

I got on East B Hill Road just about 3:30 and started heading for Andover. Andover is the town where I had my next re-supply waiting, so even though I just got back on the trail, I got off and into town again. I walked a couple miles and got a ride from the second person along right to the post office at 4:20 – they close at 4:30. I got my package, sent back what I didn't want, then went to a hostel for a room for the night. This will be only my second time staying in a room in a hostel, the first time with more than one person. We'll see how it goes.

It felt really good to be back on the trail after nearly three weeks off, I had been missing it. The legs and knees are fine, but my feet are a little tired and sore by the end of the day.

Tuesday 9/1

The hostel experience was just as I imagined it would be. Of course, because that's the way I imagined it'd be. I always suspected that I wouldn't like rooming with other folks, and I don't. One fellow was rather restless, often drinking noisily from his water bottle, then sometime later was up to go to the bathroom. This process was repeated about four times during the night. I was ready to tie him into his bed and throw away his water bottle. I got light sleep at best, but got up feeling rested anyway.

I went down to the store for breakfast, then got started for the trail about 7:00. I walked maybe half the distance, getting two rides along the way, the last one to the trailhead. I got on the trail about 8:00.

The day is absolutely clear and bright, but cool – 40ish. The trail starts pretty easy and remains so for about five miles as it winds up, down and around through varied terrain. This section is the most level I've seen in many recent miles. It is also quite muddy. I imagine it must have been horrible slogging through here a couple months ago when it was raining daily. Since things are drying out now, it's not too bad.

Today I find I'm a little out of sorts, no doubt due in part to last night's experience, but I'm also feeling a little lonely. Early on I meet three SoBos, two young guys, and a beautiful, voluptuous, friendly, chatty young woman. Needless to say, the wheels of my mind start turning and my imagination is off and running. I don't often get feeling lonely, but it does happen from time to time. This is one of those times.

The trail stays pretty easy to Hall Mt. Lean-to, six miles from the road. I arrive there about 11:30, and take a break to eat. As warming as the sun is, it's chilly in the lean-to and I don't stay long after eating. Shortly after leaving the lean-to the trail drops steeply 1500' in less than a mile to Sawyer Brook. Then the trail steeply climbs over 1300' in less than a mile up to Moody Mt. The climb up Moody Mt. is the toughest climb I've done in quite a while – it wore me down. Of course, it probably didn't help that I got side-tracked from the trail a little bit and had to bush-whack my way back to it. Once over the top of Moody, it's a gradual 1000', 1.8 mile descent to South Arm Road. At the road is – magic! Fairly cold sodas and candy bars. Thank you very much!

I've been ten miles today, and would like to go further, but it doesn't look like there'd be any good camping right away as I'd be up on Old Blue Mt. Besides, there are very nice campsites along the stream here, so I stop early. Meeg, from Japan, Walkabout and Rock Lobster, from Poland and Germany, make camp here as well. A little while later, two gals doing a slack-pack show up. A nice, friendly and relaxed group in camp tonight.

Hiking today had become work. And like any job, no matter how much you may enjoy it, there are days when you just don't want to do it. Today, there were sections where I didn't so much enjoy the work. Maine's western mountains are tough.

Wednesday 9/2

A rather restless night, maybe because it was pretty cool down here by the stream. I don't know if I ever dropped into a deep sleep, still I got up feeling pretty well rested. I was up about 6:00, packed and on the trail at 7:00. The morning is foggy, but sunshine is on order.

The trail started with a climb of 2200' in 2.8 miles. I'd heard this was supposed to be a difficult climb, but it wasn't that bad. The forest is fir and spruce with birch, maple, beech and poplar spread throughout. The trail has not changed, it is steep and rough, sometimes rooted and muddy. In any case, it's tough hiking. But that's the way it goes.

By mid-morning the sky is clear and the air is warm. This is a wonderful time to be hiking with this gorgeous weather. I'm hiking along pretty well even though my stomach is a little queasy and my right knee is somewhat swollen and painful. But I've learned to not focus on any unpleasantness of the trail.

Around 1:00 I arrive at Beamis Mt. Lean-to, eight miles from where I started. My body was sore enough that I thought I'd call it a day here instead of going four more miles to Beamis Stream. I sat around a couple hours and visited with four other hikers that stopped for water. They all left for the stream about 3:00. I walked around a bit and thought my knee felt pretty good. I put my pack on and it still felt pretty good, so I headed for the stream and campsite.

The next 2.5 miles of the trail are fairly easy as it winds over ridge tops, often on open rock. Maybe I should have stayed at that lean-to and rested my body, but I'm feeling good, the trail is so pretty, my spirits are high, besides I wanted to go on. I made the four miles in two hours, arriving at the campsite at 5:00, with my right knee feeling okay. And this campsite is beautiful in an open lowland setting with a clear, fast flowing stream right close by for water. It was a good choice to continue on.

As I walk the trails now, there is evidence of cooler weather coming on as there are a lot of gold colors showing up in the forest. I see a lot of fallen leaves on the trail, ferns and other low, leafy plants changing from green to brown, blueberry bushes becoming red, and there is a slight scent of fall in the air. It's on its way. As tough as the hiking is in these western mountains, the scenery is unsurpassed. I feel blessed to be a native of such a beautiful place.

Thursday 9/3

I stayed in bed until about 6:00, feeling a little lazy. I don't seem to be doing big miles lately, so it doesn't matter. Besides, the rest feels good.

On the trail just past 7:00 with about a mile, some parts pretty steep, up to Rt. 17. Up on the road there is a splendid view of the Rangeley lakes and mountains. I've said it before, I'll say it again – this country is gorgeous. Of all that Maine has to offer, which is a tremendous amount, I think this Rangeley region is among the finest, surpassed only by the spectacular wilderness of Baxter State Park.

Across the road the trail continues to rise, but more gently. On top of the first hill the forest opens up as there are more birch than fir trees, affording deeper views into the surrounding woods. With the morning light slanting in, it is very pretty, almost magical in its glow. Here I am, a native Mainer, having traveled and roamed around the state quite a bit, and it never ceases to astound me, leave me in awe, for the beauty of this place I call home.

Today's trail is still up and down, but the hills are smaller and, for the most part, not as steep. In a few miles I have a terrific view of Long Pond stretching out below me. A short, steep descent and soon I'm along a splendid sandy beach looking down the length of the lake. Beautiful. Stunning. Were it a warmer day, my clothes would have come off and I'd be swimming.

A short walk of less than fifteen minutes and I'm at Sabbath Day Pond. This is a much smaller pond, no camps along the shores, and a pair of loons out fishing. I sit in sunshine on this rocky shoreline taking a break and getting a bite to eat while absorbing the beauty and serenity. Heavenly. And the rest of the day follows suit. In about five miles I come to Little Swift River

Pond, another pretty pond set in the deep forest, and nothing around to disrupt the peace and quiet. 2.5 miles beyond is South Pond which appears as though it would be a good trout pond. They're all liquid gems tucked into the beautiful primeval forest.

The trail has been the same all day – level stretches, often muddy, and short ups and downs. The surrounding forest is typically fir and spruce, and grows snug to the trail. All in all, it's pretty easy hiking. In one section of the trail I spied fresh moose and bear tracks, but no sighting of the track makers.

Shortly after 3:00 I arrive at Rt. 4 and run into Featherfoot, who I'd met once at Kirkridge Shelter in Pennsylvania. He remembered me, but it wasn't until he reminded me where we'd met that I made the connection. We had a brief visit then he was off to hitch a ride as he was making for a distant rendezvous. I continue on to Piazza Rock Lean-to, wrapping up a 15.7 mile day. This is the highest mileage I've done in weeks, and I'm feeling every bit of it. After bathing and supper, I'm glad to call it an early night.

Friday 9/4

Not quite as lazy this morning, up early and on the trail by 6:30. I've hiked this section of trail a few times before, just doing day hikes, some of it I remembered, some of it I didn't. Doesn't matter, it's still so very pretty that it's like seeing it for the first time.

From camp it's four miles and 2000+' up to Saddleback. The climb was much easier than I expected, not nearly as steep or rocky as I'd imagined, and I make it to the top in just over two hours. The views from the top are wide open, unobstructed and magnificent, even with the light clouds blowing over it. As it's still fairly early and the day hasn't yet warmed up, combined with the stiff breeze, I don't want to dawdle as I'm dressed only in my sweaty shorts and t-shirt.

Continuing on, the trail drops steeply at first down the north side, then more gradually through dense softwood forest, before leveling some then climbing up to The Horn, 1.7 miles away. Views from The Horn are better than they were from Saddleback as more clouds have blown out. The day is pretty clear and is warming nicely. A wicked steep drop off The Horn before it moderates, levels, then climbs up Saddleback Junior.

On top of Saddleback Jr. the day is very nice, the breeze has died and it has warmed, making for a pleasant stop for dinner and a break. I have done 7.5 miles and three substantial peaks in five hours. I'm feeling very good, so I lie about on the top, literally, for more than an hour and a half. And enjoy every minute of it. I've got four more miles to the day's destination, so just past 1:00 I get on my way.

Another steep drop off Saddleback Jr. then pretty easy going to Poplar Ridge Lean-to. Why this is called Poplar Ridge I can't imagine as the forest is predominantly fir and spruce with some birch, but nowhere is there a poplar to be seen. A brief stop at the lean-to, and I'm continuing on my way. From here it's two miles and a 1700' descent to Orbeton Stream where I plan to make camp. The trail seems to be steadily downhill, occasionally steep, making me think I'm dropping more than 1700'. At 4:00 I come to Orbeton Stream, a rushing, tumbling, raucous stream that looks great for trout. A short, but very steep, climb brings me to an old woods road with good camping. Nearby is a nice, fast, clear, little stream coming down off the mountain – great for drinking water, bathing and laundry.

Although clouds come and go, the day is mostly sunny and warm, so I have all my gear airing out. My laundry might even be dry by morning so I don't have to start the day in damp hiking clothes!

Saturday 9/5

In a lean-to register somewhere back along, a hiker wrote, "Maine smells like Christmas all the time." Yeah, it's like that.

A gorgeous start to the day, perfectly clear and a little bit warmer. The trail starts with an easy uphill walk along a beautiful, lively little stream through an open forest of birch and fir. This early morning walk is tremendously pleasing, the forest is absolutely serene. For a while the only sound was the quiet conversation of a couple chickadees. Oh, I love these woods. It's a great time to walk and reflect.

I cross over a woods road and a couple brooks and make note that I need to remember them for fishing. Compared to what I've been over the past week, today's trail is quite easy. I've got a 1700' climb up to Lone Mt., but it isn't difficult – kind of long and gradual. The next few miles of trail seemed level; they weren't, of course, but again, by comparison to what I'd been over lately, it was quite gentle.

Lone Mt. did not provide a view, neither did Spaulding Mt. at just over 4000', as the trail is crowded by fir and spruce. Today's hike is very pretty, the trail so easy and dry, and the day so beautiful that a grand mountain vista is not necessary. It's fantastic hiking for the sake of hiking and being alive.

For five of this morning's miles, I have been walking on high ridges and mountains, the trail seeming quite gentle, though there have been elevation gains and losses of 1000' or more. Near noon I come to the half mile side trail up to the summit of Sugarloaf. This short side trail is steadily uphill, but once on top – Oh boy! – what a spectacular view! The day being so clear, I could see from Mt. Washington to Mt. Katahdin, and everything in between. Just incredible country. There was not a cloud in the sky and just a light breeze on this splendid, warm late summer day. Such a day to be alive!

The next mile after leaving Sugarloaf was more like the trails I'd been going over – roots and mud. And then I come around the side of the mountain to the steep south side. The trail dries out again as this section is fairly open being flooded with direct sunlight, and it becomes quite warm. The trail drops very steeply, losing many hundred feet of elevation in a half mile, and in sections becomes a boulder hop. This side of the mountain looks down into Caribou Valley, and as the side of it is an open rock slide, there is an unobstructed view of the valley and Crocker Mts. to the north.

After the steep, dropping descent, the trail becomes a pleasant walk through woods of birch and fir to the South Branch of the Carrabassett River, a large, clear, rushing, tumbling stream. A break for water and a snack, a no-nonsense log crossing, and another mile of a gentle but steady uphill through more birch and fir forest to Crocker Cirque camping area – a very pretty spot, with a clear, fast brook, tucked into the woods. I hiked all day with Rugged Shark, a fellow I just met yesterday; a nice guy, very easy to get along with. I suppose we will hike together into Stratton tomorrow.

Sunday 9/6

Quite chilly overnight, I never really did warm up during the night. I rested well just the same. Up and going about 7:00, I guess, with the morning being very clear and cool.

Not much easing into the trail this morning as it immediately starts to climb. Even though it's a 1300' rise, it doesn't seem that bad. In fact, it's kind of nice to have the workout to warm me up. Before very long I'm walking along the ridgeline to South Crocker. There aren't any views to speak of, it's pretty much a thick wall of trees. A little dip in the trail and a short rise to North Crocker, I arrive there about 9:30. There is a small opening in some trees providing a little view of the mountains to the north, but mostly it's a wall of evergreen trees. Even with the bright sunshine, it's pretty cool up here. I encounter quite a few day and section hikers this morning, as I did yesterday, what with it being a gorgeous weekend.

From North Crocker, it's just over a five mile and nearly 3000' descent to Rt. 27 to go to Stratton. It's a fairly gradual trail with only an occasional steep section, and even that is not bad at all. In the lower elevations, the thick, stunted fir and spruce give way to larger, taller trees of mixed hard and soft woods. A stop for a little bite to eat – the last of my food – about 11:30, and only now sitting in the sunshine can I feel any real warmth to the day. And it feels good.

The whole trail today has been quite nice – generally easy hiking, and with the blessing of gorgeous weather, it's a real pleasure to be out here. I have been hiking today with Shark, and have enjoyed his company and conversation.

Near the bottom I hike the last half mile to the highway with Daryl and her son, Ken, both from Fairfield. They ask me a number of questions about hiking the trail: pack weight, equipment, food and so on, which I am glad to answer. They're very nice folks. We get down at the trailhead parking lot about 1:30, and they give Shark and me a ride the five miles into Stratton. Living so close by, they had never been there before.

Right away I headed to the White Wolf Inn for an awesome Wolfburger (it lives up to its reputation) and strawberry shortcake. Oh boy, now that's good eating! I dubbed around for a few hours talking with other hikers before heading out of town to camp for the night along the shore of Flagstaff Lake. Since I can't get my re-supply until Tuesday, Monday being Labor Day, I have to take a zero tomorrow, and I don't want to spend two nights in town. Shark asked me if I wanted to split a room, but I told him I was going to go camp out.

So I walk out of town headed for an old camp that I know of on the side of the lake. I get there to find a couple already there – no surprise – so I head a little further down the shoreline. It's not what I was hoping for, but pretty nice just the same. Tomorrow night I'll take a room in town so I can get all cleaned up and be close to the post office Tuesday morning.

It feels very odd – in a couple more weeks I will finish hiking the Appalachian Trail. It seems so long ago, and yet almost like it was yesterday, that I started this journey. How far I've come…

Monday 9/7

A little chilly this morning, damp mostly, and I stayed in bed until 8:00 – the life of Riley! But I'm starting to get hungry, so I pack and get on my way. When I got to the diner, it looked as though it would be busy, but it was fairly quiet. I dined on blueberry pancakes and bacon, some different from my usual trail fare. I sat and read a little bit, then continued on with my day. It was near 11:00 already!

I got into my room towards noon, made a few calls, showered, then headed off about 1:30 to go do laundry. Back to the motel, laundry laid out on the railing to dry, some more reading, then to the store before 5:00 for some incidentals. To supper by 6:00 – prime rib, baked red potatoes and zucchini – all very good – back to my room by 7:00 to do my journal. It has been a very relaxing, quiet day of rest. First thing tomorrow I will do the last of the big hills for a while – the Bigelow Range.

Tuesday 9/8

An easy start to the day. I'm up at 6:00, a couple phone calls, breakfast at 7:00, packed and ready to go before 8:00. I got to the post office at 8:20, and the lady gets me my package. I square away my pack, and mail stuff back. Outside the post office I get jawing with a local, Randy – a real nice guy – and he offers me a ride to the trailhead. We talked for a few more minutes, then we're on our separate ways.

The day is sunny and warm as I start the trail at 9:00. It feels really good to be hiking again after the zero in town. The trail starts pretty easy through a beautiful, mature forest, but since I'm heading up Bigclow it's not long before I'm climbing. And since it's sunny and warm, I shed my clothes and go naked. For a while. As I get nearer the top, it gets cloudier, breezier and cooler, so I put the clothes back on.

Bigelow Mtn. overlooking Flagstaff Lake

I'd been up this trail before, but I'd forgotten how long it was, how up and down it is, or that it seemed to take forever to get to Horn Pond and the lean-to. It was now 12:00 and I'd come five miles, it was time to eat. While eating, I met Zipper, so named because she's so skinny that if she turned sideways and stuck out her tongue, she'd look like a zipper. A very pleasant woman whose brief company I enjoy.

Bigelow is one of those mountains where you're certain you're coming to the top, only to discover that the top is further and higher onward. And just for fun, in between the climbs there are small downhill sections – to be sure you get as much vertical hiking as possible. As if there's a shortage of it. Eventually you climb over the last rock scramble, navigate a craggy, wind-blown ridgeline, and you're at the summit... of the West Peak. Looking ahead, nearly a mile distant, is Avery Peak, the other high point of this massive rock pile. To be sure you get in enough climbing, you have to make a low descent to Bigelow Col so that you can make another climb again. It's all in good fun, and before you know it, you're at the second peak.

The weather up on the peaks is wonderful – clear skies, plentiful sunshine, and a light wind. There is a long view over Flagstaff Lake to distant mountains in the north and east. It's a great place to sit and gaze upon the world. I caught up with Zipper at the West Peak, and as we're going to the same camping spot for the night, we hike together. After Avery Peak, the trail makes its descent and two miles away is the day's destination. At first the trail is pretty good, but it gets steeper and rougher as it goes. We stop at an overlook for a splendid view, and I point out Katahdin, as good as it can be seen, and we sit for a brief time to take in the sights.

We proceed onward and the trail becomes steeper and rougher, eventually leading through an area of large rocks. Very large rocks. House size rocks. It is fantastically pretty in an other-worldly sort of way, very wild and primeval in appearance. Finally we arrive at the side trail to Safford Notch Campsite. It is rather crowded, but before long we find a couple spots and have our camps set up. Washing, laundry, supper, my journal, and the day is done at nightfall.

Wednesday 9/9

I sort of woke all at once this morning. I came to, a little groggy, at 6:00. On the trail just before 7:00, the weather looking promising yet again. A mile of nice, pretty walking before I come to Little Bigelow. Don't be misled by the name, even though it's only 3010' this mountain is just a smaller version of its counterpart. It has steep climbs, the trail is up and down, up and down, and seems to go on and on.

The morning is gorgeous; there are some nice views from the summit, making for a very nice climb. And once over the top the trail descends relatively gently, often crossing exposed ledges and more nice views, before depositing you in a lovely hardwood forest. Down off the mountain, the trail almost levels out, and the hiking becomes strolling. The easy trail coupled with the awesome weather – Thank You very much – and it is an absolute joy to be out here.

Before long I'm walking along the shore of Flagstaff Lake which, if nothing else, is wonderfully scenic. In a few miles I cross Long Falls Dam Road, in the middle of which is painted "2000 mi," the approximate distance to Springer Mt. in Georgia. Sometimes it's hard to believe that I am as close to the end as I am.

Across the road the wonderful, easy hiking continues through a lovely hardwood forest. And in a few miles, I am suddenly in a low, lush softwood forest as I near West Carry Pond. I walk peacefully along the shore of this beautiful, little lake thinking that this is the stuff dreams are made of. In less than a mile I come to West Carry Pond Lean-to, and there's magic! Peanut butter crackers and little Tootsie Rolls. I guess I might have had a few, and maybe a few more.

On the last 3.7 miles to East Carry Pond the walk is still easy as the trail meanders through a quiet softwood forest. There is a pleasant boardwalk around a small pond, and I'm grateful I'm not here in June as the flies most certainly would be horrendous. Today it's just a nice stroll. Near 4:30 I come to East Carry Pond, a little smaller and more developed, but still a gem. Just past a small, sandy beach, in a low softwood grove, I locate a nice spot and set up camp. I bathe and have supper started when Zipper shows up. She has supper with me, and we enjoy a pleasant conversation. She produces dessert, some home-made brownie something treats from the trail angels, then goes to set up her camp. By now there's just enough time to write in my journal, then turn in. A terrific, easy day.

Thursday 9/10

A chilly start to the day, Zipper informed me it was 42°. Well, it's getting to be that time of year. But the sky is clear and the sun is bright, promising another beautiful day. And it is. It just IS.

It's an easy, meandering trail this morning through a quiet hard and softwood forest. Early on I flushed a partridge, then another. A few more paces up the trail and I flushed another, then another, then another. I'd nearly walked into the middle of a covey of them. In all, I put up about a dozen birds. When you flush a partridge they typically take off suddenly, unexpectedly, often startlingly with a great beating of wings that, if you're not accustomed to, can leave you with a racing heart and wondering what just happened. Maybe you know, maybe you don't, but partridge is some of the best eating of nature's fare, and my mouth watered at the thought of fresh pan fried partridge.

I walked along easily, to and fro, up and down, by and by coming to Pierce Pond. From the lean-to, you look out upon a rock-lined cove of the pond, nestled in a deep green forest. Pierce Pond has long had a reputation for being a great brook trout fishery, and I imagine paddling my canoe along in pursuit of fine dining. I take a small, quick snack, and then mosey to and around Harrison's Camps. I'd hoped I'd meet someone there, I was curious about living and working at a sporting camp, but no one was around.

This section of the AT follows Pierce Pond Stream, often a cascading waterfall, occasionally a placid pool, as it makes its way to the Kennebec River. Aside from the beauty of the place, all I can think about is the trout fishing – the stream looks fantastic. Following the stream the trail is gently up and down, maybe a little rocky or muddy, but very nice in this spectacular country.

I get to the river about 1:00, the day pleasantly sunny and warm. I sit on a grassy piece of shore eating my dinner, and Zipper joins me. We chatter some, but mostly relax as we wait for the free, ATC provided canoe ferry to take us across. A quick, uneventful crossing, a very short stretch before crossing Rt. 201, and another six miles, half uphill, through beautiful, hilly forest to Pleasant Pond Lean-to.

I'm getting back into the rhythm of doing higher mileage days as the trail is now much easier than it was in New Hampshire and the hundred miles of western Maine. Two mountains to cross tomorrow, then a relatively flat run into Monson. Maine is, in my opinion – though I may be just a mite biased, the prettiest state along the whole Appalachian Trail. And for NoBos, the best for last.

Friday 9/11

A little slower going because I stayed in the lean-to, but on the trail by 7:30. The morning is starting a little overcast, so we'll see what it brings.

Right away the trail climbs, gradually at first, then steeper towards the top, as it ascends Pleasant Mt. It was an easy climb, it seems I was on top within a half hour. Pleasant Mt. is indeed pleasant. It has an open, treeless summit providing nice, pretty views of the river valley and mountains and lakes in the surrounding area. Down the other side I walk through an incredible, beautiful old-growth spruce and fir forest the likes of which used to dominate the area before the white man came along. I stand in awe and appreciation of this magnificent forest, and am pleased that it will never be cut – it will ever remain simply to be enjoyed.

A little farther on, just over a little bump and around the bend, it becomes a hardwood forest. Odd how it can change so dramatically. But that only adds to the beauty of the place. The trail is pretty much that way to the next road, six miles from the lean-to; it alternates between soft and hardwoods, and back again. At 11:30 I sit on the shore on the south end of Moxie Pond eating my dinner; the clouds have burned off and the day is warming nicely.

The next three or so miles going up to Moxie Bald Mt. are very easy hiking. At first the trail wanders through a low forest, along an old beaver bog before coming to Bald Mt. Brook, a pretty, tranquil place. Then the trail starts a gentle, steady climb up to Moxie Bald Mt. The last half mile to the summit is twisty and steep in places, but unusual and very scenic. There are large rock formations – one a giant slab lying flat on top of an upright slab so it forms a giant T – that are spectacular and pleasant to behold in this remote mountain setting.

On the summit, it being open and treeless (hence the name), there are awesome, lengthy views of mountains and lakes in all directions. This is stunning, spectacular country. The two miles down to Moxie Bald Lean-to, where I will spend the night, are quite nice. They start with a side hill meander through stunted fir and spruce between sections of exposed ledge, eventually becoming a more obvious descent. The trail is mostly gradual with an occasional, small steep spot as it winds through woods that again alternate between soft and hard woods.

I arrive at the lean-to about 3:30, and even though there is plenty of time to hike, I decide to stay put and enjoy this place. I take a swim in the pond, wash my clothes and myself, then lay everything out on the rocks, my naked self included, to dry in the warm sun. This is the stuff Heaven is made of. I gather wood for a fire, get supper and settle in. Later on, five more hikers, Zipper included, wander into the site to camp for the evening. I feel really good tonight.

Saturday 9/12

Slept great last night. Up sometime before 6:00 and went to the pond to view a gorgeous, colorful sunrise.

I got on the trail at 6:45 this morning, hiking with Zipper as she wanted to get into Monson in good time, and hiking with me sets a faster pace for her. The trail is nice, some rock, root or mud, otherwise pretty level. Weather wise, the day is undecided: it could clear right out, or cloud in and rain, so far it's just lightly cloudy. Mostly we have been following the outlet stream from Bald Mt. Pond. I often paused to admire a fishing hole, and make a mental note about fishing here in the future.

We move along well, chatting as we go, and in two and a half hours have covered the nearly six miles to the first river crossing at the West Branch of the Piscataquis River. The data book says this is a ford, but the water is low enough that I cross on rocks. The next five miles are more up and down, but still good going. Before long I lose Zipper. I guess I was feeling good and energetic, and just left her in the dust. But that's how it goes out here – unless you're intentionally hiking with someone and maintain the same pace, you either get ahead or fall behind. It's the AT version of leap-frog.

This section of the trail follows the West Branch of the Piscataquis River through very lovely, scenic country. I still keep looking at the river and think of fishing. About three miles down, the river flows through Horseshoe Canyon – a narrow, twisty cut between steep, shear rock walls. If it weren't for this canyon, the river would be fun to run in a canoe.

After the canyon, the trail drops down and runs through luxurious lowland forest. I have always known, and appreciated, the beauty of Maine, but having seen it the way I have, I have gained an even greater appreciation for this land. In another couple miles I come to the East Branch of the Piscataquis River – another walk-across ford. Then it's a small uphill followed by rolling trail for three miles until I come to the side trail to Monson.

In a couple miles I'm in the heart of town, and take a room at Shaw's Lodge. There is a hiker celebration of sorts in town this weekend, and I could have tented at the school ball field for nothing, but since this is my last hurrah on the trail, I'm going big. I dubbed around a little bit, then went over to the ballfield where a hiker feed is being held to see what's happening.

There isn't much going on until the feed starts and hikers arrive. A few hikers and the folks putting on the feed sit around on benches and chat, a few hikers are engaged in a game of Frisbee. After a bit, more hikers arrive and the meal is served. The plentiful meal consists of hamburgers, lasagna, a rice dish, potatoes, corn on the cob, watermelon, chips and soda. All you can eat, all delicious, all out of the kindness of some very nice folks. Thank you to all who presented this wonderful meal and gathering.

Afterward, hikers and helpers sit around a big fire barrel chatting, joking, entertaining each other with tales of trail and derring-do, and just enjoying a fine and pleasant evening. In the morning, these same generous folks will be putting on a breakfast. Excellent, if accidental, timing to get here for all this.

Sunday 9/13

Yesterday I thought I might get right out at 6:00 this morning to walk the three miles of trail I missed, but that didn't happen. Instead, I did my laundry then moseyed over to the hiker breakfast a little before 8:00. Breakfast came about 9:00ish, a complete, full course meal, and it was very good. Much thanks again.

After yet another plentiful, delicious feed, I rode with Holmes, a thru-hiker, and her boyfriend who came to visit her, up to Greenville to take in the annual float plane show. The weather was very nice, the show was fun and educational. Near 1:00 we rode back to Monson, and I walked the three miles of trail I missed yesterday, getting back to town about 3:30. I made phone calls, then went to supper at 5:30 at the Lakehouse, the other lodge in town. The Lakehouse also has a small pub and restaurant in the back. A number of the other hikers were there – none of them drinking, of course – and I enjoyed pleasant conversation as I dined. My last big meal on my last big night before the hundred mile wilderness and the grand finale. Back to my room for a couple chores, the journal and a little reading before turning in. Tomorrow is the beginning of the end.

Welcome sign to Maine's 100-mile wilderness

Monday 9/14

Awake about 5:30, but no need to get right up. I laid in bed and read until 7:00ish, then went to breakfast. When you stay here at Shaw's, you have the option of paying a little more and getting the all-you-can-eat breakfast. It's worth it, a great meal. I sure do enjoy eating good food, and when you're hiking the trail, there's no way you can eat too much. I went to the post office for my re-supply and warm clothing, stopped at the store for the last bit of day food, called Beck, got packed up and on the trail at 9:30.

The day is sunny and seasonally cool – perfect for hiking. The first three miles of the trail are quite nice, gently rolling and in good shape. The woods are all mixed growth, and there are four small, scenic ponds along the way, all very pleasant. But then...

The next eight or so miles I walked a roller coaster – an up and down, twisting, turning section of trail that as the crow flies would only have been about five miles. There were a couple views of distant mountains, a small, pretty pond and a couple streams, but mostly it was hilly forest. One of the streams, Little Wilson, had a nice waterfall on it with ledges right to the water's edge – perfect for relaxing. The trail with surrounding country is all very pretty.

I had two stream crossings today, Big Wilson Stream and Long Pond Stream that my data book said I had to ford. Big Wilson Stream I did, the water being about knee deep, but Long Pond Stream was an easy crossing on rocks. The last mile to Long Pond Stream Lean-to was a little aggravating, mostly because I was tired from having hiked nearly fifteen miles – some of the last of that being pretty rough – but mainly because in that last short distance I had four steeper climbs and three steeper descents. I know I was tired, but I just couldn't see the need for it. But, it is what it is. Still, I got into camp at 5:30 in good season to get everything done and turned in before 8:00.

Tuesday 9/15

A good night for sleeping last night. I woke feeling quite refreshed. I got up at 6:00, and on the trail a little after 6:30. The trail started right off going up a rocky mountainside, and that pretty well set the pace for the day.

I headed up Barren Mt. right away, stopping about half way up to go to Barren Ledges and the site of a massive rock slide, and got to the top, about four miles away, with light clouds blowing over. No view from here this morning. Then there was a steep and rocky drop down the other side, the same up and down Fourth Mt., again up and down Third Mt., yet again up and down Columbus Mt., and finally up and a very steep and rocky down off Chairback Mt. After the initial 1700' climb, I was up or down maybe five hundred feet at a time, so in the eleven trail miles, I probably gained and lost a mile in elevation.

All the mountainsides are a jumble of rock, and when the trail wasn't rock, it was root. I did 15.3 miles today, and by the end of the day I was feeling every bit of it. But despite the trail being so rough, the countryside is ever pretty, the air ever fresh, the feeling being one of deep tranquility. From the tops of Fourth, Third and Chairback mountains were great views of surrounding mountains and lakes.

Although today's trail was so difficult, I made it to the West Branch of the Pleasant River by 5:00. As I was debating a camping spot, a man and woman forded the stream to where I was; the very pleasant woman told me that they thru-hiked the trail in '02. She said when they got to this point, she just wanted to hurry up and be done with it. As she was leaving, she gave me a granola bar and a homemade brownie for my dessert, and wished me well on the remainder of my hike. The treats didn't make it 'til dessert. A ford across the river and I set up camp alongside the trail. Very soon I'll have my supper, and will be turned in before dark. I'm looking forward to resting my body as tomorrow could be another big, hard day.

Wednesday 9/16

I turned in last night by 7:00; I got up this morning at 6:00. Eleven hours of rest after the pounding I took yesterday sure felt good. The day is starting mostly clear with just a few high, puffy clouds. I got started on the trail at 6:40.

I've got four mountains to get over today, the biggest ones in the hundred mile wilderness, and if they're anything like the mountains of yesterday, I've got my work cut out for me. So I start off going as best I can so I can get the easy miles done quickly, giving me more time for the tough stuff should I need it.

By 8:00 the sky is completely clouded in and looks as though it could rain any time. I make the first six miles, after a half-mile steep climb, to the top of Gulf Hagas Mt. in a little less than three hours. Pretty good, I'm thinking. The clouds are quite low, and there is a heavy mist in the air that prompts me to cover my pack and put on my rain coat. The warm, sunny days we've had have been replaced by a rather raw day. But that's the way it goes.

Down Gulf Hagas I stop at Sidney Tappan Campsite to eat and get water. It's about 11:00, and I've done seven miles so far. From here I go up and down two more peaks before I head up Whitecap at 3650'. Despite the ups and downs and the altitude gains and losses, I think these mountains are relatively easy. Even with the downhill sides, I am making a gain towards Whitecap, so that the actual climb up that last, big hill is not so bad. Certainly not as bad as I'd imagined it would be. And the forest all along is so pleasant whether it be mixed growth, or the predominant spruce and fir. It's comforting.

On the top of Whitecap there would be an excellent view, I'm sure, if it were not clouded in. The top is mostly open, a jumble of loose rock with some stunted fir and spruce scattered about for fun. Off in the distance today is a light grey shroud. Oh well, the view will still be there for another trip. Going down the other long, steep side there are some 163,792,845 (so it seems) steps to get down, or up if that's the direction you're headed. I'm thankful I'm going down as the three young fellows laboring up the hill don't appear to be enjoying it so much.

A mile or so from the top the trail levels out, and the mostly softwood forest now has a lot of young birch trees throughout. The forest is much lighter with the increased daylight and the golden color of the turned leaves. I stopped to get water at Logan Brook Lean-to, but continue on headed for the next lean-to four miles away. It is now 2:00, and I figure I'll be at my final day's destination about 4:30.

This birch forest is very pretty with its more varied color, and a welcome change from the thick spruce and fir I have been in all day. But it doesn't last long. Two miles from the lean-to I drop into a relatively flat, quite featureless spruce forest. There are some random, round rocks, but mostly it's an extensive grove of spruce trees with a mossy forest floor for as far as you can see. There is nothing to distinguish one direction from another. If a person were to wander off the trail, and wasn't paying close attention, it would be very difficult to find your way back to it. I suppose that is why there are so many blazes along this stretch.

Gratefully, I'm at East Branch Lean-to at 4:00 as my feet and knees are sore from the day's workout. I get my water, gather wood for a fire, prepare my supper and bed, eat, write and relax by the fire, and I'm ready for bed. Just two other hikers in camp tonight, so it's a quiet respite.

Thursday 9/17

A terrible night's sleep. I'd just caught a cold, I couldn't breathe through my nose, the night turned clear and cold, and I could not warm up. But just laying at rest for eleven hours or so my body rejuvenated. I got on the trail a little after 7:00, and really had to move to warm up.

In a few miles I made the 755' climb, though it seemed like more, up Little Boardman. And there was no view. The day is absolutely clear and bright, though at this early hour has not warmed up much. Once down over the other side, the trail flattens right out, and the hiking is effortless. I've passed by a couple small ponds, so lovely and tranquil in the early morn. The morning is simply beautiful, looking so fresh and clean in the bright sunlight.

I stride along at a good pace, not so much that I'm hurrying, but because the trail is so easy – a pleasure compared to the past few days of rough rock hopping. Travel is mostly through mixed forest with some large, mature trees along the way. It's always a pleasure to see large trees that have not fallen to an axe or chainsaw. I always get imagining what it must have looked like way back before man.

About 10:30 I arrive at the next shelter eight miles from where I started. It's time for a break and a bite to eat. There, I meet an older fellow from Greene who is hiking the hundred miles. A very nice guy and we chat for a bit. He informed me that the forecast is for rain tomorrow, though the amount is uncertain.

Originally I thought I would make Antlers Campsite my destination for the night, but the trail is so easy, and I'm making such good mileage, that I decide to head for the next lean-to in case it should start to rain overnight. That way, if it did rain, I won't have to pack a wet tent tomorrow. So on I go moving at a fast pace as I have twelve more miles to go. The trail really is so easy, and the day so pretty, that it doesn't seem like work, which, of course, it isn't. Along the way I pass ponds and lakes, and streams large and small. More great fishing holes! Around 2:00 I stop for water and a little more food. I have five more miles to get to Potaywadjo Lean-to. This land is very pretty with much water hereabout. I think I'll explore this area more later on.

The last three or four miles of trail have gotten rockier with more roots. Rocks are tough enough, but the roots really seem to punish the feet, and my feet are starting to complain. The last 2 miles are torturous, but I'm nearly there. Finally I arrive at Potaywadjo Spring Lean-to about 4:00, and collapse for a few minutes before I start my chores. First, I head to the spring for water. Potaywadjo spring is a beauty – about sixteen feet in diameter, maybe ten inches deep in the center, and the sand in the middle of it is perfectly clean from the volume of crystal clear water that flows from it. It's one of the nicest springs I've seen anywhere. No need to filter this water, it's as pure as can be.

Two young fellows had come into camp shortly after I arrived, and we gathered up a nice pile of wood for a fire. As we were eating our suppers, the young fellows were talking about how hungry they get while hiking. I listened to them describe the kinds of food they supplied themselves with – a lot of snack foods, pastries and such. Yeah, those things have a lot of calories, sugar for quick energy, fats for more prolonged energy, but they do nothing to replenish nutrients burned up from the day's exertion. No wonder they're always feeling hungry. You've got to eat to put proteins, vitamins and minerals back into the body – it's not just about consuming the 7000+ calories burned a day.

My supper and chores all done, and I sit writing by a cheerful, warm fire. I figure I have three more days of trail, and then Katahdin. I have mixed feelings.

Friday 9/18

Slept well last night and woke refreshed. It was a milder night than the previous one, so I was much more comfortable. I'm on the trail about 6:30, the day being clear to start, though the forecast is for showers. Yeah, whatever.

The first few miles of the trail are pretty good – gentle and a pleasant walk. But then I get down along Nahmakanta Stream and the trail becomes a crisscross of roots, and roots, more so than rocks, are hard on the feet. As tough as it is for walking, it is equally as pleasing to behold. The forest is very lovely and lush appearing as though it would support a lot of game, but I haven't seen any. In fact, I haven't seen any game, other than partridge, since I've been in Maine. Then again, moving along as I am, and the forest as thick as it can be, I could be walking right past them and never know it.

For a few miles I walked along Nahmakanta Stream, large enough it could be a river, a splendid water body with many scenic spots, as well as excellent fishing holes. There is one spot on the stream where it curves in closer to the trail. There is a very large rock on the stream bank with a good size pine tree growing on top of it. The stream at this big rock is maybe six feet deep with a few more large rocks at the bottom. I gazed into that pool and could just imagine the trout or salmon that would be stacked up there just waiting for a worm, lure or fly to be presented to them. Later…

In another few miles the stream becomes a lake – probably because that's where it originates. Nahmakanta Lake is a gem lying there in the big woods surrounded by low mountains. I could surely enjoy having a cabin on the shore of such a lake. In time… At the south end of the lake is a sandy beach with an outdoor chair just so you can sit and absorb this wonderful environment.

The trail follows the shore of the lake for a distance before it climbs Nesuntabunt Mt. The hike up is not too long, but it is fairly steep and rocky in sections. As I was starting up, I met a SoBo thru-hiker just getting down. It seems a rather late start to such a long hike, but she appears unconcerned. On top there are nice views of the lake, surrounding forest and Katahdin – when it's not obscured by clouds. The weather today has been in and out. Sometimes it would be overcast with a pattering of rain, other times it would be sunny and nearly cloudless. All in all, pretty nice for a showery day. All over Nesuntabunt are large rocks with their tops covered by dense, lush ferns and moss giving them the appearance of giant chia pets. A very pretty and fun hike through here.

Down off the mountain and in a bit I come to Crescent Pond. I suspect there's good fishing here as well on account of the small boats and canoes on the shore. A little further on through this gently rolling forest is Pollywog Gorge – high, steep rock walls with a rushing stream at the bottom. It's wild and lovely country.

In a mile or so I cross a gravel road and large, rushing stream. On a tree at the junction of a smaller road are the letters NLC. "Some rich man's camp," I say to myself, "Well, good for him." Just up the trail is the boisterous, energetic Rainbow Stream. The water in this stream is absolutely clear with terrific pools. At one point along this stream I saw a trout leap out of the water trying to get over a small fall as he was making his way upstream – the first time I'd ever seen a trout do that.

Just past 4:00 I arrive at Rainbow Stream Lean-to where I will spend the night. I've hiked eighteen miles today, many of those miles tough, and I'm glad I'm now in camp. But as tough as the miles may have been, the scenery and forest along this entire section of trail is wonderfully pretty, really a pleasure to see.

Saturday 9/19

A nice night, not very chilly, and I sleep comfortably and restfully. Up and on the trail just past 7:00.

The trail sort of follows the stream which eventually opens to Rainbow Lake. The morning is quite breezy, some might say windy, overcast with occasional, very light rain. Fortunately any rain does not last long. Along the shore of the lake I walk through a beautiful hardwood forest as the wind-driven waves break on the shore. The wind, which doesn't feel so strong inside the trees, has a good hold on the lake – the water is slate grey and completely covered with large, frenzied whitecaps. No place for a canoe this morning. This is spectacular country.

A few miles down the lake the forest becomes predominantly softwood. This area feels really good; there is a lot of great energy here, and an explosion of life all about. There are stately old growth pines and young saplings in great abundance all along the way. As is the case, with life there is also death, and I hear a few trees cracking and falling, giving way to age and wind. Such is the cycle of life.

After leaving the lake, I start up a two-mile rise to Rainbow Ledges. This hill, with sections of barren rock and vibrant young trees, is magnificent and magical. It's a grand fairy land with a meandering trail through open fir and spruce, birch and maple and blueberry bushes. It is awesomely beautiful by itself, but with the views of distant mountains and lakes it is – well it's beautiful beyond any description. I thank Spirit for creating such a wonderful place. On top I sit and eat a bit, then lie down for a while to soak up the sun and energy of this wilderness sanctuary.

After an hour or so, I move on down the other side into predominantly softwood forest. Today's section of trail, including the gentle climb up to 1517' Rainbow Ledges, is pretty good going. Yeah, there are the rocky, muddy or rooted sections, but generally it's quite nice. Pretty soon I come to Hurd Brook and the last lean-to before Baxter State Park, and I stop for water. The wind is dying down now, and the day is warming. From here, it is a gentle 3.5 mile walk to Abol Bridge. This section of trail, occasionally not well marked and more difficult to follow, flows through luxurious softwoods, and with the bright sunshine, is terrifically vibrant with the greenest emerald greens you could imagine. In contrast, or compliment, the sky above is a deep, rich, clear sapphire blue. Early autumn in Maine – such a beautiful time of year in such a spectacular place. I'm blessed to be here – to be home.

Around 3:00 I come to the Golden Road, Penobscot River and Abol Bridge. At the east end of the bridge is a camp ground and a decently stocked little store. I dub around a while, eat a sandwich and treats from the store, chat with hikers while I decide where I'm going to spend the night. Across and just up the road is the state-maintained Abol Campground along the Penobscot River. I walked over, found a lovely, picturesque spot, and set up camp. The remainder of the day was spent in relaxation and contemplation.

Sunday 9/20

I thought I might lie about some this morning, but that didn't happen. Shortly after the sun was up I had to go to the bathroom, or in this case, the privy, and since I was already up I got going, but at a slower than usual pace. I made a call to Julie to see if she was coming by – she wasn't, and a call to Beck to see if she was able to come after me when I finish tomorrow – she wasn't. I dubbed around a bit, drank some hot chocolate and orange juice, then left for the trail about 8:30.

I come to the Baxter State Park boundary just before 9:00 under partly sunny skies and seasonally cool temperatures. The first part of the trail is literally and figuratively a walk in the park. The path is so flat and easy that it is effortless to walk it. In a short section I cross a couple little streams, and then I'm walking beside the Penobscot River. For the next three miles or more I walk along this beautiful, clear, swift river through a piney forest. The trail is very gentle and being covered with pine needles is much like walking on a rug. You really get the impression that the AT has saved the best for last.

After a bit, I come to Pine Point where Nesowadnehunk Stream joins the Penobscot. Here, the trail makes an almost 90 degree turn to follow the stream, and I figured I'd be in for some hill scrambling, but such is not the case. The trail remains fairly level, with only a few little bumps, as it shoulders the stream. The Nesowadnehunk is a lovely stream – fast flowing, clear water with occasional falls to tickle it into laughter. The thought of wetting a line does not enter my mind at all.

At one point the trail crosses the stream, but is not well marked, or I just didn't see the markings, and I continued on in the direction I was heading. A common mistake as evidenced by many other footprints here. It did not take me long to realize I missed a turn as I am suddenly scrambling up a steep, slippery hillside. A short back-track and I see where I should have crossed. At the intersection, I laid a couple logs across the trail to alert others of the change, crossed the stream, and built up the cairn on the other side to make it more obvious. Having done my good deed for trail maintenance, I journey on.

Now that the land is rising higher, I'm also having to climb a bit, but not an awful lot, and certainly with no difficulty. The gently rolling forest now is a mix of soft and hardwoods, and there is nothing to indicate that a great mountain mass is laying in wait just a few miles away as the crow flies. Some little climbs toward Big Niagara Falls, then the trail turns again heading for Daicey Pond. I met eight day hikers along this stretch, talking for a bit with the first group of five about hiking the trail and what-not. Nice folks from Bethel and Yarmouth areas. The woman in the group asked me if she could get my picture, and stood beside me while it was shot. I advised her not to stand too close as the vapors may be rather toxic. She replied that it had been a couple days since she showered, and did not seem to mind. Up the trail a ways I flushed four fat partridge, and thought about how tasty they'd be. Pretty quick I'm at Daicey Pond with Katahdin looming over the far shore. There are many people about enjoying this splendid last day of summer. I stop along the shore of the pond for a little bite to eat – such a pretty, peaceful spot. There are five folks out canoeing and kayaking, and I think of how fun that would be.

The forest now is all spruce and fir as it huddles around a couple small, tranquil ponds. And yet, even though this is excellent moose country, I have not seen one while I have been on the trail. Perhaps it's the toxic vapors? And before long I'm on the park road with just a half mile to go to Katahdin Stream Campground and trailhead up Katahdin.

The day now is partly sunny and quite mild. I dub around, gather firewood, and pretty much take it easy in camp as I rest up for tomorrow's hike up Katahdin and completion of the Appalachian Trail. In camp tonight are maybe six other hikers, all doing the same. We sit and enjoy a bright, lively campfire, eat our suppers, chatter and joke in good cheer.

It is coming quite near the end of this journey. On one hand, I'm anxious to finally see this dream come true; on the other hand, I'm feeling a little blue that the end is so near. I'd finally come to the place where I'm enjoying the hike for the sake of the hike, where just being out here is reward enough. This frame of mind, being so at ease in the forest for such an extended time, is what I originally thought I would be hiking the entire trail with. Well, I guess I had to walk all those miles to find it waiting for me.

Monday 9/21

This is it, the very last of my journey. I'm up at 6:00 and attending to business as if it was any other day on the hike. Breakfast and packing done, I'm at the ranger station before 7:00 to get a day-pack for the hike up the big hill, and I'm on the trail at 7:00 – the first one today to go up the Hunt Trail. The day starts sunny and cool – ideal hiking weather – just what you'd expect for this time of year.

In just a short bit, I come to the crossing at Katahdin Stream. I would have to say that this stream is the prettiest, cleanest stream I've ever come across. Looking into pools that must be three feet deep, I can easily discern shapes and colors of all the rocks in the stream bed. If it weren't for that the water is moving, and the ever so slightly different shade of color, you maybe wouldn't notice there was water at all – it's that pure.

I'm not pushing, but I'm not poking, as I progress uphill. As I hike along, I don't think much about where I've been, what I've done, or what's next. I simply think about the task at hand – hiking up this mountain. Occasionally I stop for a drink, take in the view, once to watch a mouse out getting some breakfast and whatever else a mouse pursues. I've been up or down this particular trail maybe six times, some parts I remember, some I don't. And it doesn't matter as this is a whole new time. The number of times I've seen this country, granted that number is not exceptionally high, I'm always impressed with the beauty and splendor of this land – it's magnificent country!

The sunny day is warming up, and I've shed my hat (fairly early on), and my pant legs. Before long I'm far enough up the mountain to where I'm having to climb up, over and around rocks large and small. In a short distance I'm into the serious rock climbing. Well, not serious in that you need ropes and high-tech hiking gear, but this part of the mountain is quite steep, a great jumble of very large rocks and open ledge. It's not what you'd call strenuous climbing, neither is it easy hiking. I just think it's fun.

Once out of the largest rocks and above the tree line, you start up a long, jagged spine of rock – surely the top is just beyond. It seems to go on and on, and when you think you've reached the top, there's another. But all good mountains are built that way. Eventually you reach the top of the spine and are deposited on the tableland. The tableland is a broad, relatively level expanse of the mountain, maybe a mile across. It is composed of small(ish) rocks, blueberry bushes, grass and various alpine plants. It's a whole different ecosystem than the rest of the mountain. There is just a light breeze here, the temperature is quite noticeably warmer than where I was just a short while ago, and the trail, delineated to a single path, is very easy – simply a delight.

And then you're at Thoreau Spring at the junction of the Abol Trail, and the last mile to the summit. From here the trail rises gently, becoming rockier; then it becomes a little steeper with larger rocks before leveling off to the summit – the very last section quite easy. And then, just like that, I'm at the summit. I've done it – I've completed the Appalachian Trail.

Until I stop to think about it, this feels like it's been every other hike up Katahdin. I eat a snack, chat with other hikers, get my picture taken, and poke around a bit. But then I walk over to and sit on a rock, and gaze down upon Chimney Pond. Here I reflect on what has happened – I have fulfilled a dream. And the emotions flow. I cry tears of joy that I have accomplished this part of my life journey – in itself quite a journey – and I thank Spirit, Mom and Dad, and myself for making it all possible.

And so I sit and reflect not so much on the physical aspect of the hike, or of the trail, but that I have fulfilled a long-held dream. That is one of the most important aspects of this journey – I've lived a dream.

As for the Appalachian Trail and the hiking of it, well, I guess I would have to say it was everything. It was beautiful, it was blah; it was exciting, it was boring; it was enjoyable, it was miserable; I loved it, I hated it, and every thought, feeling and emotion in between.

While hiking the trail, I experienced suffering and triumph, being knocked down to my lowest only to be lifted to great heights. I'd overcome adversity of my own making, and the tortures of old demons. I received tremendously valuable insights to my inner self, into long-held thoughts – "programming" – that had contributed to my life. I'd been blessed with being able to find profound joy in the simplest things. I gained an even greater appreciation for the natural world.

During the hike I went through a transformation. I don't suppose I could have experienced what I did and not have been transformed in some way. I learned many valuable lessons: the error of poor thinking, and the benefit of sound thinking; that my thoughts and attitudes, positive or negative, will make or break me; that our thoughts create our lives; to listen to my heart – to honor and cherish myself; to be more patient, compassionate and understanding – mostly with myself; to rely on myself; to not sit back and wait for "what life brings to me"; that I can achieve whatever I want; to live more fearlessly from having a better understanding of the simple process of this event called life; to feel, to love, more deeply than I ever had. I forged a deeper relationship with Great Spirit, God or whatever name you give the Creator.

Ultimately, hiking the Appalachian Trail was the best thing I could have done for myself.

And so it was that I came to the end of my journey, sitting up on a mountain top. I dared, I did. I followed my dream, I saw it through. Would I ever hike the AT again? Yes, I would. Will I? God only knows. Now I have other dreams to follow, the time is right to fulfill them. Having hiked the Appalachian Trail, I know I can achieve all my dreams. All of us can – we need only to dream, to dare, to do.

On Katahdin—end of trail

AND IN THE END

Many times I was asked, "When you're through with the trail, what then?"

My reply would be, "I don't know, something will come up."

I spent a month getting somewhat re-acclimated to the un-natural world. I felt out of place, that I had no direction. I thought about what I wanted to do, where I wanted to go. I'd always dreamed of owning a cabin on a pond in the woods. At the same time, I always have loved to travel. I could go up-country to find my place, or I could load my camper onto my truck and go see what I find. The pull to do one is as strong as the pull to do the other. What to do?

I did the only natural thing for me to do – I went for a walk.

There is a short hiking trail nearby home that is an easy, pretty walk; I went there and started walking and talking to myself. Well, to myself and Spirit. I imagined Priyadarshi, my Tai Chi instructor, talking to me. I imagined him telling me to close my eyes and let it come to me:

"What is in my heart?"

"I really want my own place now."

"Well then, there you have it."

I needed to find something somewhere, so the focus of my search was in regions where I thought I'd like to live. I'd often thought that working in a sporting camp would be a good fit for me, so that's what I sought out. I went to the town library, got online, and made a list of sporting camps that were open year-round. That was my direction. Sometime toward the end of October, I put my camper on my truck and headed up-country.

I traveled a large area of the state starting in Oquossoc and Rangeley, over to Stratton, down to Kingfield, over to Bingham, up to Jackman, over to Rockwood and Greenville, winding through the woods to Millinocket, ending up in Shin Pond. On the way I stopped at many sporting camps and lodges, meeting a lot of great folks, asking if anybody needed help.

Gradually I made my way to Nahmakanta Lake Camps. I met Don, the owner, told him what I was up to, had a pleasant visit, and left with him saying he would think things over and see if he could use me. I then went up to Shin Pond, planning on going further north and east if need be. The next morning I got a call from Don at NLC saying he could use me. We roughly worked out some details, and now being set for the winter I headed back down state for a few weeks.

I started at NLC mid-November, doing some carpentry for a couple weeks, then headed back down state for Thanksgiving. After the holiday, I went back up, coming out again for Christmas. After Christmas I went back up for the winter. Primarily I was doing carpentry at the camps, but much of what I was there for was just to keep an eye on things.

Now here's the funny thing – as pretty and serene as the place is, as much as it's the kind of place where I'd always desired to be, from just about the moment I started there I was ready to leave. I don't know why, I can't explain it, but there it is. Things don't always go as you imagine they will.

Through December and into the first part of January, I was alone at the camps, which are remote in the summer, isolated in the winter. My buddies, Stan and Jim, came up on New Year's Day for a couple days of ice fishing; at the same time, Regina and Maria were in for the weekend. On two occasions I met some ice fishermen, and two of the local game wardens. Other than that, it was just the three of us there – me, myself and I. At least I had someone to talk to. I struggled with the isolation, but stuck it out as over and over in my head played the word "opportunity." What that opportunity was, I had no idea, but I kept getting the same message. But more and more I was feeling like I was all done there, that that position wasn't taking me where I wanted to be. By and by I had come to the place where the solitude was no longer the burden it initially was, rather the solitude had become comfortable – like a warm blanket to wrap around you on a chilly night, or a close friend you can have a heart to heart talk with. I was enjoying the solitude.

I was out for a walk on the lake on one of my last nights there when I realized that I was ready to leave, that I felt I'd gotten all I was going to get from this opportunity. It wasn't the isolation that got me; in fact, I'd got to the point where I was completely comfortable with myself. With myself, by myself.

After leaving the camps I realized that that was my "opportunity;" I'd become, for the first time in my life, completely comfortable with myself. What started on the AT in April of 2008 had been completed with my 2009 winter sojourn at Nahmakanta Lake, a place I had not known existed until I walked past it while hiking the Appalachian Trail.

And now the circle is complete. I've walked home – to myself.

ACKNOWLEDGEMENTS

To Pat through whose patience and guidance this book came to be.

To all the Trail Angels, your kindness and generosity are a blessing that is truly appreciated.

To Priyadarshi who said, "You owe it to yourself to do the hike," I thank you for all your help.

To Stef whose support through love, and tremendous efforts to get my re-supplies to me – words of thanks can't possibly express the gratitude I have for you.

To Mom and Dad through whose love I came to be here. You set the mold for me to become who I am. I love you and miss you so very much.

To myself for daring to follow my dream.

To my spirit guides, angels and loved ones who helped me along the way, thank you for being here for me.

Mostly, to Great Spirit who makes all things possible – You have my heart and soul.

www.ingramcontent.com/pod-product-compliance
Lightning Source LLC
Chambersburg PA
CBHW051946090426
42741CB00008B/1291